Cultural Critique

122

Winter
2024

EDITORIAL STATEMENT

Cultural Critique provides a forum for creative and provocative scholarship in the theoretical humanities and humanistic social sciences. Transnational in scope and transdisciplinary in orientation, the journal strives to spark and galvanize intellectual debates as well as to attract and foster critical investigations regarding any aspect of culture as it expresses itself in words, images, and sounds, across both time and space. The journal is especially keen to support scholarship that engages the ways in which cultural production, cultural practices, and cultural forms constitute and manifest the nexus between the aesthetic, the psychic, the economic, the political, and the ethical intended in their widest senses. While informed by the diverse traditions of historical materialism as well as by the numerous critiques of such traditions from various parts of the globe, the journal welcomes contributions based on a variety of theoretical-methodological paradigms.

Cultural Critique appears four times a year. General issues, including essays, book reviews, and thematic sections, as well as entire issues devoted to special topics, are regularly published. The editors welcome the submission of freestanding essays, special issue proposals on topics of interest to the journal, as well as reviews of relevant, new, and not-so-new books.

In 2022, the journal launched its online section hosted by Manifold, the open-access platform of the University of Minnesota Press. *Cultural Critique Online* on Manifold expands *Cultural Critique's* existing web presence to include new open-access book reviews, short articles, interviews, and more. For more, please visit https://z.umn.edu/7p7i or scan the QR code below:

Cultural Critique Books is the companion series of the journal. It seeks to attract work by those scholars across the humanities and social sciences who continue to draw inspiration from, and seek to contribute to, the theoretical movements and debates so long nurtured at Minnesota. Book proposals should be addressed to one of the five senior editors at: *Cultural Critique,* Department of Cultural Studies and Comparative Literature, 235 Nicholson Hall, 216 Pillsbury Drive S.E., University of Minnesota, Minneapolis, MN 55455–0229, U.S.A., or via email to **cultcrit@umn.edu.**

THE CON AND THE PRIMAL HORDE

J. Asher Godley

For Don Pease

Let's face it. Despite centuries of critique, a cursory view of today's global landscape makes it painfully apparent that the seductive appeal of the tyrant has scarcely diminished. Relatively few countries today support a more than nominal democratic system, and those that do are besieged by an emboldened minority of fascist parties. One aspect of this phenomenon is all too familiar to the left: what we are seeing is widespread rage against corporate-sponsored neoliberal governments that grow more estranged from the public by the day, only for that discontent to become spitefully displaced onto minorities and migrants. One need only add what conservatives almost admit, which is that the global diasporic patterns resulting from the untrammeled reign of "free markets" force into being new forms of community that conflict with the symbolic consistency of centuries-old cultural traditions that rely upon xenophobic prejudices for their self-definition and distinctiveness. Race-baiting, identitarian, border-obsessed reactionary politics enters the breach when these tensions overflow. No surprise, then, that this situation propels some of the worst specimens of society into positions of public trust under the rallying cry of the need for "strong leaders."

But what remains perplexing is why so many supporters of these figures are seemingly unbothered when time and again their heroes fail to live up to the "masterly" image they project of themselves. How could a Jair Bolsonaro or a Recep Erdoğan benefit from so much popular support when they are so *demonstrably* inept, corrupt, and uninterested in democratic process or debate? Liberal and leftist critiques still struggle to answer that question. Listening to the pundits, it would seem we can only say so much "about" Trump even if we go on and on, when maybe there just isn't that much "there" there. Images of a shirtless Putin riding a bear are the stuff of memes, but there is little to be gained by pointing out the overwrought phallic tropes he traffics in. Given broad public awareness of the zeal with which these would-be "strongmen" pursue cliches of power only to fail to embody them, what task is left for demystifying critique? With weary yet ever-renewed surprise we keep asking: How can people not see what is so damned *obvious*?

This impasse of critical knowledge around the sticking point of tyrannic seduction resembles a scene from Herman Melville's prescient novel *The Confidence-Man: His Masquerade*. Three observers debate whether the titular charlatan, lately exposed but still at large, is a cunning knave who exploits the unwary, a fool who believes in his own myth, or a secret agent pursuing a hidden agenda (89–92). For each imagined scenario, Melville insinuates a specific supposition about the subject of knowledge: The first speaker, who believes the charlatan is a knave, assumes that he is more cunning than those he defrauds. This would be a straightforward example of what Jacques Lacan calls a "subject-supposed-to-know," a figure believed to have special access to the truth of another's unconscious. In the scenario imagined by the observer, the grifter picks up on precisely what his victim would rather not know. But the second speaker thinks that this gives the operator too much credit—what if he's just got a "cracked pate"? (91). No doubt he mostly deceives himself and only infects others by the contagion of his enthusiasm. In this case, he is a subject supposed *not* to know, but in this ignorance a different danger weighs upon the "enlightened" observer. For even if *I* know the truth, what can I do against the dupery of others? Because I am a part of the same society, their blindness is still my burden.

At this point, the third speaker steps in. According to his hypothesis, the operator is part of a Jesuit cabal that prowls the country in disguise in the attempt to pervert and enslave people. Working backward from this conjecture, it's simply a matter of seeing how well the pieces fit: "True knowledge," the theorist proclaims, "comes but by suspicion or revelation" (92). In other words, the situation is truly hopeless—the Con is *both* a cunning knave *and* part of a fanatic cult: a subject who knows and doesn't know at the same time. Reasonable and moral appeals are both in vain. With this grand gesture of conspiracy, we encounter the deadlight of critical knowledge: everything comes back to that beguiling trait that cannot be "conned" even when unmasked.

Melville's scene illustrates how critical inquiry can lurch into confusion and even impotent despair when the enjoyment that underlies the observer's certitudes is directly implicated. Likewise, the confidence-men who have come to power in recent times prey upon the palliative assurances of the nonduped as much as the naivete of the willfully deceived. With a precise perceptiveness that some have mistaken for misanthropy, Melville observes that those who think they share the inside joke or are privy to the con's schemes fast become lovers of his exploits. Do we not see a hint of this in the fact that even those who hate Trump have to admit their fascination?

In his seminar *Les Non-Dupes Errant*, Lacan makes a similar point when he compares a certain prejudice against dupes to the plight of the "hoopoe," a bird that, like the more famous dodo, went extinct because their obliviousness to danger made them easy prey for trappers. A typical misprision in reference to such victims of man's avarice is the imputation of stupidity to the prey, as if being duped were evidence of mental inferiority. According to the bird's use as a cautionary illustration, to be undeceived one should not trust too much to one's unsuspecting inclinations. Yet the sensible person who would point to such a moral is the very type of "non-duped" that Lacan singles out in the title of his seminar. By mistrusting the "erroneous" structure of the unconscious, the nonduped might be led all the more astray by his overconfidence in the alibis of consciousness. Mistaking the dupe for someone with faulty judgment, the nonduped tacitly aligns his own intellectual discernment with the deceiver's, which, in turn, makes him susceptible, because they thereby share the same axis of truth. Just as the cautionary tale of the hoopoe lends credentials to the exterminators of the *rara avis*, so cynicism naively entertains the brutal conventions of knavish "realists."

The nonduped and the duped are thus joined in a common deception, which consists in their shared assumption that the spuriousness of the leader is other than the source of his strength. Yet even in the earliest days of political theory, the autocrat's seduction was known to be based in a constitutive illusion that linked the pretensions of a would-be master with the unconscious wishes of the *polis*. In *The Republic*, Socrates defines the tyrant as he who is "awake, presumably, what we described a dreaming man to be" (576b).[1] Night after night the object of obscure desires returns with the impact of a forceful, if familiar, revelation, only to be lost again the next day. Correspondingly, the tyrant announces himself with all the fanfare of a triumphal reawakening from a long slumber, as if we had forgotten when last we closed our eyes. Indeed, Socrates understands the dream (ὄναρ) the same way Freud does, as the production of an unconscious wish. And to encounter a figure who compels the fulfillment of desire beyond one's capability of assent can only signal the very worst of predicaments.

Yet despite the demagogue's nightmarish presence, his performance is more apparitional than real. The typical scheme of an autocrat's life, according to Socrates, resembles a tragicomedy about a man who pretends to forge his own path despite having no idea what he wants and who attempts to resolve this incongruity by assuming that whatever he does is in everyone's best interest. In his youth, the budding demagogue only learns to seduce by continually being seduced himself: at first overawed by a gang of "dread enchanters and tyrant makers" who flatter him disingenuously, he later cows them with his more zealous pursuit of the same illicit pleasures they enjoined him to pursue (572e). But this only leads him to fall hopelessly in love with the mirage of himself that he finds dimly reflected in the eyes of his accomplices and sycophants. Goaded by this capricious inner monarch, he subsequently busies himself attempting to impress an ever-changing entourage (574e–575a).

Such an account, with which Socrates counters Thrasymachus's claim that only strong-willed tyrants have the aptitude to rule effectively, begs the question of how such a weak and indecisive character could convince anyone he is powerful and independent. Yet Socrates already supplies the answer: the tyrant's mystique lies at the root of leadership, in the tendency of the democratic polis to choose "some *one* man as their special leader and to foster him and to make him grow great" (565c; my emphasis). Because of this push for a single representative, a "one for all", the citizenry hardly notice his imposture since they are so compelled by the promise of an exceptional character uniquely capable of standing in for a heterogeneous multitude. For his part, the tyrant forms a pact with his followers reminiscent of the myth of Lycaon, in which a public guardian transforms into a wolf after succumbing to the temptation to taste the "kindred blood" of his subordinates (565d–e). He thereby secures from the people the promise that even his most unspeakable transgressions will remain indistinguishable from what lies at the basis of law's legitimacy: namely, the obscene enjoyment of the sovereign exercise.[2]

But the paradox of this enjoyment is that it neither "belongs" to the sovereign individual nor even to what is called his "base"; it remains the mythic accompaniment to the structure of the state, where one man is imagined to enjoy on behalf (and at the expense) of "all" the polis. Relative to this structural incommensurability, Freud in *Group Psychology and the Analysis of the Ego* ascertains a form of regressive identification on the part of each constituent member of a group—in his relation to the leader, the subject falls back on an earlier libidinal position where the father appears as an ideal who is admired, envied, and feared (*SE* 18:105, 122, 129–30).[3] This ideal has only a little to do with the father as an empirical being but much to do with the phallic function, that quantum of undiluted desirability that Freud argues secures the place of paternal authority within the structure of the family and society. That nobody in fact can occupy such an ideal position presents no difficulty. For it is only the supposition that there *could* be such an undivided subject of sovereign enjoyment that furnishes the keystone of the Oedipal drama. Holy Grail or MacGuffin, the phallic signifier is reducible to the absence that motivates the subjective quest for its acquisition.

Yet such is Freud's quandary about the profound reduction of the father to this phallic function that he resorts to a myth to explain its eldritch power. In *Totem and Taboo*, a prehistoric "primal father" is said to rule over a constituency of his sons and concubines and to enjoy their bodies without restriction, only to be overthrown and murdered by his envious progeny. After the murder, his sons eat his flesh and distribute his wives among each other, but then out of an attack of remorse, decide to deify him. Thus, the prestige of the primal father comes from a tale twice-told, both in the beginning and retroactively after his murder: he is an exceptional man who enjoys "all" and yet remains utterly removed from all others, untouched by the lack that would make him vulnerable in his desire.

In *Group Psychology*, Freud invokes this figure as the ancient prototype of the contemporary dictator, describing him in contradictory terms: coarse and brutish yet intensely cunning; ruthless and independent but crippled by his dependency on a fawning crowd; the object of intense public devotion yet coldly incapable of a meaningful bond (*SE* 18:123–24). It is hard to escape the impression that he is not actually a man but only the emblem of one, like a fixed coordinate in structural space. And in fact, Freud conceives of the identification at issue in groups as relying on a single point of inflection or unifying trait (*ein einziger Zug*), where enjoyment registers at the limits of the subject's knowledge. By grounding the illusion that a constituency hangs together as a coherent "oneness," this unary trait implies an identity that, in turn, renders conceivable a position and place from which collective enjoyment would be possible (106–7). But this "master signifier," as Lacan comes to call it, is also something that can become reinscribed differently within a social order, not as the ensign of an exceptional *being* but, beneath its mythic trappings, the marker of collective impasse.

The reinscription of this signifier of impasse within a problematic of collective desire explains why any advance in political theory today crucially depends upon the discourse that psychoanalysis makes available. Note that this does not mean we require the language *of* psychoanalysis (i.e., its specific idiom or terminology) but to know how to read from a specific orientation where unconscious desire is the bottom line. Here we can return to Melville's inquest scene, which he could not have written if he did not accommodate a fourth position, which is best approached through a slight adjustment of the conspiracist's theory. Viewed analytically, the conspiracy theorist's notion that the Con is an agent poised to unleash an *intolerable enjoyment* on the world is entirely justified. No doubt the Confidence Man does draw power from such a threat. To conform with reality, we need only observe that such a power is freely granted by the one whom it affects. That is, the Con need only hint that such an overmastering enjoyment is at his disposal in order for the would-be dupe to make use of a fantasy that will allow him to situate himself as its potential victim, deriving in this way both the means of contextualizing the danger he feels to himself arising from the "operator" and a means of obtaining satisfaction from it. As the theorist and the other two speculators excitedly speculate, so do the novel's dupes and skeptics delight at the impostor whom they eventually declare "Quite an Original" with an air of breathless pride as if they were flattering *themselves* (237).

In an effort to more clearly track the subterfuge, this essay aims to displace what usually passes for the critique of authoritarian populism, a critique that, insofar as it situates its critical gesture within the limitations of knowledge, remains susceptible to the maneuvers of the Con. As such, my argument is allied with the recovery of the power of critique by clarifying a position through which epistemological indeterminacy opens onto unconscious knowledge, as I show through readings of *The Confidence-Man*. What Melville's novel teaches is that in place of the overemphasis on the hopeless impasses that result when we try to capture the truth of the demagogue's character, deeds, or particular statements, we would be better situated to pay heed to the paradoxes of enjoyment that are crucially at work in the transactions between the Con and the *polis*, particularly those organized around the sovereign's "exceptional" impostures. Moreover, when we read these maneuvers in light of the psychoanalysis of group dynamics, we can see how Lacan's revisioning of the master as a "transfer-agent" is indispensable to an updated theory of sovereignty in our age of huckster-tyrants. In this context, Lacan's rereading of the Oedipal myth in *Totem and Taboo* furnishes a "primal" frame through which we can rearticulate the conditions for the seductive operation of contemporary authoritarian populism.

The stakes of this rearticulation are hinted at by one profound point in Freud's myth which Lacan only slightly acknowledges, which is that the primal scene of sovereignty is directly linked to the community's attitudes toward death. In the story of the primal horde, the death of the sovereign reflects the privation of the entire polis. This privation reveals an excessive dimension of longing and pain that shows how the organizing logic of community is perhaps just as closely aligned with the psychical process of mourning as the sovereign persona. When the sovereign fails to represent the excess dissatisfactions of the community, his existence is genuinely threatened. The *grief* of the primal horde thus comes to decide the fate of the master: Either collective privation is handed over to his care as the sacrificial offering to a god, or it destroys the sovereign myth by opening up a different path, namely the desire of the community to reinvent its modes of symbolic enjoyment. Darkly farcical as Melville's novel is, there are moments even in the midst of the Con's subterfuges where a different declension of the sovereign signifier lets fly the play of another satisfaction than that of falling prey to tyrants: the enjoyment of truthful fictions.

THE TRUTH OF THE IMPOSTER

The Confidence-Man, the novel itself as much as its title character, is known for playing tricks on the reader's epistemic faith. Less a traditional plot-driven narrative than a series of vignettes where strangers on a steamboat attempt to profit off one another through verbal arrangements, the narratorial focus is not on deeds but their decomposition into the gestural ambiguity of signs. Though each of the novel's episodes center on a figure recognizable by his loquacious efforts to convince strangers to give him their money and their trust, we can't know for certain that he is the same character throughout, let alone whether he can be trusted. Like the characters who encounter him, we are constantly thrown back upon our suspicions and half-aware suppositions. Under various names and guises, the spurious operator follows an errant trajectory, circulating like a fiction. In the first half of the book, the surest way the reader can spot him is by a single, identifying trait, like an *einziger Zug*—"a man in gray," "a man with a weed," "a man in a traveling cap," "a man with a snuff-colored surtout." What unites them into a group of one is the pattern of their speech, which bears upon a demand that the Other believe that the petitioner is who he says he is. He offers himself thus, and in each case, as a new reality.[4]

Written at a time when the concept of a "confidence man" and the term itself were only just beginning to appear in American newspapers, Melville was able to take advantage of the still-shifting fortunes of an emergent signifier that had not yet definitively settled into the lexicon, perhaps in hopes of influencing its semantic destiny. A further ambiguity in the novel therefore stems from the moral, aesthetic, fiduciary, and psychological properties associated with the polysemic complexity of "confidence," inclusive of an attitude of prospective assurance, an exchange of intimacies or secrets, an ideal of faith or trust, the bestowing of credit or value, or, in a negative or ironic sense, a misrecognition of appearances. The reader must decide whether the figure who espouses these significances is marked by any of them in particular, or if the swindler's deceit is the overriding and determining quality. The question is pointed insofar as it is never made materially explicit that the Con defrauds his presumed marks, though they give him their money and assurances, and most have their suspicions. The reader ascertains criminal intent only through tacit assumptions, suggestive reactions, loaded silences, a "Pentecost" of gestures, densely layered allusions, and, only very occasionally, an act—as when someone outright refuses the Con's plying with a sweeping blow (88). But even then, no lingering effects are known; we watch him recover himself and get away.

Yet these narrative evasions also have edifying implications, in that the book is largely about the movements of discourse, specifically the sense in which the authorial *place* of truth is distinct from what is true or not in a given matter at hand. Indeed, one lesson Melville teaches our moment is how the con game, like politics, depends on a severe reduction of language to its performative dimension, eliminating the descriptive and historical in favor of ever-brimming actualities. As a necessary consequence, discourse continually turns upon suppositions about the speaker's being. The audacity of the Con is that he assumes positions of authority purely by self-declaration—that is, he continually changes the place of meaning by presenting himself as its sovereign operator. These bravura performances cannot but affect the formal presentation of the novel, which takes its distinctive shape in response to the social urgencies that condition it: Melville's insouciant narration subtly teases out, with exquisite malice, the fragile state of democratic social bonds during the 1850s, a period of turbulent economic fluctuation and political volatility just ahead of the coming Civil War. Set on a Mississippi steamer ironically called the *Fidèle,* its passengers, who are always ready to talk about what they believe, both individually and *en masse* seldom prove faithful to a consistent idea. Instead, like the river below, the ship's decks are "ever overflowing with strange waters, but never with the same strange particles in every part" (8). Faith, it seems, comes from without rather than within, as stock traders, counterfeiters, charlatans, and clerics openly peddle their fetishes on the ship's promenades. The fluidifying and ultimately devaluating effects of capital on social representation are explicitly foregrounded here—beliefs, reduced to fungible signs of abstract value, "pass for whatever they may prove to be worth," as Melville titles one chapter (182).

In this flattening of representation into value, the exchanges that the Confidence Man barters all have a Pascalian implication. At stake in them is the essence of the *believing attitude*, reduced to a question of confidence in the operation that produces it. Belief collapses into the implication of its praxis; the Confidence Man wholeheartedly devotes himself to his technique as a means of producing the effects of faith in others. In a telling revelation, one of his dupes comes to realize that what motivates the Con, who scarcely manages to get more than a handful of dollars off his marks, is "more for the love than for the lucre" (130). Money is never more to him than a way of keeping score; what interests him are votes of confidence. After all, what is voting if not the materialization of faith in a gesture "freely" given by individuals through which the value of a representative is determined? This, at least, is what Melville would have us understand about the coimplication of democracy, Christianity, and capitalism—value is what can be counted on as presupposed within a series of exchanges based upon fiduciary esteem and good feeling. Whether by tallies, signatures, stock numbers, television ratings, crowd sizes, social media "likes" or declarations of piety, capitalist sociality reduces to valorization in the form of a countable accumulation of *confidences*.

There is, however, a surplus dimension to the Con's work that exceeds the goal of simply gathering assurances, which even more closely resembles the contemporary dictator. His greatest artistic challenge is to induce an attitude of faith in those who refuse to give it. This goes a step further than Pascal who, after all, only cares about fence-sitting agnostics and is content to have would-be believers adopt external forms without initially requiring inward passion. For the Con, on the contrary, ideological conviction must involve a sudden change in the energy and direction of faith, and most importantly, it must be the perceptible effect of the petitioner's presence that induces it; he must see the image of himself in the attitudinal change registered by those he affects. How this is accomplished is the essence of his calling card: the confidence trick.

The novel begins with such a demonstration, a pantomime of the effects on a group of strangers of a play of written signs. On the lower deck of the *Fidèle*, passengers gather excitedly round a bill declaring a reward for the capture of a "mysterious impostor," purportedly "an original genius in his profession" though the particulars of his art are not specified (3). While their eyes are "fixed on the capitals," the Con enters inconspicuously as a man in cream colors carrying a portable slate and quietly sets up his first act. Thus the Confidence Man is first publicized as he who cannot be known except as someone Other, someone who is singularly identifiable in not being himself and, in the midst of this undecidability, enters as sole authority on what he is.

Although in an obvious sense the Confidence Man is the epitome of grandiose egoism, it's interesting that Melville initially underscores his deliberate, even painstaking efforts of self-effacement—he comes aboard the ship almost unnoticed as a man who doesn't speak and is blandly dressed, without luggage, companions, or any hint of a past existence—a "stranger," thus, "in the extremest sense of the word" (3).[5] In introducing his master seducer this way, Melville suggests the opposite scenario of the emperor's new clothes is what works in democracy: when the sovereign wears his kingly raiment, we mockingly demand to see him stripped bare, so that only the most naked is presumptively the true ruler of men. And so the Con enters the novel without words, luggage, references, or a name, so that he is taken for what he passes for—a fool, a dreamer, a schemer, a devil, a god.

The one thing this *infans* passenger does furnish is a sign: brandishing his chalk slate before him, he writes and erases a series of phrases, each beginning with the word "Charity"—"Charity thinketh no evil"; "Charity suffereth long and is kind"; "Charity endureth all things"; "Charity believeth all things"; "Charity never faileth" (4–5). This one word "Charity," with its disappearing attributes, has a noticeable effect upon the crowd. Amused at first then gradually irritated, they respond to the mute with the ironic obverse of his message: they conduct themselves *uncharitably*, jeering and violently jostling him. Yet, rather than causing injury, the rebuke causes some passengers to sympathize with him, as he appears to them an innocent naïf, undeserving of hostility. Such a reaction, indeed, plays to his advantage, where the initial opposition not only supplies a contingent of supporters but prepares a future situation in which their latent sympathies have room to unfold. Later, in a different disguise, he encounters a "charitable lady" thoughtfully contemplating the message of the man in cream colors and applies himself to her guilt-laden sympathy to receive a generous donation to his Seminole Widow and Orphan Asylum fund (43–45). The Con's procedure thereby begins with a particular kind of inscription, an incipit and commandment whose ambiguous formality is not unlike a "presidential tweet" in that it is neither an official message nor an informal missive but something in between, which seems to issue from everywhere or nowhere. By reducing himself to the bearer of a commanding sign—a representative signifier—the Con latches on to the unconscious of the crowd of strangers and moves them suggestively in the direction he anticipates.

In another scene, the Con reverses the initial movement. Rather than eliciting the sympathy of his target, he instead effects repugnance. Dressed as a man in mourning clothes, the Con approaches a pensive young "collegian" absorbed in Tacitus. In a spasm of lachrymose sentiment, he pleads with the youth not to befoul his mind with such a heavy-hearted and bitter work lest it breed in him a despairing attitude through excessive sympathy (24–25, 27). Though the student is apparently unaware that the man-in-mourning is performing a savage caricature of his own solemnity, he is clearly unnerved by the strange encounter and the stranger's insistence that he throw away his book.

Repelled by the image of his double, the collegian now finds the characteristics and qualities represented by him distasteful. As a consequence, when the Confidence Man later reappears in the guise of a hard-nosed businessman, the collegian, recounting his earlier encounter, cynically mocks the man-in-mourning as a dreary sentimentalist and contrasts himself as an action-oriented realist (49). So when the hardy businessman casually mentions what sounds like an opportune investment in his company's stocks, the sophomore's eagerness to project entrepreneurial ambition leads him to sign for the swindler's spurious shares.

Through the Con's subterfuges, Melville makes readers aware of the narcissistic illusions that underpin claims to accurate judgment; but he also goes further than this, showing how the failure of knowledge opens onto the truth of fictitious enjoyment. The pleasures of speculating, equivocating wordplay, and other forms of idle talk that proliferate in the novel remind us that knowledge of the good and true is far from the primary motive for discourse. The Con's easygoing conviviality and genial discourse is therefore not to be underestimated: it is the portal through which the fantasies that dupe his marks are conjured. Such is what occurs when Pitch, a Missouri backwoodsman who prides himself on his shrewd powers of discernment, discovers as a consequence of getting tricked by the Con that he willingly, if unwittingly, played accomplice to the overthrow of his senses when he let himself speak freely.

Embittered from his failures as a plantation owner, Pitch is a confirmed misanthrope whose universal distrust is aptly characterized by his unnerving habit of punctuating his brusque statements with cracks from his double-barrel rifle. He is also a skilled debater who is perceptive enough to quickly spot flaws in argumentation, making him one of the Con's most formidable adversaries. His motto, "My name is Pitch. I stick to what I say" makes clear that unlike virtually every other character in the novel, he does not vacillate (117). Yet with Pitch, Melville fully tests the hypothesis that an intelligent "nonduped" can be deceived by the Con just as readily as a naive or idealistic person. The nonduped err not because they believe too readily but because they do not recognize the source of seduction in what lies closest to them.

Appearing as an agent of the Philosophical Intelligence Office, an organization whose "philosophical" mission is to train ideal servants, the Con offers to sell the misanthrope one of his best "good boys" to work on his plantation (114). Though Pitch ridicules the agent's enterprise and openly suspects him of being a cheat, he cannot resist the chance to expatiate on his favorite proof of the innate depravity of men: his experiences with a series of thirty-five "rascals" whom he had hired and fired on his Missouri farm. In each instance, the hired boy had been discovered doing things without his employer's permission, such as hoarding food, scavenging clothes or other items for personal use, or avoiding hard labor (116–18). Yet as he listens to the misanthrope's overloud griping, the PIO man detects a note of subdued longing. He drops a subtle suggestion that a boy's qualitative change into manhood is at first imperceptible, ripening in secret "like the ear of Indian corn." The erotic hint arouses Pitch's wish that he might meet a thirty-sixth boy "whose sickly, half-eaten sprouts" would one day "thrive into the stiff, stately spear of August," a clear double entendre (126). The plying of the PIO man works its charm, and the dreams of erotic domination of the would-be master take over, leading him to purchase "for the sake purely of a scientific experiment" a thirty-sixth boy who might finally be "the one" for him (128).

After the PIO man leaves him, Pitch realizes with mortification that despite having correctly surmised the falsity of the agent, he had nonetheless been made an "unphilosophical dupe" (129). How did he err? Not, he is convinced, through any failure of reason or fault of observation. Adopting his habitual stance as an enlightened philosopher, he tries to rationalize his lapsed awareness as a natural phenomenon. Surely it is part of "the mystery of human subjectivity in general" as revealed in the light of the teleological certainty of death. Just as a healthy person in the morning may "ere bedtime get under the weather, there is no telling how" and suddenly expire, so a man of reason "slow of assent, very wise and very slow, I assure you" may find himself "before night, like a trick in the atmosphere" subverted in his faculties (130). In Pitch's analogy, the precariousness of life mirrors the inexplicable fragility of consciousness, yet rather than reassure him, these explanations only leave him with even more abysmal uncertainty. They cannot tell him how the Con trespassed against his reason and knowledge, or "where was slipped in the entering wedge" (130).

It is only once he admits this ambiguity to himself that he half-realizes the "enemy" intruded not by way of his rational head but "on the castle's south side, its genial one," that is, at the level of his sex (130). Coming from someone who thinks of himself as the master of his own thought, this is a remarkable admission.

> He revolves the crafty process of sociable chat, by which, as he fancies, the man with the brass-plate wormed into him, and made such a fool of him as insensibly to persuade him to waive, in his exceptional case, that general law of distrust systematically applied to the race. He revolves, but cannot comprehend, the operation, still less the operator. [. . .] Before his mental vision the person of that threadbare Talleyrand, that impoverished Machiavelli, that seedy Rosicrucian—for something of all these he vaguely deems him—passes now in puzzled review. Fain, in his disfavor, would he make out a logical case. [. . .] Analogically, he couples the slanting cut of the equivocator's coat-tails with the sinister cast in his eye; he weighs slyboot's sleek speech in the light imparted by the oblique import of the smooth slope of his worn boot-heels; the insinuator's undulating flunkeyisms dovetail into those of the flunky beast that windeth his way on his belly. (130)

As he contemplates the scene of his humiliation ever more vividly, the stranger's "crafty process" of speech takes on a threateningly seductive hue. The operator's clever words "wormed into him," his "seedy" aspect fascinates and puzzles him, his sinuous equivocations and smooth palaver makes his obsequious tone seem serpentine and insinuating. The allusion to Satan here, oft-noted by critics,[6] should not be seen as a flat allegory but the fantasized product of these worming, winding fantasies that attract a man who fancies himself a master to one who acts like a servant, only to be overmastered by this seduction. The confidence trick here is precisely the maneuver whereby the sovereign fantasy reverses itself; the slave becomes the master through his power of erotic "seduction," an allure that Pitch associates with the "Machiavellian" power of the potentate. However fraudulent the Con's grift may have been, there was a grain of infernal truth in it. Pitch's fantasy of a suitable boy was only a cover for his desire to be overcome by a rascal, which is exactly what he played out in each prior iteration of the thirty-five. Each time, an erotic encounter that was missed resolved into the dissatisfaction that eventually led him to move on to the next one.

Freud famously likens the repetition compulsion to a "demonic" force, as if a form of possession takes hold of the subject's body, forcing it to reenact the dramaturgy of the fundamental fantasy (*SE* 18:34). Such a figuration is also not far from how Freud accounts for the continuing influence of the primal father in modern politics. Deleuze, in fact, reads Melville's *The Confidence-Man* in light of this possibility, which he associates with a quintessentially "American" dilemma, wondering if each of the passengers aboard the steamer might be "false brothers sent by a diabolical father to restore his power over overly credulous Americans?" But on the other hand, "The novel is so complex that one could just as easily say the opposite: this long procession [*théorie*] of con men would be a comic version of authentic brothers, such as overly suspicious Americans see them, or rather have already become incapable of seeing them." Whether the con men are demonic deceivers or deluded fools, whether the Americans who receive them are overly trusting or overly suspicious, the one thing for sure is that failure doesn't stop any of them from trying to manifest their myths: "Even in the midst of its failure, the American Revolution continues to send out its fragments, always making something take flight on the horizon, even sending itself to the moon, always trying to break through the wall, to take up the experiment once again" (89).

Whether from the side of the dupe or the side of the deceiver, each of the Con's routines seem to act out an encounter where more is at stake than just an artful theft. As Gary Lindberg aptly puts it, the Con is continually trying to "make belief" and to manifest something from nothing (7). We can begin to see how Melville presciently evokes a modern image of sovereignty that, unlike the classical master, does not rely on law, the legitimation of fact, or rational judgment but rather the direct transfiguration of subjectivity. Already in 1857, Melville was anticipating the mutation of the traditional paternal leader into the perverse agent of capitalist enjoyment, the incorrigible self-promoter who continually pretends to make something out of nothing. A new style of sovereign was emerging, a self-authorized leader who owed nothing to noble lineages or institutional hierarchies and whom the guardians of the latter could only view as an upstart pretender. In time, the ridiculousness of the confidence man, the patent absurdity that attached to this figure in Melville's time, would cease to be a disqualifying feature of power. This new master would retain his structural position as integral to the way enjoyment is collectively organized; but he would represent not so much society's success at managing its *Unbehagen* as the symptom of its perpetually recurring failures.

THE PRIMAL GRIFTER AND THE GRIEVING HORDE

In his seminar of 1969, Lacan had occasion to observe that the master's discourse was more "solidly established" than anyone realized (177). In several respects, the accumulation of capital has changed how we desire—it instituted a "society of permissiveness," which has flattened the field of social values and, correspondingly, installed a social imperative never to be satisfied. Against the force of these new systemic demands, the law's prohibitive restraint is no longer as strong as it used to be. It's not that the image of authority appears weaker or less forbidding, but its oppressiveness is based on an inducement to enjoy beyond a tolerable threshold for the sake of an illusory ultimate. The state of chronic dissatisfaction that results ensures that anything that society produces cannot have lasting power. Simply put, no commodity ever lives up to its "hype" but always leaves something to be desired, a void that cannot be filled.[7]

In consequence of this disjunction between the product of capital and the truth of the subject's dissatisfaction, the *impotency* of capitalism as a system that ensures desires are met becomes obvious. And yet, strangely, this doesn't put a stop to anything:

> What is striking, and what no one seems to see, is that from that moment on, by virtue of the fact that the clouds of impotence have been aired, the master signifier only appears even more unassailable, precisely in its impossibility. Where is it? How can it be named? How can it be located?– other than through its murderous effects, of course. Denounce imperialism? But how can this little mechanism be stopped? (178)

We cannot grasp the sweeping political import of this passage without distinguishing between the register of visibility, wherein the "clouds of impotence" are obvious, and what cannot be seen: the "impossibility" that grounds the master signifier. On the one hand, it's "striking" that something is not working in the social link of the master's discourse—malaise, paralytic outrage, impotency, and other morbid signs appear as endemic features. But what isn't obvious is that this dissatisfaction doesn't just express lack but actively creates something extra, a surplus enjoyment, that fuels the repetition of its discourse. The situation is hopeless not because things aren't working as they should but because we secretly require them *not to*. The very discontent that capitalist exploitation produces impels the subject to a repetition compulsion in hopes of attaining an impossible satisfaction. In the maddening cycle, this phantom keeps the subject engaged precisely where he feels most put out, a situation that remains perversely desirable inasmuch as it perpetuates the thought of its eventual transcendence.

Lacan thus gives visceral shape to what is essentially a ruse: the master's discourse functions only to mystify its own dysfunction, even when it cleverly makes use of its own dysfunction to do so. The appeal of a popular sovereign, then, has to do with his ability to cover over the brokenness of his system by declaring that the source of society's dissatisfaction can be located and redressed. If the leader is shown to be a fraud, this does not necessarily disqualify him, moreover, because his illegitimacy with respect to law reinforces the impression that he might be exceptional. He may even turn the tables and declare the law itself to be illegitimate, which, however contradictory, at least manages to name the source of discontent!

The question is, how can the law be maintained when the force of its prohibition has slackened? After all, it is not an easy thing to work around the law, especially when its effects are largely unconscious. To investigate this issue, we should first clarify how Lacan strategically revises Freud's myth of the primal horde; it is here that he attempts to theorize sovereignty and the origins of the law and, in the process, makes present a number of paradoxes. The point here is not just to rehearse certain theoretical differences between Lacan and Freud, or to show how Freud was "wrong" or inconsistent, but rather to see how Freud's insights into social organization go astray very precisely in accounting for the structural prestige of a "strong leader." Lacan's analysis, in other words, allows us to resituate a couple of persistent assumptions in political commentaries on authoritarian populism: namely, that what we've called the obscene enjoyment of the sovereign exercise is actually realizable, or that power "belongs" to anyone—sovereign, state, or people.

As Colette Soler points out, Lacan in his later teaching ultimately conceives castration independently of the father, seeing the former as the cause of desire rather than a threat connected to a paternal myth, as in *Totem and Taboo* or the Oedipus complex (145–46). As part of this shift, in Seminar XVII, Lacan criticizes the Oedipal stereotype of the father as a rival and forbidding figure, contrasting the very different view of fathers given even by Freud's own patients. Dora's father, for example, is an invalid, "strictly a castrated man," but has considerable importance for her psychical life because he is "made out of symbolic appreciation." (95) Whereas, in Freud's theory, castration is a punishment, for Lacan the father bears the mark of castration himself and passes it on to the subject he is structurally bound to. The father as agent of castration becomes little more than the operator of the social bond, an essentially "creative" intermediary that introduces a privileged signifier into the world of the subject's desire. A hint of this pure function of the master signifier is already in Freud, as when he argues in "The Economic Problem of Masochism" that in rare cases, the superego reveals itself as a categorical reason or impersonal necessity that has nothing to do with any paternal attribute (*SE* 19:167–68). But when he resorts to myth, Freud insists on the father as an essential obstacle to the subject, leaving aside the impossibility of the father's own relationship to enjoyment. *Totem and Taboo* most clearly exemplifies this evasion with a transhistorical alibi that Freud invents as a way of justifying his Oedipal version of the "strong" father (Verhaeghe, 36).

In *Totem and Taboo,* Freud attempts to theorize the origin of civilization by inventing the myth of a tyrannical father who rules over a primal horde composed of his sons and wives. This primal strongman has a "masterful character," possessing a special prestige that Freud attributes to his exclusive access to a pure enjoyment beyond law—he "keeps all the females for himself" and enjoys unrestricted use of their bodies (*SE* 18:124 and 13:141). By all other Freudian accounts, such unlimited enjoyment is impossible, a mirage of masculinist fantasy; but in the myth, the father is said to possess such exceptional capabilities, and the awe and envy of his horde is only matched by their dread of him. Only after the tyrant banishes his eldest sons is the spell of bondage finally broken, and they return to overthrow him. The lethal revolt of the horde is how Freud exemplifies the Oedipal wish at the heart of the tale—the father is construed as an obstacle who keeps enjoyment in reserve. In order to "acquire" enjoyment, the father must be removed.

Crucially, Freud attributes to the primal murder the significance of "castration"—after the sons kill the father, they become contrite and mourn him (*SE* 13:143). This makes castration synonymous with a sacrifice that involves the sense of expiation and exculpation. Yet the father in the story is never himself subject to it, nor does his murder imply that he is in fact rendered powerless or impotent. Everything in the story is designed, it seems, to conceal the fact that the father lacks, and it is ultimately because of this that even the tyrant's death does not diminish his power. On the contrary, the upshot of the primal myth is that an undivided, all-powerful male holds continuous power in both life and death. In his perpetuity, he prefigures the *aevum* of the sovereign's "body politic," as Ernst Kantorowicz construes it in *The King's Two Bodies* (84). Yet there is something marked in the implication that the father's death seals off any possible trace of his *frailty*. In other words, as Lacan observes, it's remarkable that Freud does not attribute to the death the kind of meaning it has in tragedy (Lacan 2007a, 117). Unlike Sophocles's Oedipus, who falls into destitution when he becomes aware of what he did not want to know he already knew, the sons of the primal horde know very well what they are about and afterward compulsively perform expiatory rituals that both ward off the recurrent trauma and reenact it (see Lacan 2007a, 114). After successive generations, these ritual reproductions lead to a revisionist account of the tyrant as a benevolent, loving God, while sacrifices are eventually done as if in a gratuitous spirit of honoring him (145–50).

History itself thus becomes little more than a memorial edifice to the primal father's death. Yet this event is paradoxical: before the introduction of the signifier into history, how can we say that there is such a thing as a "crime," a "murder," or even an "act" (125)? Lacan again underscores that the primal horde's transgression, like the primal father's enjoyment, is *impossible*, something that Freud can only make sense of in terms of a structure of indebtedness on the part of successive heirs (123). At a point where sense breaks down, we find a father who dies and is dismembered, yet his phallic significance (i.e., his symbolic potency) remains somehow operative even in death. Then, as if through sleight of hand, the progress of civilization makes his mortality into a guarantee of our collective indebtedness to an *immortal* tyrant.

What kind of death, or mode of thinking in relation to it, could be at stake here? For Lacan and Freud alike, the awareness of mortality is deceptively certain. Freud declares with a materialist insistence that the unconscious knows nothing of death because there is nothing in lived experience that we can be certain corresponds to it (*SE* 14:289). For Lacan, likewise, any supposed knowing of death only obscures the subject's fundamental dependency on the signifier, by substituting some metalinguistic "truth of truth" with regard to existence (Lacan 2007a, 122). There is, however, such a thing as an unconscious *thought* of death in Freud; it is what he calls the "death wish," the desire for the death of another. Often in Freud, the death wish is answered by the threat of castration, and this is one important reason why castration is for him a threat rather than the symbolic operation and structural fact it is for Lacan. We see this in the primal myth: the sons act on their death wish against the father. But notice that castration comes *in consequence* of the death wish and thereby engenders guilt. Castration has a punishing quality *because of* the thought of the Other's death, which suggests that death itself is the master insignia of the paternal function.

For Lacan, on the other hand, "death" is implied by the operation of castration but is not its ultimate meaning. The difference becomes clear when Lacan reconsiders Freud's remarks on mourning in "Mourning and Melancholia." In the burdensome guilt of melancholic mourning, Freud argues, the subject reverts onto himself his reproachful feelings toward the dead (*SE* 14:248). Lacan, however, finds this self-reproach of the melancholic mourner problematic, where the lost object is identified with on the basis of "a vengeance on the part of the griever" (2014, 111). In Lacan's view, this constitutes an aversion to the painful truth of loss. The remorse of mourning is about more than a redirected hostility felt toward the dead, but the felt effects of a devaluation "inasmuch as the object we are mourning was, without us knowing, the one that had become, the one that we had made, the support of our castration" (117). In mourning we encounter the father, the *real* father, as the agent of castration—the one who is both subject to it and who, tragically, cannot help but pass it on.

The fact that this element of tragedy is obscured in the interminable indebtedness that results from the consequences of the father's death in *Totem and Taboo* is thus very telling for the kind of structure that Freud sets out, even against himself, to elaborate. In Freud's repeated assertion that, retrospectively considered, the primal myth *must* have taken place at the origin of civilization, Lacan observes the insistence that is characteristic of the primary repressed (*Urverdrängt*), of "what has not had to be repressed because it has been repressed from the start." Unlike most instances of (secondary) repression or forgetting that can be inferred through slips of the tongue, bungled actions, jokes, and so on, this primary repressed is *irrepressible*, even locatable as both a "politically" and "structurally definable" fact (Lacan 2007a, 90). For this reason, the place of the "primary" or "primal" in Freud tends to mark a fantasy that commemorates the installation of an inaugural signifier, the means by which the subject is, right from the beginning, overcome by the Other's desire. In the relation between one signifier and another, a part of subjectivity is split off, without being fully represented in what follows. What is functionally determined in this sense is what it means that the subject is "castrated"—and it is this element of castration that Freud's primal myth refuses and that is obscured by the master signifier. As Kenneth Reinhard puts it, "The function of the obscene father of the Primal

Horde who claims all enjoyment as his alone [. . .] is thus both the agent of man's castration and exempt from its cut," with the consequence that "men submit to the conditions of the phallic signifier and accept the pittance of jouissance that it allows them only insofar as they posit a Great Father who enjoys in their stead" (153). In this way, the trace of the *urverdrängt* takes shape in a virtual enjoyment that lies beyond the reach of history and representation.

When the primary repressed signifier appears as an impossible object, an effect of "mastery" is produced. This is the rational kernel in Freud's mythic idea that the father keeps enjoyment in reserve—there is a *surplus enjoyment* that is produced *through the same operation in which a loss occurs* (93). Accordingly, the subject can get entrapped in a structure of bondage when authority is attributed to the *cause* of castration, as in the masochist's fantasy where "my father is beating me": the master enjoys *at my expense*. In the primal myth, the death of God thus turns Him into a loving sadist who torments His children with guilt for killing Him and encourages them to feel good about being punished. At the same moment that castration induces loss of enjoyment, a surplus enjoyment thus makes an appearance, and how this surplus becomes inscribed makes all the difference. When the sovereign manages to make himself appear as if *he* has induced this effect (or, what amounts to the same thing, if he appears as exempt from castration), he can create the illusion that he *is* the representative of the repressed, thus allowing for his positioning at the head of a structure of fantasy.

To better understand the "hook" or lure of this surplus enjoyment, we can compare it with an exemplary nonpsychoanalytic analysis of popular sovereignty. Friedrich Nietzsche outlines a similar alternation of dissatisfaction and surplus enjoyment in the way aristocratic *Gewaltmenschen* (violent men) made use of the desperate conditions of their supporters. As depicted in historical studies from Hesiod to Jacob Burckhardt, these demagogues "with cunning act out their comedy beneath a cloak of rough consistency" to an admiring throng that asks nothing so much of them but their performance of a sovereign enjoyment (108).

> However much utility and vanity [*die Eitelkeit*], those of individuals as of peoples, may play a part in grand politics: the strongest tide which carries them forward is the need for the feeling of power, which from

> time to time streams up out of inexhaustible wells not only in the souls of princes and the powerful but not least in the lower orders of the people. There comes again and again the hour when the masses are ready to stake their life, their goods, their conscience, their virtue so as to *acquire that higher enjoyment [um jenen ihren höchsten Genuß]* and as a victorious, capriciously tyrannical nation to rule over other nations (or to think it rules). Then the impulses to squander, sacrifice, hope, trust, to be overdaring and to fantasize spring up in such abundance that the ambitious or prudently calculating prince can let loose a way and cloak his crimes in the good conscience of his people. (110–111; my emphasis)

For all its crudeness, the prince's populist dramaturgy subsists upon a precise mechanism of identification. Unlike typical statist politicians, who portray themselves as technocratic mediators of law and symbolic norms, the *Gewaltmensch* speaks instead to a general condition of subjectivity, a "need for the feeling of power" that arises from a condition of lack and takes shape as a grand fantasy. Like his supporters, the populist prince courts this "higher enjoyment" and also, like them, he lacks it; this is the basis for their mutual identification, referred to obliquely as his "authentic" rapport with his base. Indeed, despite their vast and insuperable differences in social status, there is a strange intimacy implied here, whereby the sovereign's performance of his own enjoyment is made the basis for a spectacle of communal faith.

Yet, as Nietzsche hints, any acquisition of such a sovereign enjoyment is not just out of reach, but *unattainable*; even if the imperial objectives of the tyrant state are achieved, it only "think[s] it rules" over those it subjugates, when in reality their dreams of dominating have no direct relation to the subjectivity of the conquered. Before long, as his supporters realize he is no miracle worker, the spell is liable to fade, and the ruler's ineptitude ceases to be perceived as the charming prelude to his genius. But any danger of this happening is drowned out by the immense outpouring of faith, sacrifice, and fervent fantasizing on the part of the "lower orders of the people" whom the prince readily exploits. Indeed, here is where he makes good use of his "personal" rapport—the cunning of the prince (and this may be the one thing genuinely clever about him) is that he knows how to flick his matador's cape and "let loose a way" for the lethal fulfillment of untenable fantasies on the part of his people. Without this gesture, which lends sanction to their abandonment to enjoyment, his constituents would lose a vital support for their transgressive ambition and might even be forced to confront the bitter conditions of their deprivation, without alibi or escape.

Like a gambler whose speculative frenzy intensifies the more that he stakes on the big score, the imperialist horde puts everything on the line for the sake of an anticipated elevation that becomes more powerful and vivid the more they stand to lose (or have already invested). As in Freud's totemic horde, sacrifice has the function of denying loss its full weight or death its finality. Moreover, Nietzsche's example shows how authoritarian political theater makes "sacrifice" not an expiation but an investment in *speculative surplus*. The people who give up more and more for a chance at a higher enjoyment, Nietzsche implies, do not feel their losses as truly lost but as a necessary, even pleasurable, expenditure. The sacrifice made for the prince anesthetizes what Nietzsche calls the "need" that "streams up out of inexhaustible wells" through the belief that there will be an indeterminate gain in the speculative future. But the gain remains phantasmatic, unrealizable. At the heart of the impossible situation that structures the strongman's grand politics is a vain performance of confidence that elides the lack that the community grieves.

RALLIES

In Seminar XVII, Lacan identifies the superego with the kind of passion one finds among religious devotees in the afterlife and gamblers alike, where "one plays double or quits" with surplus jouissance. Recalling to his audience his formulation of Pascal's wager in the seminar on the object, Lacan points out that the "provisional life" that is staked in the wager has the value of an *object a*, the object-cause of desire. As such, it is only worth staking for a chance at eternal happiness if the one who guarantees this ultimate enjoyment "is not barred, in other words, if it is everything at once" (100). God in Pascal's wager—or, equivalently, fortune for the gambler—is imagined to be the guarantor of access to total enjoyment at the expense of the object of singular desire, which is repudiated and obscured.

This logic of doubling down as a denial of loss within a larger structure aimed at attaining a speculative surplus also occurs in a scene in chapter 4 of *The Confidence-Man*. Melville's titular Con, again disguised as the man-in-mourning, successfully appeals to a country merchant for a substantial sum in charity after telling the story of his (alleged) grief. In the scene, the reader is not directly privy to the details of the story but only learns about it from the effects it induces on the listener: "Judging from his auditor's expression, it seemed to be a tale of singular interest, involving calamities against which no integrity, no forethought, no energy, no genius, no piety, could guard" (26). Clearly impressed, the listener acts like a parody of Aristotle's auditor of an ideal tragic plot: "Even without the aid of the eye, he who hears the tale told will thrill with horror and melt to pity at what takes place" (*Poetics*,1453b). Except that the showing of the telling doesn't show what was told: Melville, rather, employs negation to give an impression of impressiveness. The negated predicates—integrity, forethought, energy, genius, piety—sound like empty superlatives when stated in the positive, but their cancellation slyly appends them to the speaker as if in modest disclamation of another's compliment. This incongruity between the hidden content of the sad tale and its vacuous presentation exemplifies the double sense of "vanity" featured throughout the novel: a futile and bitter situation is complemented, rather than contradicted, by an insistent self-regard.

In the attempt to turn misfortune into opportunity, the man-in-mourning sets up a scenario of playing *double or quits*. He mentions as a casual aside the recent incidence of a "spurious panic" created by "artful alarmists" on the stocks of the Black Rapids Coal Company, causing them to be momentarily devalued. Advising his benefactor to take advantage of the situation, he explains that the company wishes to sell the remaining shares discreetly at their depressed value: "For, the panic subsiding more and more every day, it will daily be seen how it originated; confidence will be more than restored; there will be a reaction; from the stock's descent its rise will be higher than from no fall, the holders trusting themselves to fear no second fate" (27). Once the truth of the market manipulation is discovered by the public, the stocks will go up again and even at a surplus value because of the confidence gained from surviving the feigned "fall." Here, again, the emphasis of this tale is on the value it yields for circulation, not its factual truth. Not only is the tale itself artfully contrived by the Con, but what it announces imparts the same. After all, as Sianne Ngai points out, even "spurious" emotions can trigger genuine calamities, and what lends the narrative its aura of believability is the regularly observable phenomenon of the stock market's reactivity to affective as well as economic factors (39). Such an episode therefore reminds us that a well-timed controversy, regardless of its initial truth, can induce an effect of affect that, in the end, makes something *seem* true after the fact in consequence of its premise being accepted "as if" true.

Such a retroactive truth-effect occurs in the case of the man-in-mourning's tale of woe, when the merchant retells the story back to the Con in disguise as the Black Rapids transfer agent. Hearing his own narrative returned to him, the Con is strangely dismissive of its import. Uncharacteristically, he advises the merchant not to put much confidence in the unfortunate man's tale: "Because, since the common occurrences of life could never, in the nature of things, steadily look one way and tell one story, as flags in the trade wind; hence, if the conviction of a Providence, for instance, were in any way made dependent upon such variabilities as everyday events, the degree of that conviction would, in thinking minds, be subject to fluctuations akin to those of the stock-exchange during a long and uncertain war" (84). In the pseudo-wisdom of the transfer agent, matters of life and death are like the ephemerality and unpredictability of the trade winds and stock markets which are misleading and unimportant insofar as they fall short of the larger scheme of Providence. Though understandable, the stock trader suggests, great passions like grief tend to diminish one's confidence and hence are harmful. What's striking about this ostensibly sanguine philosophy is that it denies loss its permanency and, in so doing, actually bars the prospect of bringing anything forth from grief. Hence despite his earlier attempt to wrest opportunity from tragedy, the persistence of the latter now appears as an insurmountable obstacle that the Con reveals he would rather strike out from reality altogether.

By now, the capitalist sounds as if he has reverted to some archaic prior form, a closeted Puritan fearful lest mournful contemplation devalue faith: "Indeed, whether in private or public, there was nothing which a good man was more bound to guard himself against than, on some topics, the emotional unreserve of his natural heart; for, that the natural heart, in certain points, was not what it might be, men had been authoritatively admonished" (86). This "unreserved heart" harbors what does not have value—grief, love, genuine feeling. Here we see the fragility as well as the "heart-felt" gravity of the novel's theme of confidence. The man in the cap even compares it to a Russian fort, the "Malakoff of confidence" (which, ironically, was conquered by the French during the Crimean War) (85). The warning having been issued, he pops open a bottle of champagne, proposing a toast "upon the playful plea that, whatever notions other than felicitous ones he might associate with the unfortunate man, a little champagne would readily bubble away" (86–87). But after only a few swigs, his companion gives sway to a sudden outburst from his unreserved heart:

> Ah, wine is good, and confidence is good; but can wine or confidence percolate down through all the stony strata of hard considerations . . . ? Truth will *not* be comforted. Led by dear charity, lured by sweet hope, fond fancy essays this feat; but in vain; mere dreams and ideals, they explode in your hand, leaving naught but scorching behind! (87)

The merchant, despite himself, gives voice to an ardent protest that loss cannot be so easily dismissed. With an inconsolable truth and "ideals" that "explode" all the matters at hand, Melville brings us before a different kind of surplus—one antithetical to profit. Something here insists, demanding to be thought, despite the vanity of the attempt or even the possibility of a violent outburst. Ashamed for his burst of unguarded enthusiasm, the merchant recovers himself and apologizes, making it utterly clear that the scene represented a momentary *lapsus,* that is, an opening of his unconscious. And what appeared in that interval was the hardest and most pitiless of truths, the antithesis of confidence in splenetic despair. In this utterance that escapes the unreserved heart, "confidence" is revealed to be the fragile and futile defense against an inconsolable real. What the merchant refuses is what the Confidence Man peddles, the self-valorization of the ego, deployed against the nihilism of an empty world, which is its mirror image and shadow.

Can grief and shame break through the shell of the authoritarian masquerade? At first, it would seem unlikely. While typical leaders avoid scandal for fear of eliciting shame, authoritarian populists such as Trump, Putin, or Modi seem to actively court notoriety, as if there were a secret benefit for their impudence. Yet this would be incomprehensible if the possibility of the mutual exposure of desire were not already at issue in the social organization of affects. In "Kant with Sade," Lacan characterizes shame [*pudeur*] as an "amboceptor" that induces the powerful feeling of a coincidence between one subject and another. This is why it's possible to feel embarrassed on another's behalf: "the one's immodesty by itself violating the other's modesty" (2007b, 651). But precisely this reaction to the conspicuous over-presence of the Other's enjoyment can foster the illusion that everything is already out in the open. This assumed transparency, especially where it concerns a leader's shameless behavior, is dangerous because it coarsens civic discourse and excises negativity from public view. The spectacle of shameless shams, in other words, diverts the subject's attention from the site of real deprivation. And that, of course, is a powerful seduction in its own right.

Yet if, by definition, the desire of a speaking being is addressed to an Other, then desire is constitutively a will-to-exposure. At the same time, there is never any guarantee that the presentation of a desire can be received by another's complementary desire. Such is the risk of shame: the failure of this meeting of desires can range from disappointing to catastrophic—one takes this risk when seeking to address oneself to another, thereby to disclose something of what one thinks or feels. Nonetheless, because shame depends upon desire's will-to-exposure, it does not always end in the abasement of the one who exposes himself, but it might lead to the articulation of a vulnerability that would strengthen communal bonds by opening them to their constitutive strangeness.

In the end, of course, *we* are the horde—and Melville both indicts and extols us as such. The possibility remains to us: What would it mean if we could admit our shame, like the merchant whose outburst let fly the truth of his grief? What if we opened ourselves to the unreserved heart wherein our suppressed grief might find outlet in a desire that, despite everything, holds up? That would amount to letting go the ghost of the dead master in favor of another truth, one that hews more closely to the loss we carry forward as a renewed desire. What if we could place our confidence in *that*?

J. Asher Godley is a lecturer in English at Dartmouth College. He has published in *Diacritics, Angelaki,* and coedited the volume *Inheritance in Psychoanalysis* (2018). He is currently completing the manuscript "Mass

Mourning: Powers of Loss and Community in Post-Civil War American Literature" and "In the Wake of the Plague: Eros and Mourning," a collection coedited with Klaus Mladek on the psychical impacts of COVID.

Notes

1. The author wishes to thank Kalliopi Nikolopoulou for her consultation on some of the Platonic passages.

2. Agamben mentions the passage on the Arcadian myth in his chapter on the propinquity of the etymology and cultural history of the "wolfman" to both the sovereign and the homo sacer. See 88–93.

3. All references to Freud are to *The Standard Edition of the Complete Psychological Works of Sigmund Freud* and are marked *SE* with volume followed by page numbers.

4. On this element of compulsive myth-making, compare Helene Deutsch's classic psychoanalytic study of the "impostor": "I believe that all impostors have this in common: they assume the identities of other men not because they themselves lack the ability for achievement, but because they have to hide under a strange name to materialize a more or less reality-adapted fantasy. It seems to me that the ego of the impostor, as expressed in his own true name, is devaluated, guilt-laden. Hence he must usurp the name of an individual who fulfils the requirements of his own magnificent ego ideal" (497).

5. For another reading of this scene that also draws on theories of popular sovereignty, see Greiman, 192–222.

6. See, for example, Foster, Parker, and Schroeder.

7. In this description, I am drawing on the work of, especially, McGowan 6, 11–18, 19–50; Tomsic 13–78; Kordela, 43–46, 163–65, and Vanheule.

Works Cited

Agamben, Giorgio. 2017. *Homo Sacer: Sovereign Power and Bare Life*. Translated by Daniel Heller-Roazen. *The Omnibus Homo Sacer*. Stanford: Stanford University Press.

Aristotle. 1903. *The Poetics of Aristotle*. Translated by S. H. Butcher, 3rd ed. New York: Macmillan.

Deleuze, Gilles. 1998. "Bartleby; or, the Formula." *Essays Critical and Clinical*. Translated by Daniel W. Smith and Michael A. Greco. London: Verso.

Deutsch, Helene. 1955. "The Impostor: Contribution to Ego Psychology of a Type of Psychopath." *Psychoanalytic Quarterly* 24:483–505.

Foster, Elizabeth. 1954. Preface to *The Confidence-Man: His Masquerade*. Vineland, NJ: Hendricks House.

Freud, Sigmund. 1900. *The Interpretation of Dreams. The Standard Edition of the Complete Psychological Works of Sigmund Freud.* Vol. 5. Translated by James Strachey. London: Hogarth.

———. 1913. *Totem and Taboo. The Standard Edition of the Complete Psychological Works of Sigmund Freud.* Vol. 13. Translated by James Strachey. London: Hogarth.

———. 1918. "Mourning and Melancholia." *The Standard Edition of the Complete Psychological Works of Sigmund Freud.* Vol. 14. Translated by James Strachey. London: Hogarth.

———. 1921. *Group Psychology and the Analysis of the Ego. The Standard Edition of the Complete Psychological Works of Sigmund Freud.* Vol. 18. Translated by James Strachey. London: Hogarth.

———. 1924. "The Economic Problem of Masochism." *The Standard Edition of the Complete Psychological Works of Sigmund Freud.* Vol. 19. Translated by James Strachey. London: Hogarth.

———.1937. "Analysis Terminable and Interminable." *The Standard Edition of the Complete Psychological Works of Sigmund Freud.* Vol. 23. Translated by James Strachey. London: Hogarth.

Gherovici, Patricia. 2007. "Freud's Dream of America." In *Dreams of Interpretation: A Century Down the Royal Road.* Minneapolis: University of Minnesota Press.

Greiman, Jennifer. 2010. *Democracy's Spectacle: Sovereignty and Public Life in Antebellum American Writing.* New York: Fordham University Press.

Kantorowicz, Ernst H. 1985. *The King's Two Bodies: A Study in Medieval Political Theology.* Princeton: Princeton University Press, 1985.

Kordela, A. Kiarina. 2018. *Epistemontology in Spinoza-Marx-Freud-Lacan: The (Bio) Power of Structure.* London: Routledge.

Lacan, Jacques. 1981. *The Seminar of Jacques Lacan, Book XI: The Four Fundamental Concepts of Psychoanalysis.* Translated by Alan Sheridan. New York: W.W. Norton and Co.

———. 2007a. *The Seminar of Jacques Lacan, Book XVII: The Other Side of Psychoanalysis, 1969– 1970.* Translated by Russell Grigg. New York: W.W. Norton.

———. 2007b. "Kant with Sade." *Écrits: The First Complete Edition in English.* Translated by Bruce Fink. New York: W.W. Norton.

———. 2014. *The Seminar of Jacques Lacan, Book X: Anxiety.* Translated by A. R. Price. London: Polity.

———. "The Seminar of Jacques Lacan, Book XIII: The Object of Psychoanalysis, 1965–1966." Unpublished typescript. Translated by Cormac Gallagher.

———. "The Seminar of Jacques Lacan, Book XXI: Les Non-Dupes Errent, 1973–1974." Unpublished typescript. Translated by Cormac Gallagher.

Lindberg, Gary. 1982. *The Confidence Man in American Literature.* New York: Oxford University Press.

McGowan, Todd. 2016. *Capitalism and Desire: The Psychic Cost of Free Markets.* New York: Columbia University Press.

Melville, Herman. 1984. *The Confidence-Man: His Masquerade. 1857.* Chicago: Northwestern University Press and the Newberry Library.

Miller, Jacques-Alain. 2006. "On Shame." *Jacques Lacan and the Other Side of Psychoanalysis*. Durham, NC: Duke University Press.

Ngai, Sianne. 2005. *Ugly Feelings*. Cambridge, MA: Harvard University Press.

Nietzsche, Friedrich. 1997. *Daybreak: Thoughts on the Prejudices of Morality*. Translated by R. J. Hollingdale. Cambridge: Cambridge University Press.

Parker, Hershel. 1971. Foreword to *The Confidence-Man: His Masquerade*. New York: W. W. Norton.

Plato. 1968. *The Republic of Plato*. Translated by Allan Bloom. New York: Basic Books.

Reinhard, Kenneth. 2015. "There is Something of One (God): Lacan and Political Theology." *Political Theology* 11:1.

Ruehl, Martin A. 2013. *The Italian Renaissance in the German Historical Imagination, 1860–1930*. Cambridge: Cambridge University Press.

Shroeder, John W. 1951. "Sources and Symbols for Melville's Confidence Man." *PMLA*. 66: 364–380.

Soler, Colette. 2014. *Lacan: The Unconscious Reinvented*. London: Karnac.

Tomsic, Samo. 2015. *The Capitalist Unconscious: Marx and Lacan*. London: Verso.

Vanheule, Stijn. 2016. "Capitalist Discourse, Subjectivity and Lacanian Psychoanalysis." *Frontiers in Psychology* 7:1948.

Verhaeghe, Paul. 2006. "Enjoyment and Impossibility: Lacan's Revision of the Oedipus Complex." *Jacques Lacan and the Other Side of Psychoanalysis*. Durham: Duke University Press.

LITERATURE NOW AND DEMOCRACY TO COME

JACQUES DERRIDA, BEN LERNER, AND *LEAVING THE ATOCHA STATION*

David Coughlan

In Ben Lerner's *Leaving the Atocha Station* (2011), Adam Gordon is a young American poet on a writing fellowship in Spain, based in Madrid from 2003 to 2004. He is there to research "the significance of the Spanish Civil War . . . for a generation of writers" in order to produce "a long, research-driven poem exploring the war's literary legacy" (2013, 23). But he is also an American abroad during the Iraq War, and he will bear witness to some of the fallout from that war in the form of the Madrid train bombings, which took place on March 11, 2004, and included three explosions at Atocha station. In total, ten bombs went off on four commuter trains between 07:37 and 07:39 that morning, killing 191 people and wounding over 1,800 more in the deadliest terrorist attack in Spain to date. The timing of the attacks was significant. They took place just three days before the country's general elections, with the governing People's Party (Partido Popular or PP), led by José María Aznar, and the Spanish Socialist Workers' Party (Partido Socialista Obrero Español or PSOE), led by José Luis Rodríguez Zapatero, vying for power. Keenly aware that these events would play a large part in determining the outcome of the election, "immediately after the bombing, leaders of the PP claimed evidence indicated that the Basque separatist organization ETA was responsible for the bombings" ("Controversies"). In Lerner's novel, Adam's friend Arturo explains, "If ETA were responsible, the Socialists, who were seen as weak on the separatists, would get destroyed. If it were Al Qaeda or other Islamic terrorists, the right-wing Aznar and his handpicked successor, Rajoy, were doomed: they had supported Bush's war" (120–21). In fact, not only had the Spanish government supported the Iraq War, they had done so against the people's wishes. Unsurprisingly, therefore,

> from the moment of the attacks, the PP argued that they were the work of the Basque separatist group ETA. Mr Aznar phoned newspaper editors, assuring them this was the case. Despite evidence soon emerging of a van containing detonators linked to the attacks and a recording of verses from the Qur'an, the PP stuck to its line. (Hamilos and Tran)

The government's reluctance to countenance the interpretation of events, later supported at the 2007 trial, that the attacks were carried out by an Al Qaeda–inspired terrorist cell provoked public outrage. Protests on March 12 against the bombings were followed the next day by nationwide protests against the government's response to the bombings, demanding that the government tell the truth about the attacks and not misrepresent them for political efficacy; as Adam's friend Teresa states, "The PP was blaming ETA when it knew it wasn't responsible. People are furious. . . . It's history in the making" (Lerner 2013, 129). The PSOE would go on to win the general election on March 14, 2004.

All of the above may make it seem that *Leaving the Atocha Station* is about the Iraq War or about the place of Americans or of American policy abroad, but the novel resists such conclusions: after all, Adam repeatedly says of his own art "that poems aren't *about* anything" (Lerner 2013, 36). The novel's interest in what poetry is or is not about is evident even in the title, which it shares with a poem by John Ashbery from his 1962 collection *The Tennis Court Oath.* In an important article on Lerner's work, Daniel Katz comments on the peculiarity of this mirroring, which means that "on the one hand, . . . a single title now announces two different works" (320) and "on the other hand, the title can be read another way: not as doubling Ashbery's title but as referring to it," effectively quoting the poem's title as if to indicate that the novel is "very much 'about' John Ashbery" (321). To say that the novel is about Ashbery, however, is to say that it is about the "about" because, as Katz shows, "it is Ashbery himself who most forcefully opens the way to a literature which does something other than refer to things, to be 'about' them" (320). In his choice of title, therefore, Lerner both refers to the Atocha station bombings and, via Ashbery, parts with that context to consider the question of a text's relation to any immediate context, leading Katz to conclude that "the book is 'about' nothing so much as the relationship between the artistic or literary on the one hand and the political or historical on the other" (320).[1]

If, as Katz argues, the novel deflates grand claims for the effectiveness of literature's direct political engagement, this aligns it with Ashbery's apparent thinking on poetry and politics also. In a review article on Ashbery's *Collected Poems, 1956–1987*, Lerner notes:

> Ashbery wrote about Frank O'Hara's poems in 1966, "[U]nlike the 'message' of committed poetry . . . it incites one to all the programs of commitment as well as to every other form of self-realization. . . ." When Louis Simpson took issue with these remarks, Ashbery responded with unusual directness: "All poetry is against war and in favor of life, or else it isn't poetry, and it stops being poetry when it is forced into the mold of a particular program. Poetry is poetry. Poetry is protest. I believe in both forms of action." (2010, 209n18)

For Ashbery, as for Adam and, it would appear, Lerner, poems and novels are not about anything in the sense that they are not reducible to a message or to the delivery of an identifiable program. But what does it mean to say that poetry is protest? And can literature that is not about anything be in any sense political? To consider the relationship between the literary and the political or, more accurately, the democratic, this essay places the concept of a literature that is not about any one thing but must still mean something in the context of a concept of democracy that, by definition and paradoxically, can mean anything to anyone but must still mean the same thing to all people. Engaging with Jacques Derrida's work on democracy to come, especially as set out in "Perhaps or Maybe" (1997) and *Rogues* (2003 [2005]), the essay shows how an experience of literature that is about the "about" is an experience of deciding the meaning of what is happening here and now, mirroring an experience of democratic politics.

"POEMS AREN'T ABOUT ANYTHING"

The relation between the literary and the historical includes the links between Adam and his author. Lerner authored three poetry collections, *The Lichtenberg Figures* (2004), *Angle of Yaw* (2006), and *Mean Free Path* (2010) before *Leaving the Atocha Station* and *10:04,* his second novel, published in 2014. In 2016, *No Art: Poems* republished the three volumes of poetry together with some new verse, and a third novel, *The Topeka School,* came out in 2019. Both Adam and Lerner are from

Topeka, Kansas; Lerner wrote *Angle of Yaw* while on a Fulbright Scholarship in Madrid; one of the sonnets from *The Lichtenberg Figures* is reproduced in the novel and ascribed to Adam (Lerner 2013, 127–28); and Adam's reading of Ashbery's poetry repeats material from Lerner's review article (90–91). Indeed, Lerner happily describes Adam as "a neurotic version of my already quite neurotic self" (Witt) so that, as Katz outlines, "the novels pointedly blur the lines between autobiography or memoir on the one hand and fiction on the other" (316).

But Adam is also a lying mess, a self-declared fraud, and something of a rogue. He tells women that his still-living mother has died, describes his gentle father as a fascist, and paints himself as the protagonist in others' stories. He is, as Gayle Rogers puts it, "a character who steals others' experiences and language and relates them as if they were his own" (220). For Katz, this is key because, in *Leaving the Atocha Station*, "the question of 'fraudulence' stands in for an extended consideration of the possibility of any form of authenticity whatsoever: artistic, but also social, amical, erotic, personal, and of 'experience'" (319). Personal and artistic authenticity are explicitly linked by Adam in a moment of self-reflection occurring late in the novel:

> But my research had taught me that the tissue of contradictions that was my personality was itself, at best, a poem, where "poem" is understood as referring to a failure of language to be equal to the possibilities it figures; only then could my fraudulence be a project and not merely a pathology. (Lerner 2013, 164)

Adam here attempts to come to terms with his fraudulence by considering it in the context of a specific understanding of poetry that is developed throughout the novel. This understanding is first outlined during a poetry event early on, as Adam waits to perform his own poems while a Spanish poet, Tomás, reads. Tomás is an award-winning poet whose work, so it appears, grants Arturo "a profound experience of art" (37). For Adam, however, Tomás is effectively a fraud, both in terms of his person and his art. Adam can hardly take seriously this mannered poet who presents only "a caricature of El Poeta" (37), or an exaggerated imitation of a true Poet, and whose clichéd work falls so tragically short of what poetry might be. Rather than being affected by the power of the poems themselves, Adam is affected by the loss inscribed in their failure, "as the more abysmal the experience of the actual the greater the implied heights of the virtual" (38).[2] Tomás's actual, written poems, therefore, are not actually proper poetry. In fact, for Adam, as for Lerner, there is actually no poetry. There never has been poetry as such, and poetry instead remains as something virtual, as an unrealized possibility: the poetry event is still to come. In that sense, despite his elements of caricature, Tomás can be understood as a representative figure also because no actual poem faithfully represents the desired "'virtual poem'—what we might call poetry with a capital 'P'" (14), as Lerner puts it in *The Hatred of Poetry* (2016). We hate poetry, he claims, because we recognize that our poets are just imitations of Poets and that a "poem is always a record of failure" (13), less a Poem and more something deserving of the scare-quoted word "poem," as in the quotation with which this paragraph started.

Lerner takes this distinction between the actual and virtual poem from Allen Grossman (with whom Adam Gordon shares his initials), for whom the virtual is authentic, ideal, imaginary, infinite, unintelligible, and impossible, as opposed to actual "artworks that are merely real, finished, final" (Rogers, 226). For both Grossman and Lerner, therefore, the virtual has to be the aim of the Poet. In Lerner's words, "Great poets confront the limits of actual poems, tactically defeat or at least suspend that actuality" (2016a, 100); they "defer actuality [as] a way of refusing closure," thereby "keeping the poem in touch with the virtual" (Rogers, 226). In Grossman's words, the great poet's difficult "poems do not anticipate 'completion' [and] are devised to postpone semantic closure" (877n10) in "an act of deferral" (843), which expresses "a radical fidelity to poetry's ends" (874). Where Lerner and Grossman appear to differ, however, is in their understanding of what the virtual means for the poet. As with Ashbery, the aim for both is to avoid reducing the poem to a finite meaning or to avoid having the poem be about something or refer to only one thing. For Grossman's poet, this must mean that "the imaginary poem . . . constructs only its own source" (865) and "the imaginary poem is the voice of the authenticity of language rather than its reference, the signless or silent voice of the thing signified" (864); whereas the actual poem can speak only of specific things, the virtual poem, in the undifferentiated silence of its origin, tells of anything and everything, altogether, at once, in "an unbroken unity" (851). The imaginary poem means "a totality of existence [in which] all relationships are condensed into one relationship, all words into one word, all moments into one moment" (862), so there is "only one moment—the present" (851). The virtual poem would mean full presence in an infinite present. But what Grossman's poet inevitably encounters is the "paradoxicality of the unqualified relationship he desired—a relationship which draws into itself, vertically, the totality of experience, admitting no secondary subject, no space of digression, no alterity" (862). The one word that says everything cannot say anything else: "The vortex has no outside" (862). Lerner's poet, by contrast, opens a space for something else to appear. "Poetry," says Lerner in discussing Adam's position, "allows us to negatively figure something beyond what passes for the real, to imagine its outside" (Rogers, 231), which seems also to invite the outside in but without then closing the door on it and sealing all inside. The poem that is not about any one thing can always be about some other thing; it is as if, at the same time, it were about less than one thing and more than one thing, as if it were always already about some other relationship, some other word, moment, experience, subject, voice, or self. Ultimately, says Lerner, "the virtual starts to stand for alterity more generally" (231). Whereas for Grossman's poet, therefore, the virtual poem would mean a final return to the source, for Lerner's poet the virtual poem accounts for that which arrives from elsewhere.[3]

In the novel, the return to the source is figured as the return home. The primary issue preoccupying Adam toward the end of Lerner's novel is whether or not he should leave Madrid and return home to the States. But the novel suspends and postpones his actual decision, refusing to identify where he ends up, as if there would be no final decision. For Katz, this is an impossible position to maintain because, he argues, the decision would have to be made in reality, and Adam would find himself living in either Madrid or America: "But every room, inevitably, is somewhere" (324). This reality, in turn, impacts all other aspects of the virtual in the novel; Katz concludes, "For a poetics—and possibly even ethics—of deferral and virtuality is itself only virtual, and always denied and negated by the actuality of the room in which one sits and writes" (324). The suspended realm, therefore, the realm of the virtual, is ultimately another lie because action, and especially the act of writing, can only occur in some actual here and now.

What this essay argues, however, is that Lerner's novel is prepared to meet Katz's challenge. The key lies in Lerner's understanding of the virtual as that which lets the other in, an understanding that does not reframe only the virtual but the actual as well: nothing can be simply or "only virtual" or "merely real" (and in his use of the word "negation," Katz also implies that it is impossible to conceive of the virtual without the actual). This makes it difficult to draw a clear line of division between the virtual and actual or even to draw a line between the room and its outside: "Alone on the porch, . . . I began to imagine my apartment in Madrid. . . . Then my other rooms. . . . And then it was Rufina's porch again, but imagined from a future room surrounded by a future dark, a room where I was writing, maybe this" (Lerner 2013, 56). It is as if every room were somewhere and some other where and as if the one who sits and writes in the room were some other one, someone more and less than one self, never truly oneself, never true to oneself, as if the self were a lie.[4] In fact, when Adam describes himself as a "poem," he recognizes that his actual self is a failed version of who he might possibly be, that he isn't actually his true self, that he is inauthentic, a fraud. But really there is no other way for Adam to be. Just as "Poetry isn't hard, it's impossible," he cannot possibly be his proper self anyway (Lerner 2016a, 14). "When are you going to stop pretending that you're only pretending to be a poet?" asks Teresa, and Adam wonders if he might indeed be "a real poet, whatever that meant" (Lerner 2013, 168), which might mean that he stops pretending that he is playing at being a poet and admits that he actually is a poet, or which might mean that he is a "poet," which would mean that he doesn't have to pretend to be a fraud because he is a fraud, truly a fraud. "Maybe only my fraudulence was fraudulent," he thinks (168), which might mean that he was only pretending to be a fake, or which might mean that being a fake is the only authentic position, and he can be only what he is pretending to be, be what he actually is not.

"POETRY MAKES NOTHING HAPPEN"

This key question of an authentic or fraudulent experience relates, in turn, back to the Atocha station bombings that the novel is about while not being about. As Rogers describes, the Madrid bombings are "an event that [Adam] wants to 'feel,' to experience as presence, but only absorbs secondhand through newspapers, others' responses, and afterimages. The major event of *Leaving the Atocha Station* becomes a nonevent" (220), rather as the title itself does when it announces the novel's arrival even as it defers to Ashbery's preexisting poem. The division between the event and the nonevent is another example of the relations in the novel that give rise to Katz's repeated use of the construction "on the one hand / on the other hand": on the one hand, the novel's title does this, and on the other hand, it does that; on the one hand, return to the States, or on the other hand, never return; autobiography on the one hand and fiction on the other; politics and history on the one hand and art on the other; or, even, Islamic terrorists on the one hand and ETA on the other. In fact, in the course of this analysis, a series of such (perhaps not unexpected) binary relations has emerged, with the terms on each hand, while not identical to each other, occupying an equivalent position in their respective oppositional pairing: on the one hand, virtual, open, original, voice, presence, life, event; on the other hand, actual, closed, imitation, sign, absence, deathly or deadly, nonevent. It is not insignificant, therefore, that Rogers observes that Adam experiences the event of the Madrid bombings only secondhand because this draws attention to the ways in which the novel, by questioning whether a firsthand experience—a direct, immediate, original experience—is ever possible, instead suggests that an experience can never absolutely be on the one hand or on the other hand, of the one or of the other, but rather remains between the two.

Rogers continues, "The major event of *Leaving the Atocha Station* becomes a nonevent; most of the novel takes place when nothing happens" (220). And a lot of nothing happens in this novel: Adam takes drugs; hangs out in parks; goes to galleries; dates first Isabel and then Teresa; drinks; fails to read, write or to answer emails; and so on. Nothing especially happens during a particularly rainy December in Madrid, when Adam's "research fell, [his] research was falling, into two equally unrepresentable categories" (Lerner 2013, 63), on the one hand and on the other. In *The Hatred of Poetry*, Lerner provides a figure for that which, like Adam's research, does not fall but is falling: the virgule or " / " that marks a line break in quoted verse. This he links to

> the meteorological phenomenon known as "virga," my favorite kind of weather: streaks of water or ice particles trailing from a cloud that evaporate before they reach the ground. It's a rainfall that never quite closes the gap between heaven and earth, between the dream and fire; it's a mark for verse that is not yet, or no longer, or not merely actual; they are phenomena whose failure to become or remain fully real allows them to figure something beyond the phenomenal. (99–100)[5]

In this rainy image, Lerner distinguishes his concept from Crane's waterspout or vortex that "is the momentary suspension of language in the human world before its descent (return) into the fundamental fluidity" (862) because his is a rain that is falling but does not finally fall into the source. Therefore, when Lerner writes that "the Spaniards seemed to suspend all nonessential activity" that December (2013, 63), or suspend all but the essential matters of life and death, then it is as if all that lies *between* the life / death (event / nonevent, virtual / actual) opposition remains suspended with the drizzling rain in (and as) this human world.

Moreover, the virga also reflects on the "moment" of suspension, a moment that is "not yet, or no longer," so that the "the poem is not yet present and will never be," as Grossman puts it (850). Lerner's language here, however, does not just recall Grossman's but also Derrida's:

> The present is what passes . . . *between* what *goes* and what *comes,* in the middle of what leaves and what arrives, at the articulation between what absents itself and what presents itself, . . . distributed in the two directions of absence, at the articulation of what is no longer and what is not yet. (1994, 25)

Like the rain that is falling but will never have fallen, the present is presencing but will never have been present. This understanding of time has near-fatal consequences for both Grossman's virtuality and Katz's actuality: because language remains suspended in its prolonged moment, then the "timeless presentness" (Grossman, 852) of the virtual poem cannot be, and "the ideal Poem we cannot write in time" remains absent (Lerner 2016a, 51); and because the present will never actually have been present, then the actual itself will never have been fully present either, with every here and now bearing the trace of what is no longer and not yet here and no longer and not yet now. The here and now in Lerner's novel are always already not here and not now and another here and another now; in other words, like the poet who is not a Poet, the actual here and now are not actually here and now, and this is necessarily so: just as the virtual Poem would have no outside but would condense all moments into one, so an actual Here and Now would have no outside beyond this one, solitary moment and there would never again be another here or now.

Like the virga, the rain that does not finally fall, the present fails to become or remain fully real, which means that all the "present" holds, all the rooms and all the writers, also fails to be fully real. So, if Adam's "research was falling, into two equally unrepresentable categories" (Lerner 2013, 63), the novel also wonders "if this division of experience . . . just *was* experience, for all people for all time" (65), so that experience itself is nothing other than the unreal experience of being impossibly divided between a one and an other that are forever out of reach. For Lerner, the important thing is that poetry preserves and makes manifest this impossible experience of living. Late in the novel, Adam declares, "Poetry makes nothing happen" (143).[6] He seems to be admitting that poetry is not the cause of anything, that the event of the poetic word is a nonevent, and that the advent of the word heralds nothing; at the same time, however, he is claiming that poetry *does* make nothing *happen,* that poetry *is* nothing *happening,* that poetry is the event of the nonevent, is actually inactual, is really unreal, is the presencing of what is not present, *is* not here and not now. In this way, poetry is the experience of mediating or falling between an unrepresentable category on the one hand and an unrepresentable category on the other hand, which is to say that poetry is the experience of experience.

A clear instance, engaging with the question of an authentic experience, with the unrepresentable, with the present moment, and with the event and the nonevent, plays out in an exchange that closes Adam's account of the "uneventful third phase" (Lerner 2013, 64) of his project. Adam is instant messaging with his friend Cyrus in Mexico, who is based on Lerner's friend, the writer Cyrus Console. Cyrus's girlfriend, Jane, wants them to go for a swim in a river, but he is concerned about the strength of the current. He is not alone. A girl stands on the opposite bank, reluctant to join her boyfriend in the water, but seeing Cyrus get in at last, and encouraged by the group, she jumps in too, only to be swept to her death. Throughout, this incident is framed in the context of "new experiences" (69) or "experience, not just the experience of experience" (68), but as Adam has found, these life and death events are unrepresentable as such: the "reality of death" becomes "an embarrassing cliché" or "some good material for [Jane's] novel" (77), and "a 'real' experience" (77) or a secondhand experience is, like a "poem," the only experience possible in time. Indeed, as Cyrus tells of the events, it is hard not to read the river (like the rain and the waterspout) as a figure for time, which bears us all toward death; in Console's own poetry, he writes, "*And time passed in streams, and while he could he watched objects borne along*" (qtd. in Rogers, 229). But the river does not just flow on undisturbed and steady but has strong currents, rapids, stones, a dam, and placid pools. And equally telling is the form that Adam and Cyrus's conversation takes. The instant message, which of course should be immediately present, is instead marked by delays, repetitions, and interruptions:

> ME: you there? what's up in xalapa
> CYRUS: Yeah. Went on a kind of trip this weekend. Planned to camp
> ME: I was going camping here for a while
> ME: hello?
> CYRUS: I remember. . . . Well we were walking
> ME: still there?
> CYRUS: along a river and
> CYRUS: I'm still here, yes. Jane wanted to swim, but I was a little worried about the current. (Lerner 2013, 68–69)[7]

The disorder of the instant messaging reflects Lerner's understanding of a present moment that is itself disjointed and never simply itself. And it is exactly the fact that nothing present is ever simply itself that means it can live on. For Lerner, what happens is not locked in a room, like a tomb, of one here and one now but remains in time and lives again for someone somewhere and somewhen else. Something survives and is transmitted between the opposing banks of the river, between Cyrus and the girl: he gives her "mouth to mouth" (73), there "was vomit in her mouth" (74), and that "taste is back" (77); Cyrus says, "I accidentally clicked my teeth against her teeth" (74), and continues, "And my teeth were chattering and each time they clicked I remembered her" (76). And of course, this is the story that Adam steals and presents as his own: "'When I am near a river,' I heard myself say, 'I think of my time in Mexico'" (95).

"LITERATURE NOW"

The centrality of time to the novel is especially evident in the novel's concluding set piece, a post–March 11 panel involving writers and critics that Adam is invited to participate in and that is "about 'literature now'" (Lerner 2013, 161). Adam is reluctant to take part because, as he says, "I have nothing to say. Because I don't speak good Spanish. Because literature isn't politics" (167), but his failure to decline the invitation in time means he ends up taking part, nonetheless. To address the first and second of his concerns, he decides to learn by heart some lines that he can be relatively sure he will be able to reproduce on demand. When asked to make some opening remarks, he concludes them by repeating, "I hope to hear from others what changed on March 11 that permits we [*sic*] to speak . . . of a new *now*, of a new period, without dislocation" (174). Adam remains to be convinced that a now without dislocation is possible, with his doubts also informing the nature of his preparation for the panel: "I might be able to produce several grammatically perfect sentences on the cuff, or is it off, but I might not; better to mimic spontaneous if oblique pronouncements than to rely on real-time fluency" (171).[8] "Real-time fluency" would presumably have Adam think and speak in the here and now, extemporaneously, something he's not prepared to do in his second language.[9] Therefore, he prepares himself to do it, preparing his "now" in advance. He is aiming for mimicked spontaneity, which is to say a rehearsed spontaneity or a practiced nowness. His "new *now*" is to be an old now, secondhand. "Literature now" is "literature that will have been."

In his preparation, Adam seems to contrast with the way in which Derrida approached a 1996 interview with Alexander Garcia Düttmann in London. In answer to Düttmann's opening question, Derrida begins by saying:

> Perhaps the choice of title for this event, *Perhaps or Maybe*, perhaps or maybe this choice had to do with this situation, that is, the necessity for me to address such an audience in English, improvising without knowing in advance what is going to happen. I think it appropriate for a discussion under this title to be almost totally improvised, just to see what may happen, in relation to this language and the fact that I speak a foreign language. (1)

Despite the similar circumstances and the fact that both Adam and Derrida are speaking in a foreign language, Derrida is prepared to improvise where Adam is not. Except, of course, not only *is* Derrida prepared to improvise but he *has* prepared to improvise. Referring to a quotation from his work that Düttmann had included in the question, Derrida remarks, "Coming here in a cab with Geoff Bennington and Alex we discussed the possible impossible translations of the . . . sentence," thereby revealing that he had been given a preview of what was "supposed to be a happening, something unpredictable" (1). But, of course, Derrida is drawing attention here to the impossibility of total improvisation; total improvisation would require Derrida not only to speak in a foreign language but in a wholly foreign language, a new language that would communicate nothing because it would be completely outside of his audience's experience.

Derrida here aims to disturb yet another binary relation, this time opposing improvisation to re-presentation. This is the lesson also of Derrida's encounters with the American jazz musician Ornette Coleman in Paris in 1997, which included Derrida first interviewing Coleman (in English) and then being invited to appear with him on stage at a jazz concert, where Derrida performed a reading (in French and English), accompanied by Coleman.[10] In the interview, Coleman describes to Derrida music that is "totally improvised, but at the same time it follows the laws" (Derrida and Coleman, 321), leading Derrida to observe, "Repetition is already in improvisation" (323), so that no improvisation is totally new.[11] In his later performance, Derrida reaffirms this insight "that unsettles our old idea of improvisation" when he states, "It is indeed necessary to improvise, it is necessary to improvise *well*," or in a practiced manner (2004, 332). But then he takes it further, making it clear that this new idea of improvisation also unsettles our old idea of what is not improvisation because it means that improvisation is already in writing and in reading, so that no repetition is wholly the same:

> As all of you see, I have here a sort of written score, you think I am not improvising, well, you are wrong. I am pretending not to improvise, **I just pretend,** I play at reading, but by improvising. . . . [T]he written parts are as improvised as the improvisations themselves. (332)

For both Adam and Derrida, therefore, improvisation (the new now) must be done well, as rehearsed. But for Adam this means pretending to improvise and not to repeat, while for Derrida this means pretending to repeat and not to improvise. The point is that these are not opposed positions. As Derrida says to Coleman, "The very concept of improvisation verges upon reading, since what we often understand by improvisation is the creation of something new, yet something which doesn't exclude the pre-written framework that makes it possible: . . . thus when people want to trap you between improvisation and the pre-written, they are wrong" (322–23).[12] For Derrida, reading always means playing at reading, or pretending to read, or pretending not to improvise but actually improvising because even the prewritten is not entirely predictable. Even as error creeps in when we improvise and fluently speak "on the cuff" (Lerner 2013, 171) in our so-called first language, so our rehearsed "grammar falter[s]" when "we to [*sic*] speak . . . of a new *now,* of a new period, without dislocation" (174). Like Adam fluffing his lines, "Derrida's performance makes evident that he, as reader, cannot fully control what is happening or what will happen during the reading," as Sara Ramshaw notes (2016, 12). The reader cannot (fore)tell what's happening, so to read is also to improvise.

Adam's and Derrida's approaches to their respective panels are not as different as they might appear, therefore, but their final aims are, and the difference has to do with "a relation to the future" (Derrida and Düttmann, 2) that is indicated by the title "Perhaps or Maybe." For Derrida, it is important to "distinguish between the future and what is to come" (2). He explains:

> The future means something which will be or shall be or should be, which will be present tomorrow. When I define a future I define something which will happen, which is supposed to happen, but in order to be, tomorrow or after tomorrow, present as such. The essence of the future is an essential relation to being, to being present. (2)

It is a relation to what "may be or not" (2). But "in perhaps or perchance the reference to the event, to what happens is more obvious," and "the event as such, that is, what is to come [*à-venir, venire*], does not necessarily come under the form of something present" but refers to "what remains to come" (2). The future is what may be prewritten, predicted, repeated, anticipated, foreseen, and (like Tomás's poetry) "totally intelligible," but the future to come is novel, unexpected, "unpredictable and profound" (Lerner 2013, 37), like imaginary poetry. "Unless the event [to come] is so surprising that I am not even prepared for the surprise," says Derrida, "it is not an event" (Derrida and Düttmann, 4). Preparing for his panel, Adam does not want to be surprised by the event to come, and so he tries to define or determine a future by prescribing what may or may not be. The goal is to minimize the chances of anything unexpected happening that would reveal Adam's "ignorance of Spanish *period*" (Lerner 2013, 171), whereas Derrida welcomes the unexpected or happenstance, as he welcomes the interruption from the audience that surprises him in the course of his interview: "Thank you for that. . . . That's the best surprise for me! I was waiting for that for a long time," he says (Derrida and Düttmann, 5). An awaited surprise might seem like a contradictory thing (and it is "a self-contradictory structure" [6]), but it means, in other words, that even as he was prepared to improvise, he was also prepared for an event that still happens unexpectedly: "For something to happen we have to await the surprise" (3), and "even if we succeed in anticipating or predicting everything, what happens is surprising" (6) because, as he says to Coleman, the predicted or "written parts are as improvised as the improvisations themselves. That is a great lesson . . . on what's happening—when it's happening: to the improviser, unforeseeably, without seeing it coming, unpredictably" (2004, 332).[13] What happens is exactly the surprise that overtakes what is expected (there is nothing happening that is not surprising), so that the future to come is the always-surprising "perhaps" that interrupts the "maybe"; like poetry, the future to come is happening.

"Perhaps or Maybe" also sees Derrida imagining something happening that would derail the writing altogether, so that nothing could move forward: "From the beginning I would say, 'well, this word . . . is totally untranslatable, . . . so let's stop it, let's end the session here.' Then perhaps we would leave, and perhaps this might be a good unpredictable event" (1–2). Here, "totally untranslatable" relates to "foreign language," "totally improvised," Adam's "unrepresentable categories," Grossman's virtual, and the Present Here and Now as forms that can accommodate no other and therefore put an end to all else. In order for things to keep happening, therefore, translation, or we could as well say improvisation (in Derrida's sense of repetition in invention), must happen. One here and now must translate into another here and now as the future translates the present. It is significant, therefore, that Adam's poems are exactly constructed through a process of quotation, editing, and translation:

> On these days I worked on what I called translation, . . . replacing a word with whatever word I first associated with it and/or scrambling the order of the lines. . . . Or I looked up the Spanish word for the English word I wanted to replace, and then replaced that word with an English word that approximated its sound ("Under the arc of the sky" became "Under the arc of the cielo," which became "Under the arc of the cello"). (Lerner 2013, 16)

The results of this method recall Lerner's own poems. In *Mean Free Path,* for example, Lerner "wanted repetition and recombination in the sequence to make a reader experience even the most personal and direct utterances as composed of found language—which of course all of our utterances are" (Rogers, 236). In this process of translation, disordering, and displacing, Adam and Lerner transform "literature now" into "literature that will have been."

Lerner sees a similar process at work in Ashbery's poetry and its "complicated play with temporality" (Lerner 2010, 201). Encountering Ashbery, Lerner argues, it is "as if the poem we have describes a poem for which we've always arrived too late" (207), a poem that will have been here but is no longer. Recalling all that has been said so far about the absent source, secondhand experiences, the never-present, the flow of time, and the apparent promise of the future to come, Lerner comments that, reading Ashbery, it is "as if we're reading a secondary text about an unavailable primary source" (206): the "'real' text is missing" (207). The reason, Lerner suggests, that we have this experience when reading Ashbery is "because Ashbery makes us read about our reading in real time" (206) and "experience the present as we read" (208), and as we have seen, the Real, ideal, imaginary, virtual Poem cannot exist in time. Lerner states that Ashbery's poetry grants us "the experience of experience" (210); he continues, "when his work manages to describe the time of its own reading in the time of its own reading, we experience mediacy immediately" (203), and he concludes with, again, a reference to the "immediate experience of mediacy, of the temporality of reading" (213; see also 2013, 90–91). An experience of the temporality of reading, however, is an experience of temporality *period,* as Derrida sets out in his discussions linking reading and improvisation, repetition and invention, the future and the future to come, maybe and perhaps. The concept of the immediate experience of mediacy, therefore, connects in the novel to the concept of spontaneous mimicking so that, it can be argued, it is not just "literature now" that requires us to mimic spontaneously but every "now." In every "now" in time we repeat as if for the first time. In the fiction of every "now" we experience mediacy (which is to say mimicking) immediately (which is to say spontaneously, or in the instant). Every "now" would be a mediation, or a translation, a mistranslation in fact, with all the possibilities that entails: for Derrida, "everything is, precisely, in the 'mediation'; . . . [there is only] translation" (Creech, Kamuf, and Todd, 14). In the end, translation becomes the default experience in *Leaving the Atocha Station.* The concluding lines, which begin with the silent translation of a line from Lorca's "Canción del naranjo seco [Song of the barren orange tree]," read, "Why was I born between mirrors? Teresa would read the originals and I would read the translations and the translations would become the originals as we read. Then I planned to live forever in a skylit room surrounded by my friends" (181).

"BECAUSE LITERATURE ISN'T POLITICS"

In the now that will have been, the virtual (the new, other, event) always seems to arrive or, more accurately, return hand in hand with the actual (the repeated, same, nonevent), both surviving in the very failure of the other to be wholly present or fully real. This understanding reframes Grossman's and Lerner's account of the virtual as that which suspends, postpones, or defers the actual. Because it no longer seems possible simply to divide the actual from the virtual or the present from what is no longer or not yet present, it no longer seems possible either to speak of deferral simply in terms of a delay. The virtual is not something with which to occupy time until the actual takes place; it is not a placeholder for an impending actual that will be present, maybe tomorrow. The virtual does not defer the actual to a later period but perpetually interrupts, unsettles, or suspends what might be taken to be fully or actually real or present. Conversely, and thinking of Grossman's idea of a return to the source, the virtual itself is not something that is perhaps set to come at some later, as-yet-unforeseen date; the virtual is not "of the *possible,* an ideal possible that is infinitely deferred" (Derrida 2005b, 84). The virtual event to come, the future to come, has not just been put on the long finger; in fact, it cannot be put on the long finger because we cannot even point to its approach, and instead it is what is happening without us having seen it coming. As such, the virtual event is impossible. For Derrida, the impossible is not what cannot happen but what "I" cannot possibly see happen, and he continues:

> This im-possible is not privative. It is not the inaccessible, and it is not what I can indefinitely defer: it announces itself; it precedes me, swoops down upon and seizes me *here and now* in a nonvirtualizable way, in actuality and not potentiality. It comes upon me from on high. . . . This im-possible is thus not a (regulative) *idea* or *ideal.* It is what is most undeniably *real.* And sensible. Like the other. (2005b, 84)[14]

What is perhaps impossible is happening here and now, to us, so that "we are exposed to the perhaps, . . . we remain exposed to what is coming" (Derrida and Düttmann, 6).

"Otherness and death are of course the main examples or figures of this 'to come'," says Derrida (4), and a third example is democracy. Why would democracy be impossible? On the one hand, Derrida argues, "Anyone must be able to understand, in democracy, the univocal meaning of the word and the concept of democracy" (2005b, 71), as if all the "*voices* or *votes* [*voix*] in democracy" could represent the one thing (30); but the meaning of democracy (a meaningful democracy) can hardly speak to or be available to everyone equally, as if democracy were deaf to its own differing conditions, laws, powers, or rights. On the other hand, "a democratic freedom or license . . . would authorize . . . every interpretation," so that a democratic democracy would invite every meaning; but the end result would leave us with "no *idea* of democracy" (37). Translating this dilemma into the language of literature, the one democracy that is democratically equal to everyone is akin to Grossman's virtual poem because it can admit no difference, it is closed to any outside, and it cannot mean any other thing for anyone else; a freely and democratically interpreted democracy, open always to accommodating some other idea of democracy, is akin to Lerner's virtual poem because it never equates to one democracy, to democracy as such. Either way, the concept of true democracy is paradoxically undemocratic because it excludes others and is itself lacking. As if swept up in a vortex flowing continuously about its axis, democracy's "freedom and equality are reconcilable, so to speak, only in a turning or alternating fashion, . . . only in the space-time of a 'by turns'" (24) that turns Democracy into "democracy," a democracy made possible because made suicidally worse: "Democracy protects and maintains itself precisely by limiting and threatening itself" (36) (by "delimitation . . . in the singular urgency of a *here and now*" [Derrida 2005a, 105 qtd. in 2005b, 90]), so that democracy is "equal and proper to itself only insofar as it is inadequate and improper" (2005b, 38). Like hated poetry, democracy cannot possibly be its proper self but only ever a failure of sorts, a fraud. Even where Derrida might be said to distinguish between a democratic politics and a possibly impossible democracy to come, and the temptation might be to understand these respectively as a present imperfect democracy and a future perfect democracy to come (maybe tomorrow), Derrida makes sure to remind us that "democracy will never exist, in the sense of a present existence: not because it will be deferred but because it will remain aporetic in its structure (force *without* force, incalculable singularity *and* calculable equality)" (86). Democracy is and never will be present, never itself, because it promises itself to "*the other to come*" (xiv), "to the to-come, to the future" (4), to the future to come, to the perhaps, to what is happening (see also Derrida and Düttmann, 2).

We are exposed to what is happening, and this state of exposure to what may perhaps be coming is, says Derrida, "not something we decide" (Derrida and Düttmann, 7). Nor can we decide in advance what we will be exposed to, we "cannot decide what or who is coming" (10) or whether it is good or evil, but we can "prepare ourselves for the other" (8). In fact, "we have to do this, master the surprise, without, if possible, erasing the heterogeneity, the alterity of what is coming, and that is the political and ethical challenge" (7). Politics and ethics are a response to the undecidable freedom of the democracy to come: because we can see that virtually anything can happen, then in order to be responsible, democratic politics and ethics must prepare for the singular event, or prepare not just for any thing but for this or that actual, unforeseen, undecidable, other thing that demands a decision from us; Matthias Fritsch, accordingly, states that "not seeking to anticipate the future, or not attempting to prevent this or that from happening, is manifestly irresponsible" (456). We have a responsibility to what is to come. Facing the undecidable, therefore, is not an excuse for "suspending any decision" (Derrida and Düttmann, 10) but is rather the condition of any concrete political or ethical decision, which must be made in the here and now. The freely interpretable democracy meets the "freedom [that] is essentially the faculty or power to do as one pleases, to decide, to choose, to determine *one-self*, to have self-determination, to be master" (Derrida 2005b, 22). Derrida explains that "democracy would be precisely this, a force *(kratos)*, a force in the form of a sovereign authority (sovereign, that is, . . . having the power to decide, to be decisive)" (13), so that here and now, in "the finite space and time of a democratic politics" (9) or "in the instant proper to it, the act of sovereignty must and can, by force, put an end in a single, indivisible stroke to the endless discussion. This act is an event" (10), and this "event of the interruptive decision" (35) is what makes democratic politics possible.

Given the political and ethical challenge of the here and now, it is clear why a poet might argue that allowing us to attend to what is happening is the political function of literature: "For Ashbery, the intensification of the experience of the present is the true political function of poetry" (Lerner 2010, 209n18). Lerner aims to achieve a similar heightening of experience in his own work, so that *Mean Free Path*, for example, is meant "to shift attention from the finished and polished artefact to the process of thinking and feeling in time" (Rogers, 236), which poses a particular challenge to the reader: "Lines are often out of order or belong to several possible orders simultaneously: there's a kind of choose-your-own-adventure element to most stanzas, enlisting the participation of the reader in the structuring of the poem" (226). We have already seen how, in a choose-your-own-title way, it is up to the reader to decide if *Leaving the Atocha Station* names the novel, cites Ashbery's poem, or refers to a relation between the two, and in *Mean Free Path*, Rogers notes, Lerner disrupts "the linear, sequential reading process. . . . The reader must choose and question herself in choosing" (235). Lerner's virtual poetry, the path of which cannot be calculated but instead exposes its readers to an undecidable future to come, places responsibility for the poem in their hands as they have to decide what to make of it as it happens: for Lerner, literature isn't politics—it is democracy. Another name for virtual poetry, therefore, would be *literature to come*, which would be a literature that promises itself to a future that may perhaps be and that does not commit its audience to a determined reading, look to program a particular response, or deliver a calculated message; in response, the reader of literature to come must decide what it is actually about here and now. Literature to come remains faithful to the future to come and to the future readers to come, for whom literature now is an experience of freedom and responsibility.

The literature to come shows faith in its readers and empowers them, but perversely, it also has them share in the responsibility for the hated failure of the poem because the reader reads all Literature as "literature": readers of literature to come freely betray what they freely read. In *Leaving the Atocha Station*, the political and ethical dimensions to the responsibilities of reading crystallize in the course of Adam's rehearsed comments at the panel about "literature now":

> Ortega y Gasset wrote "By speaking, by thinking, we undertake to clarify things, and that forces us to exacerbate them, dislocate them, schematize them. Every concept is in itself an exaggeration." . . . My fear about this panel is that we are in a hurry to define a period, to speak of literature *now;* every period, like every concept, is in itself an exaggeration. I hope to hear from others what changed on March 11 that permits we to speak . . . of a new *now,* of a new period, without dislocation. (174)

At this point, "literature now" becomes a near-tautological phrase because these lines further reinforce the idea that an experience of the temporality of reading is an experience of temporality period. If, as seen, Lerner admires the way Ashbery makes the reader experience thinking and speaking in time, here Lerner, by way of Ortega, equates the dislocation of speaking and thinking and of every concept with the dislocation of the now of every period. An experience of the here and now, therefore, is an experience of decision making, which is an experience of clarification and definition but also of dislocation, schematization, exaggeration, and exacerbation. Katz identifies that one of the novel's key arguments hinges on this quotation from Ortega, which links to two earlier statements on politics via the word "exacerbate." In the first, Adam learns that a Marxist acquaintance of his will vote for the conservative PP because he "votes to exacerbate the system's contradictions," which for Adam means, "He votes to make things worse" (138). Only a few pages later, however, when asked if "poetry can change the world," Adam says, "It can exacerbate the world's contradictions" (143). Katz wonders if this is meant to imply (disingenuously) that poetry can change the world for the better or if it means only that poetry's role is "one of negativity" (323). But for Lerner, understanding this negativity is vital. If poetry is understood as an experience of what is happening here and now, and if reading poetry is understood as an experience of deciding what is actually happening here and now, then poetry is an experience of a Present accommodated within scare quotes, of Poetry as "poetry," of a virtual made actually inactual, of immediate mediacy, of an improvisation in re-presentation, of the perhaps that may be, or, in other words, is indeed an experience of making things worse. As an experience of the undecidable, poetry invites its reader to take sides and to decide if it is about one thing or the other, just as if the reader were voting between, on the one hand, yes and, on the other, no, or between left and right, or blue and red. The responsible reader votes or decides to master what is surprising about the poem, but in doing so, the responsible reader risks erasing or betraying all other readings to come. Literature does not need to be about politics or ethics, therefore, in order to be political or ethical because to read is to experience and to decide what is happening with and to others. The reader who responds to the challenge of literature now learns that every reading does violence to others.

Translating every Poem into a "poem" and all Literature into "literature," the reader is responsible again and again for the failure but also for the survival of writing "now." Every decision threatens to bring closure a step closer, but what is to come grants literature meaningful closure without closure, never ending the endless discussion or closing the open debate. Because the event to come is what is happening, it asks for repeated commitments: "a political decision, an ethical decision, calls for another one. . . . Responsibility implies that we make another decision after the first, and again and again" (Derrida and Düttmann, 11). The matter is never settled and no decision ever final because the decision arises in the undecidability of the singular here and now. Responsible readers must be prepared to read well, which means they must improvise well, mastering what is happening in a way that remains unavoidably open to the other. Swept up in the flow of the poem that mirrors the happening of time, any reader—

"you / Pinned to the moment" (Ashbery qtd. in Lerner 2010, 202)—that does not still welcome the future to come "threatens to arrest the flow of language and fix its source" (Lerner 2010, 202).[15] Whatever the reader decides the poem actually means now, there must remain the possibility that they will decide otherwise next time. The reader who decides that the poem is about one thing here and now must expect that it will be about some other thing at some unforeseen date. A fixed and final decision, if it could be called a decision and if it could be communicated, would permit no other decision but would side with, on the one hand, say, only yes, and on the other, only no. It would be wholly a matter of life and death. Take, for example, the decision that Adam faces toward the end of the novel as to whether he should remain in Madrid or return to America. The novel leaves the question suspended, and instead the reader is responsible for any actual decision; the novel calls the reader to make a decision without arriving at a conclusion. A final decision, decided forever, which would mean Madrid forever or America forever, is couched in life-and-death terms by the novel's final line: "Then I planned to live forever in a skylit room surrounded by my friends" (Lerner 2013, 181). In this scene, the plan aligns itself with the calculable, which means no more future to come; and because only the dead cannot die, to live forever means to be "dead—immortal," as Maurice Blanchot writes (5); this is then not a life but an afterlife in a skylit room, which is to say (because the Spanish *cielo* translates as both "sky" and "heaven") a heaven-lit room; and all the while, it is as if his friends sit in vigil around Adam's body. Translation—between Spain and the States, between *cielo* and cello, between sky and heaven, by turns—must survive so that this is not the very end.

"NO DEMOCRACY WITHOUT LITERATURE; NO LITERATURE WITHOUT DEMOCRACY"[16]

In "Perhaps or Maybe," Düttmann ponders the effects of an experience of a relentless undecidability, asking Derrida,

> Isn't there a risk of paralysis involved? Rather than exposing us to a democracy to come, the awareness of an irreducible and necessary undecidability would immobilise us, would prevent us from taking a deci-

> sion. A decision always calls for a new decision, the undecidability reproduces itself incessantly—a paralysing thought. (10)

It would help if we could tell which decisions would be the right decisions, so that no matter what happened we would have the right response, even if it were one we had to make again and again. But of course, this would be no decision at all. If we can tell or foretell which so-called decision, made in advance of the event according to some predetermined or programmed calculation, will deliver the right or desired outcome, the "decision then no longer decides anything but . . . is simply deployed, without delay, presently. . . . There is no longer any place for justice or responsibility (whether juridical, political, or ethical)," says Derrida (2005b, 84–85). Martin Hägglund clarifies that "one has to make decisions *because* it is impossible to calculate what will happen, . . . [and] one always is forced to make decisions even though the consequences of these decisions cannot be fully established" (81). Because the laws and rules that would determine the right course are not equal to what is happening, we can say in fact that a decision is always improvised. A decision is improvised, and Lerner's and Derrida's great lesson is that a just and responsible decision is improvised well, in the sense that we are prepared to follow the laws and the rules but expect that no one law can survive exposure to the undecidable even as no one law can stem from exposure to the undecidable. Hägglund contends that "no norms or rules can be derived from the constitutive condition of undecidability" (232n4), and instead, Derrida warns, the decision means that an "always perilous transaction must thus invent [improvise], each time, in a singular situation, its own law and norm, that is, a maxim that welcomes each time the event to come. There can be responsibility and decision, if there are any, only at this price" (2005b, 151).[17]

As Düttmann observes, this risks being a paralyzing thought. In *Leaving the Atocha Station,* Lerner explores experiences of exposure and paralysis and attendant decisions that cannot simply be defined as, on the one hand, good and, on the other, evil but are more or less worse or better, more or less violent or nonviolent, more or less a betrayal or faithful, more or less closed or open, with no one term providing the principle to assure a good outcome.[18] Take openness, for example, which may have assumed a positive charge in the context of this discussion of a democracy or literature open to the future. Hägglund argues that "there is no guarantee that it is better to be *more* open rather than *less* open to the future" (232n4), and he concludes, "Deconstructive thinking enables a new understanding of the inherent contradictions . . . that ha[ve] haunted politics from the beginning. But it does not necessarily make us better at dealing with the political problems that constantly emerge as a result of these inherent contradictions" (171). Indeed, he takes Derrida to task for using "an opposition between attempts to close down the future and attempts to keep it open . . . to draw a distinction between democratic and nondemocratic systems" given that "*everything* . . . necessarily is open to the future" (231n4). However, when Hägglund notes that "the concept of democracy more evidently than other concepts takes into account the undecidable future" (171), he also makes clear that it is possible to have a different account of the future or to conceive of a different relation to the future, as something, maybe, that can be closed off. This closing off is what Derrida condemns in, for example, his opposition to the death penalty:

> The point is that it belongs to life . . . to have a future, thus some life before it, some event to come only where death, the instant of death, is not calculable, is not the object of a calculable decision. Where the anticipation of my death becomes the anticipation of a calculable instant, there is no longer any future. (2014, 265)

The calculating decision "masters the future" (except that "it only seems to do that, for this calculation, this mastery, this decidability, remain phantasms" [258], as they cannot be final). Perhaps and maybe, therefore, can be thought of in terms of what Fritsch terms a "double future" (456) that, he argues, can be understood in a normative sense: "I cannot do otherwise than in fact be exposed, unconditionally, to what will happen . . . and yet, I also must not do otherwise" (463). For the sake of "my life" (Derrida 2014, 256), I must accept (the gift of) life.

Given this, how do we judge Adam's decision to prepare for the "literature now" panel as he does, in a way designed to limit his exposure to the unforeseen and so to do violence to the event, close down what may happen, and betray the future to come? Adam does so because he knows that being open to the possibility of surprise also means being open to the risk of embarrassment or shame or worse, and so he decides against it. In fact, Adam's attitude to the panel continues a pattern of behavior that, throughout the novel, suggests a man who has often been wounded by events and who therefore shields himself from what is happening through alcohol, caffeine, and prescribed and unprescribed drugs. Early on, he insists, "I didn't need to establish a life in Madrid beyond the simplest routines; I didn't have to worry about building a community" (Lerner 2013, 15). Derrida would understand, observing, "We try all the time to resist the perhaps, to protect ourselves against the absolutely unpredictable coming" (Derrida and Düttmann, 6), but he would also suggest that a life of only simple, calculable routines is no life at all. For Derrida, "Deconstruction is always on the side of the *yes,* on the side of the affirmation of life" (2007, 51), just as all poetry is in favor of life, and he would advise Adam not to settle for being "a reader who has already been programmed" (31) but to remain open to a future that "will determine the reader, who will learn to read (to 'live') something he or she was not accustomed to receiving from anywhere else" (31).

We must make a "commitment to an open future . . . as part and parcel of the emergence and maintenance of a world" (Fritsch, 465), and we must do this even though "there is no life without the risk of losing oneself" (459). This is very apparent in Lerner's account of Cyrus's experience in Mexico, which sets out various degrees of what might be termed "openness." The girl who follows Cyrus in jumping into the river exhibits a reluctant openness to what may happen, and still in doing so she invites a future that extinguishes her life. The event itself, however, is not closed to the future, and something survives her death: she haunts Cyrus's memories; Jane, it is expected, will channel the experience of the incident into her fiction; and Cyrus decides to share the story with his friend Adam. In this, Cyrus also shows faith in the future and is open to it, but both he and the drowned girl are betrayed when Adam represents the story as his own: "'When I am near a river,' I heard myself say, 'I think of my time in Mexico'" (Lerner 2013, 95). Adam exemplifies Derrida's warning that "the threat remains. That this good friend may become the devil" (never forgetting that "if we exclude the mere possibility of such a radical evil, then there will be no event at all," so that "the good event . . . could not happen either") (Derrida and Düttmann, 9). One self here has been erased by the other self, and Cyrus is displaced from his own story by Adam, the future reader who takes possession of the narrative and makes it all about him through a perverse mistranslation, an excessively violent recontextualization, a lie. Improvising his response to the incalculable singularity of the other, Adam proves himself ill-prepared to read ("to live") well. And yet, throughout the novel, Adam is (slowly) learning to live well: learning that he "can live in this [second] language" (Lerner 2013, 168), admitting that "this is wonderful, the life I lead here, no matter if it's mine" (171), not wanting his tranquilizers, and giving the final word to his community of "friends" (181).

Adam's behavior in relation to Cyrus's story can also be framed in terms of freedom, which, like openness, is never simply good. As Derrida observes, "It has always been difficult, and for essential reasons, to distinguish rigorously . . . between the good of democratic freedom or liberty and the evil of democratic license" (2005b, 21). If a text, like democracy, is by definition freely interpretable, Adam in this instance has licensed himself to interpret Cyrus's story as he sees fit, or he has taken liberties with freedom in order to determine who or what the story is about. The excessive force of democratic license was evident also in the actions of the governing People's Party after the Madrid bombings on March 11, 2004, when they decided or determined, unilaterally, that ETA was responsible. But knowing that they would be judged to be taking liberties with their interpretation of events, the leaders acted as if this decision were no decision at all. As reported, "immediately after the bombing" ("Controversies") and "from the moment of the attacks" (Hamilos and Tran), the party identified those responsible, as if the event were totally intelligible and a ready response could be "simply deployed, without delay, presently" (Derrida 2005b, 85). Like Derrida at Coleman's concert, the government was pretending not to improvise by playing at reading but reading absolutely correctly. It interpreted the event as if it were an example of "the poems of tradition [which] are themselves 'readings' and administrations of . . . states of affairs" (Grossman, 846) and thus arrive to us as if already and conclusively read. And of course, the aim of this effort to present an incontrovertible reading of the events of March 11 was to make the result of the elections of March 14 similarly a foregone conclusion and to return the PP to power. If "there is no decision without interrupting the usual course of history" (Derrida and Düttmann, 11), the government's interruptive, unspoken decision on March 11 was intended to forestall interruptions on March 14, to "contradict the eventfulness of what comes" (Derrida 2005b, 128), and to determine that the future course of the elections would not turn up any surprises because the voters' decisions would effectively decide nothing, with the result already legible in the account of ETA's culpability and in line with the government's program. Exercising democratic license, therefore, the government decided to act as if nothing outside of the norm had happened in Madrid and therefore acted as if there was not anything happening, in the sense of anything surprising or unpredictable, anything that called for a decision, or politics, or democracy. This silent and silencing decision seems an instance of "sovereignty itself [which] (if there is one and if it is pure) always keeps quiet in the very ipseity of the moment proper to it" (100), as if it speaks in the "silent voice" of imaginary poetry (Grossman, 864), removed "from time and from language" (Derrida 2005b, 101). But this can only mean that, like virtual poetry, "pure sovereignty does not exist": "To confer sense or meaning on sovereignty . . . is already to compromise its deciding exceptionality, to subject it to rules, . . . to take into account the part played by sovereignty" (101). Sovereign power cannot not account for itself and cannot not be held to account for decisions that will always remain open to reading and reinterpretation. Decisive events turn history into a difficult poem, in which "there is no intratextual interpreter" (Grossman, 850) and that instead "situates the reader internal to the poem, and assigns him the task of completing rather than deriving significance" (846) and holds him to account for his reading (his "living").

Lerner sets out an alternative approach to the events of March 11 in *Leaving the Atocha Station*'s opening scene. By the end of the first page, an account of Adam's daily routine has brought him to the Prado Museum, standing before Rogier van der Weyden's *Descent from the Cross,* in which the two major figures, Jesus and Mary, seem suspended between heaven and earth, "forever falling" (Lerner 2013, 8), like virga. One particular morning, Adam arrives "to find that someone had taken [his] place" in front of the painting, heralding a "turning point" in Adam's project that hinges on an interruptive event that is very different to the train bombings but through which, nonetheless, the novel reflects on the relationship between democracy and literature: "The man broke suddenly into tears. . . . Was he . . . having a *profound experience of art?*" (8). Given Lerner's later reference to "unpredictable and profound" (37) virtual poetry, which links the profound and the unexpected, it is clear that the man is overtaken by an event for which he is unprepared, by the future to come, by a bolt from the blue ("the blues of [Mary's] robes are unsurpassed in Flemish painting" [8]). The man cries again before Paolo de San Leocadio's *The Saviour* before moving to consider Hieronymus Bosch's *The Garden of Earthly Delights,* where he "totally lost his shit" (9). This scene is strategically important in three ways. The first is that the experience of the event (or events, if considering the man's experience of art and Adam's experience of the man's experience) is immediately mediated because, as recounted, the event itself is never present as such but always re-presented: the man's "*profound experience of art*" (8) is immediately interrupted on the page by a discussion of mediation, with Adam admitting, "I tended to find lines of poetry beautiful only when I encountered them quoted in prose, . . . so that what was communicated was less a particular poem than the echo of poetic possibility" (8–9); Adam is left with "a profound experience of the absence of profundity" (9) or with what Lerner and Ashbery would term the "experience of experience." This necessarily reframes the man's profound experience of art also as a profound experience of mediation: Lerner says of the reproduction in the novel of a detail of a weeping mourner from *Descent from the Cross,* "It's hard not to see it as an image of the museumgoer who burst into tears before that painting; . . . the beheld becomes the beholder" (Rogers, 228).

The second is the way in which the scene of mediation appears to take place in a room of mirrors: Adam looks at the man "as if beholding myself beholding the painting"; the man looks at the mourner and the beheld becomes the beholder; and in the painting, Mary's "posture is almost an exact echo of Jesus's" (Lerner 2013, 8). This mirroring or internal quoting can be read in relation to Lorca's line "Why was I born between mirrors?" (181) or to Lerner's observation, discussing Ashbery, that "it's as if the 'real' poem were written on the other side of a mirrored surface: when we read, we see only the reflection of our reading" (Lerner 2010, 209). With no immediate contact with the real poem, which is never present at hand, we can only ever be struck by a bolt from the blue, or as if from an absent source; in the context of the van der Weyden, the bolt is thrown by no hand of God because the heavenly Father is himself absent and is instead represented by the mother and son, forever suspended between. No final sovereign power has entered the frame, therefore, to determine or decide whether the painting is about Mary or Jesus or both, echoing and mirroring each other. The painting is, at the same time, about less and more than one thing, even as the man who views it is less and more than himself; he is Adam and a reader and what is read, by turns, and in turn he is also "this great artist" (Lerner 2013, 10), the author, the creator, the sovereign authority who responds freely in the face of what is happening—even as it turns out that his response will always already have been accounted for in the mistranslation of the here and now.

Every event, including the interruptive event of the improvised decision, is immediately open to interpretation, and no democracy or sovereignty or revolution can silence itself or the readings of it, for good or evil. The opening scene's third strategic importance is in representing official authorities, in the form of the museum guards or "security force" (Lerner 2013, 10) or *kratos,* who must decide how to respond to the man's outburst. Again, they are falling between two unrepresentable categories because they "spend much of their lives in front of timeless paintings but are only ever asked what time is it," so that they are caught between the virtually timeless and the actually present, both finalities that would see the "museum close" forever (10). And again, the experience of art exacerbates contradictions because the man "force[s] the institution to face its contradictions" (10) as the guards are asked to decide "whether the man was crazy . . . or if the man was having a profound experience of art" (9): in other words, "on the one hand," they could welcome an experience of art that could result in damage to the art; "on the other hand" (10), they could interrupt an experience of art and so betray the very spirit of the art. Unlike the PP, who quasi-silently decided immediately between ETA and Islamic terrorists, the guards exhibit a paralysis of "indecision" (10), but Derrida asks, "What is paralysis? There is a paralysis which consists in keeping immobile, and that's a necessary moment for reflection. You must at some point stop acting in order to act" (Derrida and Düttmann, 10). The guards do not fix on an interpretation of the man's experience but reflect on their reading, and their decidedly indecisive response is in turn read by Adam, who found "pathos in the indecision" and "found their mute performance more moving" than any painting, so that he "felt like one of their company as we trailed the man" (Lerner 2013, 10). These figures of authority, therefore, witnessing people respond to an event, assume responsibility for a decision they do not make and, reflecting, invite further reflection in a shared sovereignty. But this necessary moment was denied to the Spanish people by their own government in March 2004. Even as Ashbery says poetry is protest, the demonstrations by the Spanish people on March 13 were protests for poetry, for the challenging responsibility of deciding in the face of an extraordinarily difficult event what was actually happening, and for the responsibility of remaking history together.

David Coughlan is associate professor of English at the University of Limerick, Ireland, and the author of *Ghost Writing in Contemporary American Fiction* (2016). He has published on contemporary fiction, graphic narrative, and critical theory in *Parallax, ImageTexT, Derrida Today, College Literature, Critique,* and *Modern Fiction Studies.*

Notes

1. Ashbery, whose *Selected Poems* are referred to on the very first page of Lerner's novel, has himself described the work as "an extraordinary novel about the intersections of art and reality in contemporary life" (qtd. in Rogers, 220).

2. These words appear also in Lerner's *The Hatred of Poetry* (43), but they are not attributed to Adam even though an earlier passage reflecting on "the echo of poetic possibility" is presented as a quotation from the novel (2016a, 32; 2013, 8–9).

3. It is worth noting that a different conception of the virtual and actual, but one which also reconfigures "what passes for the real," is key to Gilles Deleuze's philosophy, in which both the virtual and actual are fully real and the real always partly virtual and partly actualized (260–64).

4. Any lie must contain some truth in order to be believable, and what is true or is a lie here and now will change with time, so that "the true could be false, the false could be true" (Derrida and Düttmann, 3); Adam laments that "when something did in fact happen to my mother, as happen it must, I would always feel and be at least in part responsible" (Lerner 2013, 29) because his lie will one day be true.

5. "All December," writes Adam, "there was rain" (Lerner 2013, 63). In *Angle of Yaw,* Lerner writes, "WE DREAM OF RAIN that, in lieu of falling, moves

parallel to the earth. Sheet after sheet of rain. Then an upward rain that originates a few feet off the ground. You can get under the rain and watch" (2016b, 103). On sheet after sheet of poetry, rain can fall up or crossways or fall for all time.

6. The unacknowledged reference is to W. H. Auden's "In Memory of W. B. Yeats": "For poetry makes nothing happen: it survives / . . . it survives, / A way of happening" (lines 36–41). Culler discusses these lines in the context of "the power of poetry to make something happen" (240); Derrida sees "survival as a complication of the opposition life/death" (2007, 51).

7. Lerner explains that this use of "the technology of Internet chat [that] allows for a conversation to unfold haltingly in real time" (Rogers, 234–35) is a response to the question of how best to "represent the simultaneity or fragmentation of actual speech" (234).

8. The erroneous "on the cuff" nevertheless rhymes obliquely with the synonymous "on the hoof."

9. Lerner won the 1997 National Forensic League National Tournament in International Extemporaneous Speaking.

10. Derrida notes that the "brief 'rehearsal' that preceded the improvisation, Coleman's or my own, in no way resembled what took place before the audience" because, infamously, he was booed offstage about halfway through his reading of "Play—The First Name" (Malabou and Derrida, 97n14). For an excellent account and analysis of the "non-event" of this jazz event, see Wills, 41.

11. As Ramshaw puts it, "Improvisation can be neither purely spontaneous nor completely determined by the musical structures with which it engages. It must be both responsive to otherness *and* have some stable or determined dimension in order to endure *as* jazz improvisation" (2006, 3). See also Lane, 323.

12. Derrida's criticism of the opposition between improvisation and the "pre-written framework" reflects also on the opposition between the virtual poem and the "structures of well-made and decorous poems" (Grossman, 874). For Ramshaw, "Derrida's performance highlights the impossibility of a purely improvised (or unimprovised) event" (2016, 12).

13. Words in bold were in English in Derrida's multilingual performance. The word "improvise," of course, derives from the Latin *improvisus,* meaning "unforeseen" or "unexpected."

14. See also: "But the impossible is not nothing. It is even that which happens, which comes, by definition" (Derrida 2005b, 172n12).

15. But Lerner observes of these lines from Ashbery's "The Thousand Islands," "It isn't clear who or what is being pinned—you? the depths? a miracle?" (2010, 202). Relating to a closure without closure that welcomes the future, Derrida notes, "While naming [the session]—without naming it—*Perhaps or maybe,* we left everything suspended" (Derrida and Düttmann, 4).

16. Derrida 1995, 28.

17. For more on the law and improvisation, see Ramshaw.

18. Following the ideas developed in Richard Beardsworth's *Derrida and the Political* (1996) and Fritsch's "Derrida's Democracy to Come" (2002), Hägglund

argues that "all decisions made in the name of justice are made in view of what is judged to be the lesser violence" (170) but that it cannot be said "that the desire for lesser violence answers to a normative ideal or that it is inherently good" (83).

Works Cited

Auden, W. H. 1991. "In Memory of W. B. Yeats." *Collected Poems*, 247–49. Edited by Edward Mendelson. New York: Vintage International.

Blanchot, Maurice. 2000. "The Instant of My Death." In *The Instant of My Death. Demeure*, by Maurice Blanchot and Jacques Derrida, 1–11. Translated by Elizabeth Rottenberg. Stanford: Stanford University Press.

"Controversies about the 2004 Madrid Train Bombings." *Wikipedia: The Free Encyclopedia*. https://en.wikipedia.org/wiki/Controversies_about_the_2004_Madrid_train_bombings. Accessed July 15, 2018.

Creech, James, Peggy Kamuf, and Jane Todd. 1985. "Deconstruction in America: An Interview with Jacques Derrida." *Critical Exchange* 17 (Winter): 1–33.

Culler, Jonathan. 2015. *Theory of the Lyric*. Cambridge, Mass.: Harvard University Press.

Deleuze, Gilles. 2004. *Difference and Repetition*. Translated by Paul Patton. London: Continuum.

Derrida, Jacques. 1994. *Specters of Marx: The State of the Debt, the Work of Mourning, and the New International*. Translated by Peggy Kamuf. New York: Routledge.

———. 1995. "Passions: 'An Oblique Offering'." Translated by David Wood. In *On the Name*, edited by Thomas Dutoit, 3–31. Stanford: Stanford University Press.

———. 2004. "Play—The First Name: 1 July 1997." Translated by Timothy S. Murphy. *Genre* 37, no. 2: 331–40.

———. 2005a. *The Politics of Friendship*. Translated by George Collins. London: Verso.

———. 2005b. *Rogues: Two Essays on Reason*. Translated by Pascale-Anne Brault and Michael Naas. Stanford: Stanford University Press.

———. 2007. *Learning to Live Finally: An Interview with Jean Birnbaum*. Translated by Pascale-Anne Brault and Michael Naas. Hoboken, N.J.: Melville House.

———. 2014. *The Death Penalty, Volume 1*. Edited by Geoffrey Bennington, Marc Crépon, and Thomas Dutoit. Translated by Peggy Kamuf. Chicago: University of Chicago Press.

Derrida, Jacques, and Ornette Coleman. 2004. "The Other's Language: Jacques Derrida Interviews Ornette Coleman, 23 June 1997." Translated by Timothy S. Murphy. *Genre* 37, no. 2: 319–29.

Derrida, Jacques, and Alexander Garcia Düttmann. 1997. "Perhaps or Maybe." In *Responsibilities of Deconstruction*, edited by Jonathon Dronsfield and Nick Midgley, 1–18. *PLI: Warwick Journal of Philosophy* 6 (Summer).

Fritsch, Matthias. 2011. "Deconstructive Aporias: Quasi-Transcendental and Normative" *Continental Philosophy Review* 44, no. 4: 439–68.

Grossman, Allen. 1981. "Hart Crane and Poetry: A Consideration of Crane's Intense Poetics with Reference to 'The Return'." *ELH* 48, no. 4: 841–79.

Hägglund. Martin. 2008. *Radical Atheism: Derrida and the Time of Life*. Stanford: Stanford University Press.

Hamilos, Paul, and Mark Tran. 2007. "21 Guilty, Seven Cleared over Madrid Train Bombings." *Guardian*, October 31. https://www.theguardian.com/world/2007/oct/31/spain.marktran. Accessed July 15, 2018.

Katz, Daniel. 2017. "'I Did Not Walk Here All the Way from Prose': Ben Lerner's Virtual Poetics." *Textual Practice* 31, no. 2: 315–37.

Lane, Jeremy F. 2013. "Theorising Performance, Performing Theory: Jacques Derrida and Ornette Coleman at the Parc de la Villette." *French Cultural Studies* 24, no. 3: 319–30.

Lerner, Ben. 2010. "The Future Continuous: Ashbery's Lyric Mediacy." *boundary 2* 37, no. 1: 201–13.

———. 2013. *Leaving the Atocha Station*. London: Granta.

———. 2016a. *The Hatred of Poetry*. London: Fitzcarraldo Editions.

———. 2016b. *No Art: Poems*. London: Granta.

Malabou, Catherine, and Jacques Derrida. 2004. *Counterpath: Traveling with Jacques Derrida*. Translated by David Wills. Stanford: Stanford University Press.

Ramshaw, Sara. 2006. "Deconstructin(g) Jazz Improvisation: Derrida and the Law of the Singular Event." *Critical Studies in Improvisation / Études critiques en improvisation* 2, no. 1: 1–19.

———. 2016. "The Paradox of Performative Immediacy: Law, Music, Improvisation." *Law, Culture and the Humanities* 12, no. 1: 6–16.

Rogers, Gayle. 2013. "An Interview with Ben Lerner." *Contemporary Literature* 54, no. 2: 218–38.

Wills, David. 2006. "Notes Towards a Requiem: Or the Music of Memory." *Mosaic: An Interdisciplinary Critical Journal* 39, no. 3: 27–46.

Witt, Emily. 2015. "Ben Lerner: 'People Say, "Oh, Here's Another Brooklyn Novel by a Guy with Glasses"'." *Guardian*, January 3. https://www.theguardian.com/books/2015/jan/03/ben-lerner-1004-novel-books-interview. Accessed July 24, 2018.

RURAL REVOLT

THE SCALE PROBLEM IN HOUELLEBECQ AND NORRIS

Roderick Cooke

A group of economically beleaguered farmers is slaughtered in a gun battle with agents of the state. The shooting starts because of a tragic misunderstanding. The carnage takes place along an axis of transportation and is witnessed by a friend of the farmers, who is also the novel's protagonist. The above description applies equally to pivotal passages from two novels that otherwise appear to be quite dissimilar, by authors with (ostensibly) very different outlooks on life and literature. They are Frank Norris's *The Octopus* (1901) and Michel Houellebecq's *Sérotonine* (2019). I will argue here, however, that these remarkably similar events should alert us to a more extensive range of parallels between the two texts. In particular, the two fictional farmers' revolts, taking place in the late nineteenth and early twenty-first centuries, respectively, are born from the two novelists' preoccupation with the relationship between giant organizations and the individual producer under capitalism. Although the organizations the farmers hold responsible for their plight, respectively the Pacific and South Western Railway and the European Union, seem at first glance to have little in common, Norris and Houellebecq use those bodies' effect on the rural economy to confront questions of globalization, masculinity, the sociological meaning of place, and the relationship between the natural and mechanized worlds. Famously, another farm novel, Steinbeck's *The Grapes of Wrath* (1939), has a similarly distressed farmer ask: "Who can we shoot?" (39) The subtly different answers that Norris before him and Houellebecq most recently give to this question reveal the differences between the two men's visions of society and capital in their times.

FROM MUSSEL SLOUGH TO *THE OCTOPUS*

The Octopus was the first of Norris's planned trilogy, *The Epic of the Wheat,* which proposed to study the commodity's global circulation from production in California (*The Octopus*) to financialization in Chicago (*The Pit*) to consumption in Europe (the unwritten *The Wolf*). His untimely 1902 death curtailed the trilogy at two. *The Octopus*'s principal character is Presley, a young poet staying at the Derrick ranch at a time when the San Joaquin Valley's farmers are expecting both a bonanza crop and the opportunity to purchase their lands outright from the P.&S.W. Railway at the originally proposed price of $2.50 an acre. The novel's central conflict turns on the gap between this expectation and the reality that the railway will demand $27 an acre, asking the farmers to pay for the improvements they themselves have made to the land since first taking up the corporation's offer to farm it a few years earlier. Norris draws on the historical shootout at Mussel Slough, in which five settlers and two "railroad men" died on May 11, 1880. Railroads were granted land adjoining the roads built during the period as a government incentive, and Norris's novel transposes the history of pricing conflicts between the corporation (in reality the Southern Pacific) and the settlers.

After forming a league and unsuccessfully attempting to lower the price by fighting railroad corruption with corruption of their own directed at the Railroad Commission, the farmers nearly all meet their end in the skirmish with railroad operatives led by the embodiment of its greed and graft, the agent S. Behrman. Critics have discussed both the anti-Semitism inherent in Behrman's portrayal, and the fact that he gives literary-fictional form to a new legal fiction with damaging consequences to Progressive Era America: corporate personhood. In the wake of the *Santa Clara County v. Southern Pacific Railroad* Supreme Court decision of 1886, as Daniel Mrozowski puts it, the "Court interpreted the due process clause of the Fourteenth Amendment to mean that corporations held legal personhood and rights protection [. . .] the corporate entity became an economic being independent from its individual members [. . .] the inability to ascribe responsibility to a "real" person provoked an immense and continual cultural crisis" (164). Although Norris's novel does not resolve this crisis, it offers both Behrman and, later, the railroad president Shelgrim as partial embodiments of the corporate person, giving both readers and characters focal points for their affective and intellectual response to the economic conflict in the San Joaquin Valley.

But what are these responses, and what did Norris intend for them to be? *The Octopus* is a novel often interpreted as displaying a divided consciousness, oscillating between admiration for the colossal reach of the railroad corporation and the mechanistic potency of its locomotives, on the one hand, and horror at the physical and financial carnage that both train and corporation leave in their wake. Attempting to resolve these oscillations has provoked a wealth of critical discussion, not least because the protagonist Presley, despite both being a writer and himself seeming to vacillate between the extremes of revulsion and enthusiasm, does not clearly align with Norris, his creator. Clare Eby has argued that "by exhibiting Presley as his negative example of a would be epic writer, Norris redefines the role of the modern American author facing capitalism" (35). In other words, because Presley allows himself to be economically and aesthetically browbeaten by Shelgrim when meeting the latter in his office, and because he fails to understand the parallels Norris himself drew between literary production and corporate production ("Presley's continual mis-reading of business results from his refusing to accept that literature and capitalism have much in common" [Eby, 36]), the author's ambivalence toward the world of capital operates on a higher plane than does the protagonist's. More recently, Russ Castronovo has advanced a similar argument in the context of the developing discipline of global literature, suggesting that Presley "exemplifies the connection between world markets and world literature forecast by the *Communist Manifesto* a half-century before" (82) and that Cedarquist's final prediction of American consumer goods flooding the Indian market in the wake of the wheat shipment in the novel's final pages "looks to substitute wheat and other commodities to which everyone is forced to have access for an aesthetic culture where shared feelings for the beautiful create social cohesion" (84).

On these and similar readings, the corporate apparatus and the novel's own literary apparatus work together to create a totality whose outside cannot be located. Divisions or contradictions found within *The Octopus*'s pages are subsumed by the colossal global scale of the ending, in which Presley boards a ship bound for India with grain to relieve starvation. In the process, the reader observes a global circle in which the old-world crop, reinvigorated by the young Californian soil, finds hungry mouths in perhaps the oldest civilization of all. And on a related note, the Mussel Slough–inspired shootout has typically been read as a conflict internal to rival sectors of the capitalist order, rather than as the oppression of individuals or of a marginal group by the corporation. Both Donald Pizer and June Howard have emphasized that the farmers led by Magnus Derrick are "capitalists who have large investments in the land and equipment and who are competing with the railroad for the riches of the land" (Pizer 1966, 120), "gentlemen ranchers, employers of farmhands who [. . .] scarcely get their hands dirty" (Howard, 121). In a recent book, Terry Beers has expanded on this point, similarly asserting that "the growers themselves are complicit in the capitalist ideology that leads to their ruin," and that consequently the novel should be read as "a lesson in what happens when Jeffersonian agrarianism [. . .] is forsaken in pursuit of raw material power" (134–35). Norris's narrator foregrounds the farmers' indifference to their own land, the same land for which they ultimately give their lives, saying of the patriarch Magnus Derrick that

> without knowing it, he allowed himself to work his ranch much as if he was still working his mine. The old-time spirit of '49, hap-hazard, unscientific, persisted in his mind. Everything was a gamble—who took the greatest chances was most apt to be the greatest winner. The idea of manuring Los Muertos, of husbanding his great resources, he would have scouted as niggardly, Hebraic, ungenerous. (628)

However, just as with Presley's inconstant views on capitalism, the idea of profligate, profit-seeking farmers is also subject to challenge and ambiguity. Before we meet Magnus and read the above description, his younger, better-educated neighbor Annixter has already indicted the attitude of "the Governor": "'That's right, there's your Western farmer,' he exclaimed contemptuously, "get the guts out of your land; work it to death; never give it a rest. Never alternate your crop, and then when your soil is exhausted, sit down and roar about hard times'" (599). As is true of the function and ethical polarity of the railroad, the farmers' approaches to their work and perspectives on the land are polyvalent and resist simple categorization. Their formation of the League glosses over these distinctions but does not erase them from the text.

Yet do such distinctions matter? Whatever the approach to farming espoused by individual Leaguers, they are united on the questions of scale and of profit, and it is precisely these questions that bring them into unwinnable conflict with the railroad. Annixter's more modern, scientific approach to husbandry nevertheless leaves him dead in the irrigation ditch alongside Magnus's son Harran. The central problem in *The Octopus,* then, is one of scale. The Leaguers die because they have attempted to match the scale of the railroad corporation in both their agricultural and political activities but have been dwarfed by it.

Magnus Derrick sees the possibilities of global scale when the manufacturing magnate Cedarquist, a sympathetic observer of the League's battle against the P.&S.W., evokes the opening of Asian markets for American wheat (Cedarquist's grain ship, completed by the novel's end, will offer passage to Presley in the concluding chapter): "We *must have new markets, greater markets.* [. . .] Why, Mr. Derrick, if only one-half the population of China ate a half ounce of flour per man per day all the wheat areas in California could not feed them. Ah, if I could only hammer that into the brains of every rancher of the San Joaquin [. . .]" (819). Derrick's silent response is telling:

> He saw a vision [. . .] The torrent of wheat was to be diverted, flowing back upon itself in a sudden, colossal eddy, stranding the middleman [. . .] thousands upon thousands of men set free of the grip of Trust and ring and monopoly acting for themselves, selling their own wheat, organising into one gigantic trust, themselves, sending their agents to all the entry ports of China. (830)

Magnus's thoughts instantly undercut themselves, in a manner of which the character himself appears to be unaware. The words "one gigantic trust, themselves" signal the true nature of his design: not to achieve emancipation from the railroad in the name of economic justice but to replace one monopoly with another. Derrick is describing a project of vertical integration, in which production and distribution of the wheat are both handled by him and his associates. The League's conflict with the railroad thus sparks the desire to supplant a gargantuan trust with a still more gargantuan successor, one that grips not just the state of California but the entire world in its tentacles. In the process, the reader's sympathies for the farmers' plight are likely to be vitiated.

The above passage is particularly significant because critics have tended to focus on the farmers' practice of agriculture itself rather than their future plans, and it is in the combination of the two that their convergence with the logic of the railroad trust becomes clearest. While Pizer, Howard, Beers, and others such as James K. Folsom, Brett Zalkan,[1] and Florian Freitag agree that "the monopoly of the railroad complements rather than contrasts with the reckless monoculture of the farmers" (Freitag, 106), the desire to supplant that monopoly, rather than the false consciousness of suffering under it, has gone overlooked. In this sense, Presley's boarding of the ship is an unconscious act of solidarity with his fallen friends rather than the betrayal it might appear to be. He is aligning himself with Derrick's dream of flooding Asia with American grain, albeit with the fig-leaf of charitable famine relief overlaid on it.

Presley's shifting poetic projects afford us another means of analyzing the scale problem in *The Octopus.* Where Magnus will come to form the project of emulating the railroad trust, his literary houseguest begins the novel with his own mimetic dream: that of emulating Homer. Although his interlocutor Vanamee is the first to put the word in his mouth, the poet instantly and enthusiastically agrees:

> Presley caught at the word. It had never before occurred to him.
>
> "Epic, yes, that's it. It is the epic I'm searching for. And *how* I search for it. You don't know. It is sometimes almost an agony. Often and often I can feel it right there, there, at my finger-tips, but I never quite catch it. It always eludes me. I was born too late. Ah, to get back to that first clear-eyed view of things, to see as Homer saw, as Beowulf saw, as the Nibelungen poets saw." (609)

Presley aspires to match the Homeric scale of epic poetry just as the Leaguers will aspire to equal the economic scale of the railroad in their turn. In both cases, the projects will be doomed by the impossibility of scaling up their work to the epic predecessor (in the case of Homer) or antagonist (in the case of the P.&S.W.). The scale of Presley's literary dream is expanded by two influences; not only the literary monoliths he harkens back to but also the vast expanses of the Californian landscape. Norris fuses the two, along with Vanamee's insight, into a single passage combining the descriptive work of Presley's view over the valley with the intertextual work of alluding to *The Odyssey:*

> Presley climbed to the summit of one of the hills—the highest—that rose out of the canyon, from the crest of which he could see for thirty, fifty, sixty miles down the valley [. . .] he shifted his position and, drawing from the pocket of his shooting coat his little tree-calf edition of the Odyssey, read far into the twenty-first book, where, after the failure of all the suitors to bend Ulysses's bow, it is finally put, with mockery, into his own hands. Abruptly the drama of the story roused him from all his languor. [. . .] The epic defiled before his vision like a pageant. Once more, he shot a glance about him, as if in search of the inspiration, and this time he all but found it. He rose to his feet, looking out and off below him. (611–12)

Just as the extraordinary abundance of their crop, fed by the Californian soil, induces the poet's agricultural friends to expand their commercial horizons, so the sixty-mile view of the valley entwines with Ulysses's story to kindle Presley's literary project.

Yet Vanamee's literary criticism is but the first of several nonprofessional opinions that Presley will be susceptible to as the novel unfolds. In the abovementioned conversation with Cedarquist, which prompts Magnus's own expansion of scale, the manufacturer simultaneously has some literary advice for Presley:

> "We are both of us fighters, it seems, Mr. Derrick," said Cedarquist. "Each with his particular enemy. We are well met, indeed, the farmer and the manufacturer, both in the same grist between the two millstones of the lethargy of the Public and the aggression of the Trust, the two great evils of modern America. Pres, my boy, there is your epic poem ready to hand." (818–19)

And, indeed, the narrator quickly informs us that Presley has already begun paralleling Cedarquist's advice before it was given, although in so doing he explicitly abandons the epic mode. Continued exposure to his friends' struggles turns his mind toward socially conscious art: "He flung aside his books of poems—Milton, Tennyson, Browning, even Homer—and addressed himself to Mill, Malthus, Young, Poushkin, Henry George, Schopenhauer" (821). In place of Homer and Milton, he produces "a comment upon the social fabric [. . .] inspired by the sight of a painting he had seen in Cedarquist's art gallery" (872). The poem is entitled 'The Toilers' and, as Beers points out, was almost certainly suggested to Norris by Edwin Markham's 1899 poem 'The Man with the Hoe,' which "made a deep impression" (128) on him.

Once more Presley experiences Vanamee's influence, publishing "The Toilers" in a San Francisco daily in order for it to be read by "the People," who briefly take over from "the Wheat" as the object of the poet's enthusiasms. Intradiegetic reader response to the poem mirrors, in a kind of proleptic *mise en abyme*, the contradictory and perplexed judgments that *The Octopus* itself has elicited: "It was discussed, attacked, defended, eulogised, ridiculed. It was praised with the most fulsome adulation; assailed with the most violent condemnation. Editorials were written upon it. Special articles, in literary pamphlets, dissected its rhetoric and prosody" (890). The spectacular success of "The Toilers" briefly appears to give Presley the opportunity to solve the scale problem through his notoriety, offering the prospect of a national lecture tour through which he might coalesce opposition to the various trusts exerting their grip on the States. Yet the chance vanishes almost as quickly as it arose, since "Presley was essentially a dreamer, not a man of affairs" (891).

Paradoxically, then, scale is for Norris the preserve of those who act in the world, the "men of affairs," not those who dream of a better one. Where our intuitive understanding would be that it is easier to achieve colossal scale through word rather than deed since the imagination outstrips the possibilities of action, *The Octopus* inverts this relationship. It first delimits Presley's literary project from the West as a whole to "his People, the community in which he lived—the little world of the San Joaquin" (890) then, by the end of the novel, undermines even this project by voicing incisive criticism of the poem in the words of Shelgrim. The railroad president avers that he preferred the painting to the text Presley composed in response, offering the almost Platonic critique that "The Toilers" is a copy of a copy, and that "I would rather listen to what the great French painter has to say, than to what *you* have to say about what he has already said" (1036). Ironically, where Presley's first literary reflections in the novel consisted in the urge to emulate Homer, Norris closes the loop toward its end by having Shelgrim revive the most stringent denunciation of poetry to emerge from ancient Greece.

Presley's response is bewilderment and uncertainty at finding in Shelgrim not "an ogre, a brute, a terrible man of blood and iron," but instead "a sentimentalist and an art critic." The next thoughts that the narrator relates are particularly telling: "No standards of measurement in his mental equipment would apply to the actual man, and it began to dawn upon him that possibly it was not because these standards were different in kind, but that they were lamentably deficient in size" (1035–36). Just as his first attempt at a "Song of the West" was defeated by the scale of the landscape, his faith in the quality of "The Toilers" is shaken by a man whom Presley's mental apparatus is incapable of measuring. The scale problem bedevils the poet at every turn, just as it had the Leaguers. As a result, the professional wordsmith is reduced to stuttering "'I believe,' answered Presley, 'I am persuaded—'" when Shelgrim challenges him. His submission to scale is such that a single complete sentence now eludes him.

Shelgrim's philosophical disquisition to Presley further allows us to gauge that the scale problem is also a problem of agency. The president famously instructs the young man that neither Shelgrim himself nor the farmers are ultimately responsible for the operation of the railroad or the farms and, by extension, the tragedy of the shootout is essentially no one's fault:

> *Railroads build themselves.* Where there is a demand sooner or later there will be a supply. [. . .] *the Wheat will be carried to feed the people* as inevitably as it will grow. If you want to fasten the blame of the affair at Los Muertos on any one person, you will make a mistake. Blame conditions, not men. (1036–37)

This argument takes the common but by no means universal[2] association of the naturalist novel with philosophical determinism and pushes it to an extreme. It also turns Presley's poetic inspiration against him, turning "the People" into *the people* and making their aggregation into a commodity market the hypostasis for the immediate and personal bloodshed at Los Muertos. Even on his chosen ground, Presley is outmatched, as Shelgrim scales up the toilers from the individuated characters of the San Joaquin into a faceless, distributed mass rendered in italics. The commodity market inflicts a new defeat on the farming community in word as it already had in deed during the shootout.

The paradoxes of Shelgrim's reasoning neatly echo the paradoxical development of Supreme Court interpretations of corporate personhood as it entered the laissez-faire, pro-business *Lochner* era at the tail end of the nineteenth century. As Adam Winkler explains, the

Santa Clara decision that has come to be known as providing the chief precedent for the establishment of the corporate personhood doctrine actually offered no such basis. Instead it was a tendentious, inaccurate headnote added by the Court's Reporter of Decisions, J. C. Bancroft Davis, which asserted that "corporations are persons within the meaning of the Fourteenth Amendment to the Constitution of the United States" (cited in Winkler, 151): constitutional concerns had, in fact, explicitly been excluded from the Court's deliberations by Chief Justice Morrison Waite. And yet, once Davis's misreporting became published reality, "*Santa Clara* would take on sweeping importance as the justices repeatedly cited and relied on that case for authoritatively deciding that corporations were entitled to the Fourteenth Amendment's guarantees of equal protection and due process—legal principles never endorsed by the decision itself" (157). Where the Supreme Court would rely upon a distortion of a narrowly determined decision to roll out a legal doctrine with profound implications for American society over the succeeding decades, Shelgrim uses his individual executive voice to paint a picture of distributed, amorphous economic decision-making. He thereby absolves both himself and the corporation he directs of any culpability for the farmers' deaths and overthrows Presley's recriminations with a total deconstruction of the poet's intellectual apparatus.

The conclusion, with its much-critiqued dismissal of the manifold human suffering that has preceded it, can equally be read as a surrender to scale. Presley, with the help of Vanamee's mystical final words to him, finds an answer to the despairing questions: "Was good to be thus overthrown? Was evil thus to be strong and to prevail? Was nothing left?" (1097). The novel's final sentence explicitly derives moral value from the notion of scale, asserting that "the larger view always and through all shams, all wickednesses, discovers the Truth that will, in the end, prevail, and all things, surely, inevitably, resistlessly work together for good" (1098). The words of an almost penniless itinerant shepherd, motivated only by communion with the Western landscape and the miraculous reunion with his dead love Angele, appear to be twisted into a defense of the railroad's depredations and Cedarquist's still-larger hunger for financial gain, using charitable wheat shipments to India as a gateway drug to "carpet-sweepers for their harems and electric light plants for their temple shrines" (1095).

The poet's moral compass has recalibrated itself from the individual and local (the stories of his friends in and around Bonneville) to the transnational and impersonal (sailing to Calcutta while affirming that "the individual suffers, but the race goes on"). He has thus ended up where he began, in the sense that the opening chapter saw him marinating in the transnational literary tradition of the epic and steeped in the immensity of a Californian landscape that dwarfed the humans trying to improve their lot from its soil. Yet, in between, at least two things have been lost. The first is literature, since all semblance of being a writer appears to have vanished from Presley's mind in the wake of Shelgrim's critique; there is no further mention of his writings or his literary projects in the novel's remaining pages. The second is sympathy, since his initial project was to describe "a new people—hardy, brave, and passionate—[. . .] building an empire" (584). Leaving aside the morality of becoming the bard of empire, Presley's initial intent is to capture the emotions of the West's people, anchoring his writing in their striving.

We can thus observe a sequence of concatenating ambiguities and oppositions in *The Octopus.* Neither Presley nor Norris himself, in their different ways, appear able to decide whether the railroad is a monstrous local enemy to the valley's residents or the herald of a glorious, globalized twentieth century. The farmers are divided over both agricultural praxis and political strategy, and the League's uneasy alliance ends in bloodshed. Equally, the novel writhes with the paradoxes of corporate personhood identified by readers like Mrozowski: to use the repetitive phrasing Norris places in Annixter's mouth, in a way, Behrman and Shelgrim give physical form to the amorphous corporation, and then again, in a way, they don't.

EUROSCEPTIC NARRATIVE IN *SÉROTONINE*

It has become commonplace to discuss Houellebecq's literature in political terms, with many commentators in the media outside France emphasizing both the frequent controversies and the air of prescience surrounding his novels. Although perhaps less pronounced than in the case of its predecessor, *Soumission,* which imagined the accession of an Islamist to the French presidency and appeared on the same day as the *Charlie Hebdo* massacre in January 2015, the novel that interests me here, *Sérotonine,* has perpetuated these trends. It coincided with the rise of the *gilets jaunes* protest movement in France, and as such its portrayal of rural economic despair and revolt struck many observers as similarly synchronized to the zeitgeist as *Soumission* before it. Typical headlines include *The Economist*'s "Michel Houellebecq's New Book Is Eerily Prescient," *Deutsche Welle*'s "Prophet of Depressing Times: Michel Houellebecq Releases 'Yellow Vest' novel," and, in *Foreign Policy,* "Michel Houellebecq Hated Europe Before You Did."

It is the latter that will prove most relevant to the present discussion. I suggest that Houellebecq's use of the European Union in *Sérotonine* provides the closest point of contact with the problematics of *The Octopus,* since it figures a large-scale, impersonal, economically dominant, politically inexorable, networked entity that brings wealth to some but destruction to the band of farmers who organize to oppose it. As we have seen, *The Octopus* portrays such a body in profoundly conflicted fashion. It vacillates between sympathy for those who lose their lives and livelihoods to it and the two distinct claims that the losers were both outcompeted at a game they chose to play and that their defeat is, on a larger scale, of benefit to humanity as a whole. Is the same true of Houellebecq? Does the portrayal of dairy farmer Aymeric d'Harcourt-Olonde and his comrades contain similar equivocation? What differences in the European Union's operations demarcate it from the P.&S.W. of *The Octopus?* And does the change in professional status of the protagonist (Florent-Claude Labrouste is an agronomist, not a poet) bring concurrent changes in Houellebecq's portrayal of scale when his work is contrasted with Norris's?

If one takes the author's recent public declarations as reliable, there would seem to be little ambiguity in the valence of the European Union (EU) in *Sérotonine.* Collecting the Oswald Spengler Prize in Brussels three months before the novel's publication,[3] Houellebecq expressed a point of disagreement with another controversial French media pessimist (and 2022 presidential candidate), Éric Zemmour:

> Pourtant, à ma propre surprise, je n'avais pas été d'accord avec le titre de l'avant-dernier livre d'Éric Zemmour, *Le Suicide français.* Parce que dans l'histoire récente de la France, il y a quelque chose qui relève non pas du suicide, mais bel et bien de l'assassinat. Et le coupable de cet

> assassinat n'est guère difficile à découvrir: c'est l'Union européenne. Quant aux complices en France, ils sont nombreux.[4]
>
> (And yet, to my surprise, I didn't agree with the title of Éric Zemmour's second-to-last book, *The French Suicide.* Because in France's recent history, there is something that bespeaks not suicide, but outright murder. And the culprit of the assassination is hardly difficult to identify: it's the European Union. As for its accomplices in France, they are many.)[5]

Ironically given the pivotal role that Aymeric's suicide will play in *Sérotonine*'s plot, Houellebecq here presents France's cultural and economic decline not as a narrative of suicide as Zemmour does but rather as a murder perpetrated by the EU and abetted by numerous unnamed accomplices from within. Yet this murder is itself merely a specific case of continent-wide suicide, with the following unique characteristic: "à l'intérieur du monde Occidental, l'Europe a choisi un mode de suicide particulier, qui inclut le fait d'assassiner les nations qui la composent" (within the Western world, Europe has chosen a distinctive form of suicide, which includes assassinating its constituent nations). In his speech, Houellebecq thus personifies the EU, portraying it as committing suicide by slow destruction of its constituent parts, a form of transnational self-mutilation. On the train ride to Brussels to collect the award, he declared to a *Valeurs Actuelles* journalist that "je suis prêt à voter pour n'importe qui pourvu qu'on propose la sortie de l'Union européenne et de l'Otan, ça, j'y tiens beaucoup" (I'm ready to vote for anyone so long as they propose to exit the European Union and NATO, that's what's really dear to me).[6]

Derrida's treatment of sovereignty and of auto-affection connects to Houellebecq's Euroscepticism in the sense that the former's "aporetical relation between sameness and otherness" (Lawlor, 136) finds echoes in the latter's metaphor of continental self-murder. As Leonard Lawlor summarizes it, in Derrida's later political writings "sovereignty is incompatible with universalization [. . .] and yet [. . .] sovereignty must communicate its power, its freedom, its decisions" (137). The gap between the singularized, aloof power of the EU and its distributed effects on member states—as well as individual citizens such as the dairy farmer—creates the conditions for the tragedy played out in *Sérotonine.* The abolition of the milk quotas takes place in an instant, the hallmark of Derridean sovereignty, but its effects spread out across time and place from that day in Brussels. Where, in a Derridean perspective, "the event of sovereign power is always to come" (Lawlor, 137), Houellebecq too implies that the events of his novel are merely signposts along the road to a greater superstate cataclysm.

The Brexit vote of June 2016, whose consequences were fully consummated on December 31, 2020, seems to have exacerbated Houellebecq's Euroscepticism. Beginning in the second of half of 2016, he began making repeated prophecies of the EU's collapse and approvingly invoking the possibility of a "Frexit." Even when speaking to non-European interlocutors, the author often chose to foreground the topic. For instance, in a November 2016 interview with Argentine journalist Gonzalo Garces, he declared that

> La France est très proche de quitter l'Europe [. . .] Les Français sont dans l'Europe contre leur volonté [. . .] Il est dommage que le Brexit n'ait pas fait abandonner l'idée d'une Union européenne définitivement [. . .] L'Union européenne n'est qu'une idée de technocrates qui ne saisissent pas pleinement les spécificités de chacun [*sic*] pays. (cited in Gary)
>
> (France is very close to leaving Europe [. . .] The French are part of Europe against their will [. . .] It's a shame that Brexit hasn't led to the definitive abandonment of the idea of a European Union [. . .] The European Union is nothing more than the idea of technocrats who have no true understanding of each country's specificities.)

The accusation of failed technocracy leveled at the EU is a staple of Euroscepticism across the continent and beyond; it appears to confer no specificity or originality on Houellebecq's position, but it does point toward one of the salient features of *Sérotonine* that has particular significance for my reading of the novel. Houellebecq combines his preliterary career as an agronomist with his hostility to the EU in making the protagonist, the aforementioned Florent-Claude Labrouste, a member of the same profession. Florent-Claude has spent long years fighting what he portrays as a prolonged losing battle against members of his own trade who are in thrall to French and EU bureaucratic mandates and errant thinking.

In the years prior to writing *Sérotonine,* Houellebecq confessed to having lost touch with "la France périphérique" (peripheral France),[7] by which he meant those of his compatriots voting for Marine Le Pen but who could also be seen as close kin to "la France profonde," its more rural, more geographically and culturally marginal elements. In previous novels, where Houellebecq had considered "la France profonde" at all, he did so in a more postmodern fashion. Notably, in the Prix Goncourt–winning *La Carte et le territoire* (2010), he "shows that it is paradoxically under neoliberalism's conditions of throw-away production and consumption" that sectors enrolling rural France in their products and marketing, notably "the leisure industries of niche tourism and gastronomy" (D'Arcens, 264) will be able to prosper in the globalized twenty-first century. Joshua Armstrong has argued that *La Carte et le territoire* relies on "the comingling of cartographic and television aesthetics [. . .]" with a protagonist, Jed Martin, who is "singular in his lack of attachment to people, to the local, to—in a word—the *territory* and the things that make it a place of human inhabitation and attachment" (43). In such a landscape, the scale problem does not exist: "incredibly complex and consequential decisions [. . .] turn out to be no more complicated than changing the television channel." In a similar vein, Agathe Novak-Lechevalier says of the same novel that "le langage nous condamne à vivre dans un simulacre, un vaste plagiat du réel, et un plagiat volontairement truqué" (133; language now condemns us to live in a simulacrum, a vast plagiarism of reality, and a deliberately rigged one at that).

Sérotonine shifts focus, showing the human cost of the rural economy's transformations, emphasizing the individual actors at play rather than the pseudo-nostalgic products of corporations under foreign ownership, the seamless confusion of scale introduced by television, or the Baudrillardian entanglements of contemporary discourse. Houellebecq's engagement with the Norman countryside thus introduces a genuinely novel note into his writing and, in so doing, also introduces a version of the scale problem that had structured *The Octopus* over a century earlier. Florent-Claude's long professional experience, coupled with his friendship with Aymeric (which will be the particular focus here), provides a form of remediation to the author's real-life declaration of inadequacy.[8]

The relationship between the two men rests on the mutual exchange of advice and expertise. From Aymeric to Florent-Claude, this consists primarily in shooting lessons, along with the related loan of a Steyr Mannlicher rifle:

> Il étala la couverture sur le sol herbeux et me désigna une barque enfouie dans le sable [. . .] "Tu vois l'immatriculation peinte sur le flanc, BOZ-43? Tu vas essayer de placer une balle au centre du O [. . .] avec la Steyr

> Mannlicher, un bon tireur y arriverait sans problème à quinze cents mètres; mais bon, on va commencer avec ça." (Houellebecq 2019, 233)
>
> He spread the blanket across the grass and pointed to a small boat half-buried in the sand [. . .] ("You see the license number painted on the side, BOZ-43? You're going to try to hit the middle of the 'O' [. . .] with the Steyr Mannlicher, a good shooter hits it no problem from a mile away; but anyway, let's start small.")

The exchange is doubly significant, prefiguring both characters' later actions. It announces both Aymeric's violent death and Florent-Claude's abortive attempt to assassinate the young son of his ex-lover, Camille.[9] Where Aymeric's suicide is driven largely by economic despair, Florent-Claude's turn toward gun violence has no such cause; he is not in financial distress and has had a successful career first at the agribusiness behemoth Monsanto and then as a contractor for the French agriculture ministry. Instead, his midlife crisis manifests as depression rooted in his failed romantic relationships, with Camille the most painful of those failures. This explains his pedicidal intent with regard to her son: "Pouvait-on imaginer que Camille mette en danger pour moi cette relation parfaite et fusionnelle qu'elle vivait avec son fils? [. . .] La réponse [. . .] était passablement évidente, et la conclusion inéluctable: c'était lui ou moi" (299; was it conceivable that Camille would endanger the perfect, symbiotic relationship she had with her son? [. . .] The answer [. . .] was pretty obvious, and the conclusion inescapable; it was either him or me). Just as prolonged contact with his farmer friends in *The Octopus* powerfully affects Presley's worldview, inspiring him to write *The Toilers*, so Florent-Claude's time with Aymeric shifts his depression into an almost-deadly fixation with instrumentalizing violence: "le tir le plus important de ma vie, le seul objectif au fond de mes mois d'entraînement" (303; the most important shot in my life, the only goal at the end of my months of training).

Where the plight of France's agricultural sector is a new theme in Houellebecq's corpus, even those who have never read him may well recognize existential pessimism over the possibility of romantic and sexual fulfillment as a perennial theme in his fiction, simply from the labels attached to him in media and/or academic discussion. Carole Sweeney captures this prevailing mood in the author's work: "Beneath the graphic descriptions of sex and the deadpan humour, lies a profoundly melancholic despair; a poignant sense of loss that something has passed away in human relations" (43). Florent-Claude stands in a long lineage of avatars of this pessimism stretching back to the unnamed autodiegetic protagonist of *Extension du domaine de la lutte* (1994) and perhaps most clearly exemplified by Bruno Clément, one of the two brothers at the center of *Les Particules élémentaires* (1998). Whereas Bruno ends up in a mental asylum after a lifetime of sexual disappointment and obsession, Florent-Claude will end *Sérotonine* shut in his studio with the blinds down, contemplating a plunge from the balcony:

> J'avais l'intention d'opérer de nuit, pour ne pas être arrêté par la vue du béton de l'esplanade, je croyais peu en mon propre courage. [. . .] Il y aurait certainement bien davantage de suicides si les gens connaissaient ce simple chiffre: quatre secondes et demie. J'attendrais le sol à une vitesse de 159 kilomètres/heure [. . .] (342–43)
>
> (I'd planned to do it at night, so as not to be deterred by seeing the concrete walkway below, I had little faith in my own courage. [. . .] There would certainly be a lot more suicides if people knew this simple figure: four-and-a-half seconds. I'd hit the ground at a hundred miles an hour [. . .])

As Karl Ågerup has pointed out, Houellebecq's standard protagonist "is a depressed solitary middle-aged male whose pleasures are basically limited to having sex with prostitutes, consuming lots of bourbon, and formulating one-liners that capture mankind's decrepitude" (198).

Yet this familiar protagonist trajectory does not mean that *Sérotonine*'s thematics of despair will be divided into two variants, assigning the romantic strain to Florent-Claude and the economic one to Aymeric. Instead, both characters inextricably combine sexuality and economics in their analysis of Aymeric's plight. As a result, Houellebecq opens his fictional world up to a discussion of rural tragedy by interweaving it with other themes familiar to readers of his six previous novels.

Aymeric's romantic and economic plots operate in parallel throughout the novel. One of the many analepses Houellebecq employs (as Florent-Claude casts his mind back over the events of previous decades) describes the protagonist's first visit to his friend's farm a few years after their graduation: in other words, it occurs around fifteen years prior to the main narrative. With his hypertrophically aristocratic double-barreled surname and dilapidated thirteenth-century chateau whose walls are studded with ancestral portraiture ("un incohérent assemblage de bâtisses, dans un état de préservation variable, on avait du mal à reconstituer le plan initial de l'édifice" [143; an incoherent assembly of structures, in varying degrees of preservation, it was hard to reconstitute the original layout in my head]), Aymeric simultaneously incarnates two different aspects of French decline in Houellebecq's presentation. He combines the vanished power and pride of the landed aristocracy with the more modern and pervasive financial plight of the small-scale farmer, his gleaming metal silo being "le premier bâtiment récent que je voyais depuis une cinquantaine de kilomètres" (144; the first recent building I'd seen in the last thirty miles). This almost self-contradictory architectural congeries gives tangible form to the quixotic nature of Aymeric's project, in which he has forsaken the promise of a lucrative career at dairy giant Danone for a doomed attempt to resurrect his family's agrarian traditions.

On Florent-Claude's first visit, Aymeric's wife Cécile has embarked on the venture of turning the chateau into a hotel, in response to the dairy farm's inability to generate a profit. Signs of strain are already apparent, as the protagonist's narration combines appreciation for her looks with the symptoms of chronic stress: "une jolie brune, mince et élégante, mais son visage était marqué par la tension, la souffrance presque" (148; a pretty brunette, slim and elegant, but her face was marked by stress, perhaps even suffering). Meanwhile, his time surveying the farm with Aymeric brings a foreshadowing of the key event in the novel's economic plot, which will then occur elliptically:

> je n'avais pas osé le dire à Aymeric mais [. . .] j'avais entendu des rumeurs selon lesquelles, à Bruxelles, on commençait à agiter l'idée d'une suppression des quotas laitiers—cette décision qui devait plonger des milliers d'éleveurs français dans la misère, et les réduire à la faillite [. . .] (151)
>
> (I hadn't had the heart to tell Aymeric but [. . .] I'd heard rumors that, in Brussels, they were starting to mull the idea of abolishing the milk quotas—that decision which would later plunge thousands of French herders into poverty, and reduce them to bankruptcy [. . .])

Through Florent-Claude, Houellebecq ties the abolition of EU milk quotas, a cornerstone of the Common Agricultural Policy enforced between 1984 and 2015, to the fictional catastrophes he visits on the farmer characters of *Sérotonine.* In other words, a single, centralized decision by the hegemonic economic power of the EU has the same ruinous consequence that the P.&S.W.'s enforcement of high land prices on the farmers of the San Joaquin Valley does in Norris's novel. In both cases, it is this single decision that sets in motion a narrative syntagm, culminating in public, collective bloodshed.

This combination of aristocratic decline, struggling small dairy farms, and EU top-down rulings sets up the problematic of scale in *Sérotonine* years before the period of the primary narrative is reached. Aymeric is suffering the indignities of scale twice over, a man not only afflicted by supranational mandates that will make his economic survival impossible but also a pale shadow of the illustrious forebears who bequeathed him his name. Furthermore, as will become clear below, the scale disparity between the farmer and his economic antagonist is greater still in *Sérotonine* than in *The Octopus;* rather than a single US state, an entire continent squirms in its grip. The additional complexity inherent in the political economy of the early twenty-first century, as compared to the turn of the twentieth, intensifies the scale problem and renders it still harder for individual human minds to resolve.

Does Houellebecq's fictionalization of the quota abolition correspond to its reality? The few short years that have passed mean that definitive analysis is still lacking. It does seem to be the case that French producers with small herds, of which Aymeric and his colleagues serve as imagined counterparts, were among the hardest hit in Europe. Reflecting on the change in policy five years on, agricultural news organization Agra reported that "malgré la volatilité des prix et la dégradation du rapport de force des producteurs face aux laiteries en France, le prix moyen ne s'est pas dégradé sur l'ensemble des cinq années" (despite price volatility and diminished bargaining power for producers in their dealings with dairies, the average price has not decreased over the last five years [*AGRA*]). Yet this overall equilibrium masks the fact that "les exploitations se restructurent. Elles grossissent ou disparaissent—à un rythme de 3 à 4 % par an. Les grandes exploitations de plus de 100 vaches représentaient 3 % du cheptel en 2000, 11 % en 2010 et 33 % en 2019, note l'Idèle" (farms are restructuring. They either expand or disappear—at a rate of 3–4% per year. Large herds of over 100 cattle represented 3% of the national stock in 2000, 11% in 2010 and 33% in 2019, according to the French

Livestock Institute [*AGRA*]). Academic research supports the claim that "the changes had a negative impact on smaller dairy farms, while benefiting the larger ones" (Bórawski, Pawlewicz, Parzonko, Harper, and Holden 3). Thus, in service of his narrative of decline, Houellebecq has highlighted (or cherry-picked, depending on one's perspective) one of the most distressed segments of the European agricultural sector, exploring the collateral damage of an EU policy that has brought greater wealth to those already possessing capital and often insurmountable hardship to those operating on a smaller scale.

Sérotonine is far from the only French cultural product of recent years to explore the challenges of the nation's farmers. Films such as Hubert Charuel's *Petit paysan* (*Bloody Milk,* 2017) and Edouard Bergeon's *Au nom de la terre* (*In the Name of the Land,* 2019) have trodden similar ground and garnered significant critical and / or commercial success. *Petit paysan* took home three Césars, including Best Actor for its lead Swann Arlaud, while *Au nom de la terre,* which Bergeon based on his own family's experiences,[10] sold over two million tickets in France.[11] In reviewing *Au nom de la terre* from across the Atlantic, *The Hollywood Reporter* situated it in a recent French trend of *cinéma du mal de terre,* a term that appears to have been coined by journalist Jordan Mintzer. In parallel with these fictional treatments of the problem, French media have begun to discuss elevated suicide rates among agricultural proprietors more frequently, with major outlets such as *Le Figaro, Franceinfo, LCI,* and *France Culture* devoting pieces to the phenomenon. *France Bleu* describes farmers as "la catégorie socioprofessionelle la plus à risque" (the most at-risk socioprofessional category) and highlights that "la production laitière et l'élevage bovin sont les secteurs les plus touchés" (milk production and cattle herding are the worst-affected sectors, Jocteur Monrozier). Houellebecq's novel thus reflects a growing preoccupation in France with the manner in which its agricultural sector as a whole, and its cattle farmers in particular, have been afflicted by despair.

In *Sérotonine,* the despair is expressed through confusion. Despite his experience operating in both the French and European systems, Florent-Claude at times expresses a similar degree of incomprehension and incommensurability concerning the economy to that evident in Presley's reaction to Shelgrim in *The Octopus.* Reflecting on his discussions with Camille's father, he claims that:

> Les conversations sur l'économie sont un peu semblables aux conversations sur les cyclones ou les tremblements de terre; on finit assez vite par ne plus comprendre de quoi on parle, on a l'impression d'évoquer une divinité obscure et on se ressert du champagne. (187; conversations about the economy are a bit like conversations about hurricanes or earthquakes; you quickly end up not understanding what's being said, you start feeling like you're invoking an obscure deity and you help yourself to some more champagne.)

It is noteworthy that this conclusion immediately follows the other man's expression of sympathy for "la détresse de plus en plus criante des agriculteurs de sa région" (186; the increasingly deafening distress of his region's farmers). Houellebecq's choice of metaphor, painting local farmers' economic hardship as akin to the survivors of a natural disaster, contributes to the book-length extended metaphor of agricultural economics under the EU's stewardship as a force beyond individual or even collective control. The follow-up image of a "divinité obscure" adds an element of sacred terror that, while distinct from the almost pantheistic ending of *The Octopus,* nevertheless similarly serves to emphasize the radical disproportion in scale between the toil of the individual farmer and the larger mechanisms and organizations Houellebecq and Norris set against them. Both writers allege an absence of human agency in the forces acting against their agricultural characters, likening them instead to uncaring entities from the natural world.

As in *The Octopus,* the farmers' fictional insurrection is a product of the scale problem. Their inability to protect their interests in the face of top-down changes to the CAP is what drives them to attempt armed resistance to state power. In this case, however, and unlike in *The Octopus,* the French state serves as an agent of the European superstate, meaning that Houellebecq's treatment of the scale problem is still more telescopic than Norris's, reflecting the increasingly networked and globalized world he is attempting to describe. Symbolic of this nested approach to scale, and more specifically to the deployment of economic and police power, is the fact that the term "Union européenne" appears only once in the entire novel. Before discussing the passage in which it occurs, it is necessary to return to Aymeric's romantic plot.

When, in the main narrative, Florent-Claude meets up with his friend after fifteen years, he finds him bereft of both Cécile and the two daughters they had been raising in the intervening period. Aymeric now haunts his ancestral castle with a "regard qui était effrayant, un regard creux, mort, qu'il semblait impossible de distraire, davantage que quelques secondes, de la contemplation du vide" (195; a terrifying gaze, hollow, dead, which seemed impossible to distract from staring into the void for more than a few seconds). The two men have different interpretations of her departure, Aymeric's being economic ("je l'ai trop fait bosser, le gestion de la ferme c'était déjà énorme mais avec les bungalows c'est devenu dingue" [204; I made her work too hard, managing the farm was already huge but it got crazy with the holiday bungalows on top]), Florent-Claude's sexual ("elle n'avait qu'à épouser quelqu'un d'autre, la salope [. . .] Il aurait pu ajouter [. . .] qu'ils ne baisaient plus, et que c'était là le cœur du problème, les femmes sont moins vénales qu'on ne le prétend parfois" [205; she should have married someone else, the whore [. . .] He might have added [. . .] that they weren't fucking any more, and that that was the root of the problem, women are less materialistic than you'd think sometimes]). Despite apparently having no evidence, the protagonist projects his sexual preoccupations onto his friend's marriage, convincing himself that a lack of erotic fulfillment was the cause of Aymeric's solitude.

Florent-Claude's casually derogatory branding of Cécile as a "salope" returns with ideological force later, at the moment of Aymeric's death. In the process, it collapses the apparent initial distinction I have just highlighted between economics and sexuality. The farmer's suicide occurs as follows. Aymeric and many of his regional colleagues, in order to protest falling milk prices, have blockaded Pont-l'Evêque, the town having been chosen "parce qu'elle était à l'intersection de la branche de l'A132 venant de Deauville et de l'A13 Caen-Paris" (252; because it was the intersection of the A132 highway from Deauville and the A13 from Caen to Paris). They choose to position themselves at a node in the French transport network, a motorway junction whose visibility and economic importance will draw maximal attention to their cause. (Their apprehension of milk tankers headed for port at Le Havre had already made the news station BFM the previous day.[12]) Confronted by a deployment of the CRS (French riot police), whose excesses have been heavily chronicled during the real-life *gilets jaunes* protests Houellebecq has been credited with anticipating,[13] Aymeric's previously closely guarded depression suddenly takes on very public form. He begins aiming his assault rifle at the massed CRS, then, after a pregnant pause, "quelque chose de différent passa alors sur son visage, comme une douleur générale; il retourna le canon, le plaça sous son menton et appuya sur la détente" (262; something different flashed across his face then, like a generalized pain; he turned the barrel around, placed it under his chin and pulled the trigger). The other farmers, believing that the CRS have gunned him down, open fire, which precipitates a shootout that leaves ten of their number dead along with one officer.

How does Florent-Claude's misogyny toward Cécile inform the tragedy? As he watches Aymeric's final moments before the gunfire begins, realizing that the death of his friend's dreams has left him beyond saving prompts the thought that

> Cécile s'était avérée une grosse salope passionnée par la vie à Londres avec un pianiste mondain, et l'Union européenne elle aussi avait été une grosse salope, avec cette histoire de quotas laitiers, il ne s'attendait certainement pas à ce que les choses se terminent ainsi. (259)
>
> Cécile had turned out to be a massive whore living the high life in London with her fashionable pianist, and the European Union had been a massive whore too, with the milk quota business, he surely hadn't expected that things would turn out this way.

The narrator's final judgment on the farmer about to end his own life intertwines sexual abandonment by the latter's wife with economic abandonment by the CAP. Where, on first presenting Cécile's flight to London, the narrative offers two viewpoints that place economic and sexual logic at odds with each other, by the time of the farmers' insurrection the distinction between the two has been erased. The absent wife and the delinquent EU become twin "grosses salopes" whose concerted efforts have, on Florent-Claude's analysis, dictated a good man's death. In the process, Houellebecq switches metaphors for the transnational body: from natural disaster to harlot. In a recent reading, Amaury Dehoux takes *Extension du domaine de la lutte* as typifying the limits of the "roman occidental contemporain, qui se trouve donn[*é*] dans son incapacité à proposer une alternative à l'*anthropoïesis* de l'individualité" (222–23; contemporary Western novel, which is given in its incapacity to offer an alternative to the *anthropoeisis* of individuality). The farmers' insurrection in *Sérotonine* prolongs this perspective, showing the limits of scale far more dramatically and spectacularly than the narrative of *Extension* does. Although the bloodshed leaves eleven dead and involves both the French state's monopoly on violence and, behind it, the EU's technocratic decision-making, it stems from the individual act of Aymeric choosing despair over life. The disjunction in scale between this deed, on the one hand, and the vast political forces at work—the farmers confronting riot police at the motorway junction—on the other, precipitates the plot resolution.

This solitary direct invocation of the EU in *Sérotonine* in fact represents the culmination of a pattern running through the novel, one that associates foreignness with both economic and moral corruption. Cécile's derided pursuit of better economic and sexual rewards in London accompanies two earlier incidents that imply a related perspective. The first comes in Florent-Claude's analeptic explanation of his breakup with Camille years earlier. At the time, his work often took him to Brussels, which gave him "l'illusion d'être un homme important" (182; the illusion of being an important man). This hubris leads him to sleep with a member of the British delegation, Tam, with whom Camille later discovers him in Paris.[14] The diegesis of his lapsarian moment immediately follows a reflection on the economic and political lessons learned from his time in Brussels: "le budget agricole européen [. . .] avait beau être le premier budget européen, et la France le premier pays bénéficiaire [. . .] je conclus peu à peu que les agriculteurs français étaient simplement condamnés" (even though the European Union's agricultural budget [. . .] was its largest expenditure, and France the greatest beneficiary [. . .] I slowly concluded that French farmers were simply doomed).The agronomist's response is telling: "aussi je me détachai de cet emploi, comme des autres" (182; so I disassociated from that job, like all the others). His series of detachments from professional commitments mirrors his lengthy sequence of romantic abandonments, of which that of Camille is the most profound. Each of the other lovers named in the novel, from Yuzu to Kate to Claire, is forsaken in turn, albeit that circumstances sometimes complicate the picture (notably the discovery of Yuzu having used their apartment to create an impressive collection of sex films).

Florent-Claude's narrative thus combines economic and romantic detachment more often than Aymeric's, which centers on a single incident of each, but the other difference between the two men lies in their agency. Florent-Claude is perennially the agent of abandonment, while Aymeric is its victim. Their mirrored depressions thus have similar thematic roots but different psychological mechanisms as a result of the disparity in agency; Florent-Claude is driven by guilt, Aymeric by despair. To return to the former's betrayal of Camille, it is presented as inspired by the technocratic environment of Brussels (he makes a pass at Tam on a night out as part of "un groupe d'eurocrates relativement jeunes" [182; a group of relatively young Eurocrats]), marking a slippage between the character's loss of faith in European institutions and his faithlessness toward the woman waiting for him in Paris.

Another form of corruption awaits Florent-Claude immediately before the fatal farmers' insurrection. The only other winter guest staying at Aymeric's holiday bungalows is a German ornithologist, whose increasingly eccentric avoidant behavior fascinates the protagonist. On seeing a little girl arrive at the German's residence, he immediately suspects pedophilia: "quelle raison pouvait bien avoir une petite fille de dix ans pour frapper à la porte d'un quadragénaire misanthrope et sinistre, allemand de surcroît?" (212; what possible reason could a ten-year-old girl have for knocking at the door of a sinister, misanthropic forty-year-old, and a German one to boot?). When the opportunity to break in presents itself, Florent-Claude's suspicions are confirmed by the discovery of a video whose viewing Houellebecq narrates in blackly comedic style ("tout de suite je sentis que j'allais souffrir de l'amateurisme de la prise de vue" [214; I could tell right away that I was going to be distressed by the amateurish camera work]). A tense confrontation between the two puts the German to flight, never to reappear.

The choice of the pedophile's nationality is unlikely to have been a coincidence, given the novel's overarching anti-EU slant. In France and beyond, Euroscepticism regularly targets Germany and its purported economic and political dominance of the union: mainstream opinion writers on both the left and right of the French press have harshly critiqued German political gambits in recent years.[15] The German pedophile thus incarnates another form of malign European influence extending its tendrils onto Aymeric's farm. Where the abstract, remote EU will ruin his agricultural project, the birdwatcher brings a personal note of sexual depravity directly onto the premises, another means for Houellebecq to interweave the two thematics and to characterize France's integration into Europe as a double disaster.

It is important to note that Houellebecq's and *Sérotonine*'s hostility to the EU is not reflective of a more general discomfort with transnational identity in the author's work, which makes the particular vitriol directed at the union more striking. Jacqueline Dutton has argued that Houellebecq's previous novel, *Soumission,*"predicts the coming transnationalism as overwhelmingly Islamic, hegemonic, yet perceived by his protagonist as positive. [. . .] Some transnational identities must fall away for the dominant transnational dynamic to change France and Europe in the future" (218). Where the imagined winner of the 2022 presidential election, Mohammed Ben Abbes, remakes France into the hub of a transnational, Mediterranean-centered new order in *Soumission,* the EU operates in *Sérotonine* without the cult of personality or imperial vision that had proved successful in its predecessor. In other words, the political-science-fiction premise of *Soumission* enables Houellebecq to propose a solution to the scale problem that *Sérotonine*'s reversion to a more realist premise then banishes. This serves as a reminder that the difficulties posed by scale in the latter novel are not pervasive across the author's entire corpus. As in Norris, the defining characteristics of modern farming make for an especially acute statement of the scale problem in fiction.

The plight of both Norman cattle herders and San Joaquin wheat growers reflects four of the five features given to the concepts of "natural and social commons" by Michael Hardt and Anthony Negri. In Christian Fuchs's summary, these are:

1) The earth and its ecosystems;
2) The "immaterial" common of ideas, codes, images and cultural products;
3) Tangible goods produced by co-operative work;
4) Metropolitan and rural spaces that are realms of communication, cultural interaction and co-operation;
5) Social institutions and services that organise housing, welfare, health, and education (459)

Leaving aside the fifth category, Aymeric's farm in particular combines the other four in a single locus with particular force. The earth and its ecosystems are transformed into tangible goods, synthesizing points one and three, and the collapse of Aymeric's marriage also serves to underline the loss of work's cooperative aspect underlined by Hardt and Negri. Meanwhile, and as seen in countless narratives such as the films discussed above as well as in the French educational system going back centuries, farm life undoubtedly provides one of the country's major repositories "of ideas, codes, images and cultural products." A clear example of this is the mythic status afforded in more recent centuries to the Duc de Sully's early seventeenth-century pronouncement that "labourage et pâturage sont les deux mamelles dont la France est alimentée" (tilled soil and pastureland are the two teats that nourish France).[16] Indeed, when it comes to smallholdings, the fourth aspect of the commons provides a hypostasis for the second; it is precisely because the specific mode of life led by people such as Aymeric has (an often distorted and romanticized) appeal to those with more urban, sedentary existences: their spaces serve as "realms of communication," which feed the entire nation's cultural codes as much as its hungry mouths. Of course, all of the above points hold, albeit that Norris may emphasize them less, for the Californian farmers of a century or more earlier.

As a result, the economic failures that spark the gun battles in both *The Octopus* and *Sérotonine* can be read as symptomatic of real subsumption, in which "ever more spaces that were autonomous from capital have come under its influence and control and have been turned into spheres of capital accumulation, commodity production and the exploitation of labour" (Fuchs, 457). The precapitalist age of Aymeric's ancestral home, and his explicitly contra-capitalist motivations for returning to it rather than working for Danone, testify to a geographical and cultural resistance to accumulation that is overcome by the end of the EU milk quotas. Thrown to the vagaries of the market, the herder becomes incapable of keeping these spheres separate. Cécile's departure for London similarly demonstrates that the affective, private space of marriage has succumbed to real subsumption. It is no accident that her new husband is a concert pianist, representing the fungibility of a cultural product that, thanks to the globalization of taste alongside capital, is as marketable in, say, East Asia as it is in Western Europe. Although culture functions somewhat differently in *The Octopus,* creative activity there too either aligns itself with global capital or perishes. Where Cécile's pianist appears to thrive, Presley abandons his poetic aspirations because he cannot equal the railroad's scale in verse; here, we observe capital stifling an autonomous space rather than re-creating it in its own image.

If we return to Shelgrim's obfuscation of agency in the sermon to Presley that produces the above result, the still-greater work of scale on Houellebecq's part in *Sérotonine* is thrown into its clearest light. There is no such equivalent figure in the French text. In discussing European decision-making and economic markets more generally, Florent-Claude repeatedly employs the impersonal third-person singular pronoun "on," thereby disembodying the operation of both spheres. The question posed by Steinbeck in *The Grapes of Wrath,* therefore, can only be answered with a reflexive pronoun. Aymeric's decision to turn the gun on himself is the logical outcome of an economic narrative in which no personal antagonist appears.

Both *The Octopus* and *Sérotonine,* then, conclude their agricultural plots with a submission to scale. In other words, the remarkably similar features of their fictional farming insurrections are a clue to the deeper parallels between the two novels rather than mere happenstance. The submission takes different forms, with Norris's tempered optimism writing out the tragedy of the shootout in favor of Presley's Panglossian globetrotting in the conclusion. Fed by Houellebecq's bleaker perspective, Aymeric's response to being defeated by scale is almost diametrically opposed, rooted to his native soil rather than setting forth across the ocean, dying from "douleur générale" instead of affirming that "all things [. . .] work together for good." Yet these are different answers to the same underlying problem; neither the wheat farmers of the San Joaquin nor the dairy farmers of Normandy are capable of scaling up their political or armed resistance to the large, impersonal entities that threaten them. The choice of farming characters adds urgency to this problematic by wedding them to the land in a manner that makes their economic failure existential in nature. Unlike the protagonists who observe them, Norris's and Houellebecq's farmers cannot move beyond the horizon of their property.

Roderick Cooke is associate professor of French at Villanova University. A specialist of modern French and comparative literature, he has published articles on writers such as Zola, Baudelaire, Tanizaki and George Eliot. He is the author of *The Dreyfus Affair's Literary Politics* (2023).

Notes

1. In "Social Darwinism or Social Protest? The 'Philosophy' of *The Octopus*" (*Modern Fiction Studies* 8 [1963]: 393–400), and "Automation and Apocalypse in *The Octopus*" (in *Science, Values, and the American West*, edited by Stephen Tchudi [Reno: Nevada Humanities Committee, 1997]: 27–51), respectively.

2. Notably, the doyen of critics of American literary naturalism, Donald Pizer, has spent decades contesting the claim that naturalism and determinism are synonymous. He defines the movement instead through "an author's struggle to confront the conflict between old values and new experience in his time, a struggle which usually resulted in a vital thematic ambivalence. [. . .] it was this very ambivalence, rather than the certainties of the convinced determinist, which was the source of the fictional strength of the naturalistic novel" (6).

3. The image of Michel Houellebecq accepting the Oswald Spengler Prize might strike one as the invention of a particularly heavy-handed satirist, but the event did, in fact, occur.

4. The full speech is reproduced in an article by *Valeurs Actuelles* titled "Houellebecq recevant le prix Oswald Spengler: 'L'Occident est dans un état de déclin très avancé.'" *https://www.valeursactuelles.com/clubvaleurs/culture/houellebecq-recevant-le-prix-oswald-spengler-loccident-est-dans-un-etat-de-declin-tres-avance-100202* (accessed March 4, 2021).

5. All translations from French are my own.

6. *https://www.valeursactuelles.com/clubvaleurs/culture/leurope-la-droite-macron-le-foot-une-journee-dans-les-pas-de-michel-houellebecq-100203* (accessed March 7, 2021).

7. See his appearance on France 2's *L'Émission politique* between the first and second rounds of the 2017 French presidential election. A video and text summary can be found in Sgherri.

8. In the same TV interview with *L'Émission politique*, Houellebecq acknowledged his unfamiliarity with 'la France périphérique' as "une faute professionnelle grave" (a serious professional failing).

9. Houellebecq 2019, 303.

10. See, for instance, Camille Labro's article ""Au nom de la terre," l'hommage poignant d'Edouard Bergeon au monde paysan," *Le Monde*, September 20, 2019, *https ://www.lemonde.fr/m-le-mag/article/2019/09/20/au-nom-de-la-terre-l-hommage-poignant-d-edouard-bergeon-au-monde-paysan_6012428_4500055.html* (accessed March 11, 2021). Bergeon's father, himself a farmer facing bankruptcy, killed himself when the director was sixteen.

11. *https://www.allocine.fr/article/fichearticle_gen_carticle=18687225.html* (accessed March 11, 2021).

12. Houellebecq 2019, 250–51.

13. See, notably, Robert Chalmers, "The Real Victims of France's 'Yellow Vest' Revolution," *GQ*, August 19, 2019, *https://www.gq-magazine.co.uk/politics/article/les-gilets-jaunes*.

14. Florent-Claude's descriptions of Tam's Black body add another layer of bigotry to his more generalized misogyny: "elle était ravissante cette petite black, surtout son petit cul [. . .] J'ajoute quelle suçait "comme une reine"" (182–3; she was gorgeous, that little Black chick, especially her little ass [. . .] I should add that she gave heavenly blow jobs).

15. See, as an example on the left, Jean Quatremer's piece "Au sein de l'Union européenne, l'appétit sans fin de Berlin," *Libération,* June 19, 2019, *https://www.liberation.fr/planete/2019/06/19/au-sein-de-l-union-europeenne-l-appetit-sans-fin-de-berlin_1734932/*. For an example on the right, see Maxime Tandonnet's "L'Impasse d'une Europe sous domination allemande," *Le Figaro,* July 8, 2015, *https://www.lefigaro.fr/vox/politique/2015/07/08/31001-20150708ARTFIG00256-l-impasse-d-une-europe-sous-domination-allemande.php*. German-led responses to the economic struggles of EU countries such as Greece in the wake of the 2008 financial crisis have led some policy experts and historians both in France and in the Anglosphere to revive the old problematic of the "question allemande," driven by worries over how to curb German power within European structures. For a summary of the discourse on this point, see Hans Stark, "De la question allemande à la question européenne," *Politique étrangère* 81, no. 1 (2016): 67–78.

16. For an examination of how Sully and his agricultural advocacy have been represented in French textbooks between 1873 and 1973, see Amalvi.

Works Cited

Ågerup, Karl. 2020. "*Submission* beyond Islam: Yielding as Organizing Principle in Michel Houellebecq's Novels." *The Comparatist* 44:196–214.

Amalvi, Christian. 1997. ""Labourage et pâturages sont les mamelles de la France": le mythe scolaire de Sully, de la Troisième à la Cinquième République." *Tréma* nos. 12–13:143–54.

Armstrong, Joshua. 2019. *Maps and Territories: Global Positioning in the Contemporary Francophone Novel.* Liverpool: Liverpool University Press.

Beers, Terry. 2018. *The End of Eden: Agrarian Spaces and the Rise of the California Social Novel.* Reno: University of Nevada Press.

Bórawski, Piotr, Adam Pawlewicz, Andrzej Parzonko, Jayson K. Harper, and Lisa Holden. 2020. "Factors Shaping Cow's Milk production in the EU." *Sustainability* 12, no. 1, Article 420.

Castronovo, Russ. 2017. "Transnational Aesthetics." In *The Cambridge Companion to Transnational American Literature,* edited by Yogita Goyal, 72–87. Cambridge and New York: Cambridge University Press, 2017.

"Cinq ans après la fin des quotas, le marché laitier (était) stabilisé." 2020. *AGRA,* April 3. *http://www.agra.fr/cinq-ans-apr-s-la-fin-des-quotas-le-march-laitier-tait-stabilis-art461249-2496.html?Itemid=344.*

D'Arcens, Louise. 2018. "Nostalgia, Melancholy, and the Emotional Economy of Replacement: Feeling for *La France Profonde* in the Novels of Michel Houellebecq." *Exemplaria* 30, no. 3:257–73.

Dehoux, Amaury. 2020. "Globalisation du roman et figuration de l'agent: considérations anthropologico-littéraires à partir de M. Houellebecq, A. Ernaux, P. Grace et A. Kourouma." *Neohelicon* 47:217–29.

Dutton, Jacqueline. 2020. "Writing French in the World: Transnational Identities and Transcultural Ideals in the Works of Michel Houellebecq and Boualem Sansal." In *Francophone Literature as World Literature*, edited by Christian Moraru and Nicole Simek, 209–26. London: Bloomsbury Academic, 2020.

Eby, Clare Virginia. 1994. ""*The Octopus:*" Big Business as Art." *American Literary Realism, 1870–1910* 26, no. 3:33–51.

Freitag, Florian. 2009. "Naturalism in its Natural Environment? American Naturalism and the Farm Novel." *Studies in American Naturalism* 4, no. 2:97–118.

Fuchs, Christian. 2018. "Universal Alienation, Formal and Real Subsumption of Society under Capital, Ongoing Primitive Accumulation by Dispossession: Reflections on the Marx@200-Contributions by David Harvey and Michael Hardt/Toni Negri." *triple* 16, no. 2:454–67.

Gary, Nicolas. 2016. "Selon Houellebecq, "la France est très proche d'une sortie de l'Europe."" *Actualitté,* November 12. *https://actualitte.com/article/30606/international/selon-houellebecq-la-france-est-tres-proche-d-une-sortie-de-l-europe.*

Houellebecq, Michel. 2018. "Houellebecq recevant le prix Oswald Spengler: 'L'Occident est dans un état de déclin très avancé.'" *Valeurs Actuelles,* October 25. *https://www.valeursactuelles.com/clubvaleurs/culture/houellebecq-recevant-le-prix-oswald-spengler-loccident-est-dans-un-etat-de-declin-tres-avance-100202.*

———. 2019. *Sérotonine.* Paris: Flammarion.

Howard, June. 1985. *Form and History in American Literary Naturalism.* Chapel Hill: University of North Carolina Press.

Jocteur Monrozier, Anne. 2018. "Le suicide des agriculteurs en chiffres." *France Bleu,* February 5, *https://www.francebleu.fr/infos/societe/le-suicide-des-agriculteurs-en-chiffres-1517491824*

Kürten, Jochen. 2019. "Prophet of Depressing Times: Michel Houellebecq Releases 'Yellow Vest' Novel." *Deutsche Welle,* January 8. *https://p.dw.com/p/3B9F7.*

Lawlor, Leonard. "Auto-affection." 2015. In *Jacques Derrida: Key Concepts,* edited by Claire Colebrook, 130–38. London and New York: Routledge, 2015.

Lejeune, Geoffroy. 2018. "L'Europe, la droite, Macron, le foot . . . Une journée dans les pas de Michel Houellebecq." *Valeurs Actuelles,* October 25. *https://www.valeursactuelles.com/clubvaleurs/culture/leurope-la-droite-macron-le-foot-une-journee-dans-les-pas-de-michel-houellebecq-100203.*

"Michel Houellebecq's New Book Is Eerily Prescient." 2019. *The Economist,* January 19. *https://www.economist.com/books-and-arts/2019/01/17/michel-houellebecqs-new-book-is-eerily-prescient.*

Mintzer, Jordan. 2019. "'In the Name of the Land' ('Au nom de la terre'): Film Review." *The Hollywood Reporter*, October 3. *https://www.hollywoodreporter.com/review/name-land-au-nom-de-la-terre-review-1244512.*

Mrozowski, Daniel J. 2011. "How to Kill a Corporation: Frank Norris's *The Octopus* and the Embodiment of American Business." *Studies in American Naturalism* 6, no. 2:161–84.

Norris, Frank. 1986. *The Octopus.* In *Novels and Essays*, edited by Donald Pizer, 573–1098. New York: Library of America, 1986.

Novak-Lechevalier, Agathe. 2019. *Houellebecq, l'art de la consolation.* Paris: Stock.

Pizer, Donald. 1966. *The Novels of Frank Norris.* Bloomington and London: Indiana University Press.

———. 1993. *The Theory and Practice of American Literary Naturalism.* Carbondale and Edwardsville: Southern Illinois University Press.

Sgherri, Marie-Sandrine. 2017. "Houellebecq: Macron, c'est "une thérapie de groupe."" *Le Point*, May 5. *https://www.lepoint.fr/presidentielle/houellebecq-macron-c-est-une-therapie-de-groupe-05-05-2017-2125116_3121.php.*

Steinbeck, John. 1939. *The Grapes of Wrath.* New York: Viking.

Sweeney, Carole. 2013. *Michel Houellebecq and the Literature of Despair.* London and New York: Bloomsbury Academic.

Winkler, Adam. 2018. *We the Corporations: How American Businesses Won their Civil Rights.* New York and London: Liveright.

Zaretsky, Robert. 2019. "Michel Houellebecq Hated Europe Before You Did." *Foreign Policy*, January 5. *https://foreignpolicy.com/2019/01/05/michel-houellebecq-hated-europe-before-you-did/.*

IMPLICIT POSSIBILITY
STUPIDITY AND SPORT "WITHOUT QUALITIES"

James Dutton

Above all: only grant the suspicion that sport is a pastime for the most stupid as much space as it deserves.

—Peter Sloterdijk, *You Must Change Your Life*

Are sports stupid? Whatever your thoughts on this question, in this article I want to consider how the will to total explication shown by industrial sports limits their potential for thought. My hope is that by doing so, we can notice the necessity of pressing the limits of what we too readily call "stupid"—especially in cultures increasingly bound up in utilitarian thinking and just-in-time production. Robert Musil's sprawling, unfinishable novel *Der Mann ohne Eigenschaften* (1930–43), composed as the industrial sporting phenomenon began asserting intellectual and financial hegemony, frequently scrutinizes both ideas of sport and stupidity, resulting in reflections on the nature of performativity, the relation between thought and action, and the "genius" of rule following. Such attention demonstrates Musil's interest in the limits of thought and identifies apparent stupidity's residence at these limits (as well as what might happen when we are forced to contemplate something instead of simply defining it as stupid and moving on). Increased interest in Musil's work[1] is illustrative of his incisive analysis of modernity's stupidity and the definitive role it plays in cultural life. One of Musil's preferred tropes when exemplifying this stupidity is modern cultures' increasing industrialization of sport and physical culture, where metrics and statistics hollow out the potential latent errors and uncertainties, working to capture even the most unpredictable event as anticipated, as already part of the game. In this essay, I want to take up Musil's comments to ask serious questions about the relation between sports and stupidity from modernity onward, to argue for the latent possibility in immediately resisting assigning something as "stupid," and attend to it for a little longer. To do so, I will follow Peter Sloterdijk's critique of modernity's mania for explication at all costs—to the detriment of the fundamental underside of thinking, or what he calls the "implicit." Importantly, Sloterdijk attributes critique of this oversight to Musil, while also showing how industrial sporting systems typify this insistent prioritization of the explicit. Interestingly, however, little commentary exists on Sloterdijk and Musil's accounts of the role sports have played in popularizing explicative logic.[2] This relation is, I claim, one that can offer instructive responses to contemporary enthusiasm for automation, curation, and "algorithmic governmentality," which seeks to limit or overlook the possibility implicit in what it constricts as "stupid" by relentlessly predicting, or disavowing through explication, the future's potential for alterity. Sloterdijk's reading can show how such productive elision is always rediscoverable within Musil's enormous novel, which resists finishing ideas, dialogues, characters, and indeed, the novel itself: insofar as Musil died without completing the novel or even envisioning a structure that might lead to its end.

The relationship between stupidity and explication is a prominent theme in Musil's writing. It features in many of his texts and lectures, typified by the address he gave to the Austrian *Werkbund* in 1937 entitled "Über die Dummheit [On Stupidity]." One of his founding contentions in this rather long talk—his "Achilles' heel" in presenting it, he tells his audience—is that he doesn't in fact know what stupidity is (1990, 270). From this enticing, potentially confused beginning (how can someone discuss a subject by openly noting, at the beginning, that they have not the slightest idea as to what it is?), Musil goes on to draw attention to the fact that most of his listeners are probably in the same position: stupidity, from his point of view, is relative, dependent on the moral and emotional circumstances around it. He cites numerous examples, among them "business relationships in which a person who is not cunning and ruthless is considered stupid" and concludes that "every intelligence has its stupidity" (1990, 276). Here, stupidity or intellect—intention, desire, will, and all of the attached schema from which we might, anecdotally or precisely, refer to something as "stupid" or "intelligent"—are always dependent not only on the environment in which its performance is being observed but also the discursive expectations set up within the judgment and by those who do the judging.[3] In this respect, the explicative *judgment* of stupidity is, and can only be, a product of a shortened attention. The willingness to judge an act or an individual as stupid is to limit the possibilities within that judgment: What happens when the judgment is wrong, or overlooks the actual intention—or misinterprets an intention that only comes to light much later? Apparent stupidity is the ballast of a society increasingly structured around (indeed profiting from) limited attention. Alternatively, a willingness to follow through with stupidity's emergent possibilities could provide a richer future than the one reduced to merely "stupid."

This much Musil concludes in his talk: insofar as we are all occasionally "stupid," if we wished not to be, the best advice would surely be to reserve "judgment and resolution in everything you don't know enough about" (1990, 286). As Sloterdijk observes, synthesizing work on stupidity by psychoanalyst Ernst Weiss and physiologist Charles Richet—whose aphorism concerning stupidity ("We are all the more stupid in our actions the less ignorant we are") resounds here—stupidity "is an act of defiance, a refusal, a not-wanting-to-be-otherwise that advances parallel to enlightenment" (1987, 495) and all of the definite, normative "reason" stowed away along with it. The thinking-through of what an instantaneously calculative culture might determine as an inevitable stupidity opens up possibilities; it is an opportunity to learn *from* the premature and erroneous judgments made by this culture and therefore to develop us as thinking beings. Following Musil, if everyone were always right and never *appeared to be* stupid, no one would ever learn, develop, or change: the world would consist as a kind of "pure presence" and extinguish itself. What I find most interesting about Musil's awareness of how judgments of stupidity can short-circuit attention (overlooking the potentially fruitful differences and potentials this greater attention can draw out) is the prominent role this plays in his theoretical approach to writing and philosophy and especially its formation into his masterwork, *Der Mann ohne Eigenschaften*. This novel's enormous material length immediately suggests some kind of attentional experiment and implies a reservation with regard to judgment: to apply the finite judgment Musil speaks of as belonging to the classification of either stupid or intelligent acts would undoubtedly lead to a much shorter text. Musil's celebrated "essayism" is, following this reasoning, a protracted liaison with the possibility of stupidity, leaving open the individuating potential of any possible judgment.[4] While this risks the essayistic thinker *appearing* stupid, Musil's thinkers retain freedom in their resistance to definitive judgment—privileging the act of think*ing* over the closure of knowledge, directing it toward a future that is always to come. This resolves into the kinds of stupidity that Musil refers to as "active" or "intelligent" (1990, 284), ones that motivate, indeed extend, his interminable novel—and much of the attentional richness of modernist art in response to "public life's" increased instrumentality and bureaucracy.

Andreas Gailus argues that perhaps "no other twentieth century writer has done more to unearth the 'silent' history of ideas and the 'anonymous constraints' that invisible structures of thought exert on modern individual and collective life than Robert Musil" (1–2). As these silent traffics increase with unscrutinized force in our century, it is useful to consider Musil's thoughts on some forms of stupidity as offering escape from such constraints. His novel is an apparently concrete manifestation of the tension between the implicit and explicit—as the critic with enough stupidity to try and discuss it discovers. And as this reasoning is encouraged by the novel's unfinished *form*, much of the novel's "action" is guided by his famed essayistic technique, where events undo their possibility of being explicated as such—*as* anything. Indeed, the novel's unfinish*ability* is one of its most important features: in calling it perhaps "the most unfinishable novel ever written," James Ramsay Wallen asserts that Musil in fact had to "compromise his artistic vision by finishing parts of it" (138–39). His resistance to completing thought creates formal difficulties that only reinforce his philosophical position—and this is constantly staged, often frustratingly, in the novel. Notably, it opens by unlacing readerly expectations as to setting and character: it seems to begin describing Vienna but argues that "we should not place any value on the city's name." This is because, we are told, we too often "overestimate the importance of knowing where we are because in nomadic times it was essential to recognise the tribal feeding grounds" (Musil 2011, 3–4). Musil's narrator suggests that a modernity evolved beyond such base imperatives can afford the conditional or the undetermined. In this light, literary fiction of this nature can open itself out to the speculative realm of imagination, a virtual space of creativity that avoids the didacticism of "knowing where" we are, or indeed, exactly *what* is being described. This continues as characters are introduced into the novel. The narrator describes two people whose "names might have been Ermelinda Tuzzi and Arnheim—but then, they couldn't be, because in August Frau Tuzzi was still in Bad Aussee with her husband and Dr. Arnheim was still in Constantinople; so we are left to wonder who they were" (2011, 4). Even as these characters go on to become key figures in the novel, this introduction provides no clarifying commentary other than these names. We are left to wonder who they were and who they are: this is precisely the creative gambit Musil opens up with his novel's decidedly virtual beginning—an opening with ("written") form, but without (closed) qualities.

THE POSSIBILITIES OF THE IMPLICIT

Sloterdijk, a thinker interested in modernity's explicative mania for recording and "statisfaction," argues that attempts to quantify the "real" world in increasingly unrecognizable ways end up deforming it. For Sloterdijk, Musil was a rare thinker who resisted modernity's *passion du réel*,[5] its obsession with deriving and quantifying a reality that then goes on to be identifiable only through those stratified terms. Rather than attend to possibility, modernity's thinkers tie down and inscribe the "real" world in the finite forms they (re)produce.

> Very few of them acknowledged, like Musil, that a serious rival to the sense of reality had emerged and was reaching its explicatory form by crystallizing into the realm of the virtual. Who would have been willing to admit that a mutation in the experience and concept of the real itself was underway? The message of the century found no one to proclaim it. It could have been this: "We have risen again from the real"—or, with less pathos: "We will keep the real at a distance in future." (Sloterdijk 2016, 647)

This explicatory form that believes it can keep reality at a distance is the kind I am identifying with modernity's attribution of what cannot be quantified as "stupid." Perhaps typically, though, this makes for a complicated moment in Sloterdijk's study. The "real," as well as the "realm of the virtual" he describes here, cannot be captured in neat or discrete binaries. Instead, the mutation in the real that Sloterdijk highlights, and what he next calls "Operation Enrichment," is "so expansive, and so pervaded by counter-tendencies and paradoxical effects" (2016, 647) that modernity's measures for discerning it are largely inadequate. The only way to acknowledge, like Musil, the permutations, "ambiguities and exceptions" of this manipulated "reality" was to meet it in the "realm of the virtual" where it seeks to crystallize itself through explication, supplanting and colonizing the material, and phenomenological—immediate—"*sense* of reality." More and more we are convinced to ignore the virtual's ability to house (often contradictory, productive, and multiplied) possibility; in seeking to define and exact the myriad, and formerly indeterminate, flows of reality, modernity dams its currents into manipulable pools.

For Sloterdijk, the quantified "reality" that begins to speak over the possible world in the form of the piling up and incontestability of "results" goes to the heart of what we've come to call "modernity." "The true and real basic concept of modernity is not revolution but explication" (2016, 82), he writes, in what becomes a key motif in *Foams*, the massive final volume of the *Spheres* project. Modernity's will toward explication and extracting finite details and data out of the material world, no matter how wildly deformed it becomes in doing so, sets out a new realm of the virtual: under the shadow of this enormous accumulation, we are much less willing to draw attention to its motivation. Sloterdijk argues here that "the Vesalian 'revolution' was of far greater consequence for the self-relationships of Western people than the long over-cited and misunderstood Copernican one" (2016, 66–68). Where once embodiment was experienced through the phenomenal reality of sensation instead of extracted, verifiable symptoms stored somewhere far beyond that sense, Vesalian objectivity gave us a normative, compartmentalized "body" against which these senses could be proven. Gone was the *feeling* of embodiment, replaced by the symptomology and ratifiable "truth" of external, predictive, and intersubjective medical analysis applied to it from the outside. Sloterdijk describes this as "part of the great rotation that altered the angle (*klima*) of knowledge about things and circumstances" (2016, 68). The "darkness of [. . .] corporeality" has ever since been blasted with blinding light, where explicatory practice's hall of mirrors is the inevitable progenitor of malaise, hypochondria, and trauma resulting from the twentieth century's *passion du réel*. The reality of sensory experience is supplemented by a radical doubt.[6]

Indeed, the bright lights of "explicatory practice" highlight the impossible task of explication: an unending or unendable zooming-in, where the identification of defined body parts only reveals more parts and more bodies.[7] But what Sloterdijk rightly notes about explication is the inverse: that explicatory modernity's mania for the apparent productivity of zooming-in invokes a massive oversight: "Seemingly self-evident things [. . .] only mature to the point of conspicuity the moment they are lost: and they are usually lost from the moment in which they are used for comparisons, which robs them of their naïve givenness" (2016, 61–62). The apparent paradox of a loss becoming conspicuous is the driving force of modernity, transfixed by the snake charming of any number of disasters (climate change, global pandemics, nuclear armament, neoliberalism) but only willing to "undo" the apparently simple answer (growth?) to the problem *after* loss becomes so conspicuous that its explication is total. The stupidity here is that what explication explicates is fundamentally different from the naïvely given, precisely *because* of its explication. The knowledge—or the *klima* that bends toward it—that gives us biological, neuro-, or life sciences "was not of a 'reflective' or mirroring character; it only performed the auto-operative rotation after which knowledge reached behind the mirror, or to the 'reverse' of subjectivities" (Sloterdijk 2016, 79). Molding them in its own image, the Vesalian body bears only a tenuous—Sloterdijk would say "monstrous"—relation to yours or mine as apprehended by our senses. And as Musil "acknowledged," the realm of the virtual where these apprehensions take place has been almost entirely refigured by auto-operative rotation; despite all experiential evidence to the contrary, to suggest that my body is in some way different from the Vesalian model is ridiculous, or utterly stupid—try suggesting so to your doctor.

The deformation this brings about, the lasting effect of the auto-operative rotation, is cultivated by the normativity that seeks *only* explication at all costs, typified by the Vesalian body. However, Sloterdijk notes that this valorization of the explicit overlooks the necessarily *implicit* part of knowledge that the explicit relies on, "which indicates a place in the existent where the bud is located for the purpose of an unfolding, an articulation, an explication." The implicit is the ungraspable *sense* through which articulable thought can emerge, call it context, discourse, transcendence, ideology: without it, thought is literally meaning-less. More pointedly, the implicit is what is "presupposed in a non-unfolded state, left in cognitive retirement, freed from the pressure of comprehensive mention and development and given in the mode of dark proximity—not already on the tip of one's tongue, not already available the next moment, not mobilized by the discursive regime and not incorporated into procedures" (2016, 72). This murky—virtual—depth and *possibility* of thinking can never be explicated as thought without losing it. It is the hothouse of thought whose temperature must remain of an uninhabitable (inexplicable) degree. "That is why the form of the true history of knowledge is the becoming-phenomenon of the previously unmanifested," *not*, as Sloterdijk and Musil are at pains to point out, the always-already present phenomenon, the total presence of what has never been *un*manifested (Sloterdijk 2016, 72). Despite the popularity of accelerative, "stop-motion" footage, plants never grow before one's eyes. In seeking only to explicate at all costs, and to pile explication onto explication (in the manner of algorithmic or machine knowledge, which represents *post*modernity's universal uptake of explicatory practice), modernity loses contact with the implicit; its knowledge emerges by substituting the always-already explicit in place of this "previously unmanifested," truly implicit thinking. What results is the stratification of the auto-operative rotation as, and *in place of*, the true history of knowledge: the realm of the virtual is totally colonized by *an* objectivity.

Musil's interest in this rotation is implicit as early as his novel's open opening, where he considers the virtual manipulation of the real that occurs through intense explication. Just after we meet our possible or quantum Frau Tuzzi and Dr. Arnheim, we follow the couple as they are stopped by a traffic accident—a man struck down by a truck. But instead of helping the victim, the gathering crowd—"bees clustering around the entrance to their hive"—hear the driver's account, unanimously agree that it was by the victim's "own carelessness that he had come to grief" and perform meaningless gestures, propping "him up, then laying him down again [. . .] really only marking time while waiting for the ambulance to bring someone who would know what to do and have the right to do it" (Musil 2011, 4–5). The mechanisms of appropriate society are well oiled here; nothing can *explicitly* be done to help the victim, and the waiting crowd know it. During the performance, the gentleman from our couple exacts reason onto these events. "The brakes on these heavy trucks take too long to come to a full stop," he expostulates, instantly accounting for, and certifiably collapsing the enormous, potentially contradicting—even stupid—contingencies contributing to this event.

> This datum gave the lady some relief, and she thanked him with an appreciative glance. She did not really understand, or care to understand, the technology involved, as long as his explanation helped put this ghastly incident into perspective by reducing it to a technicality of no direct personal concern to her. (Musil 2011, 5)

Transforming, explicating a certain "reality" folded together to bring about this event as merely the technical functioning of a great, totally present machine, makes it acceptable. But where does "the technology involved" begin and end? Can it be *explicitly* limited only to the length of the heavy truck's brakes, the angle of the curb, the speed and posture of the victim's gait, the temperature of the day, the bystanders' comportment, the time each of them spent in their previous locations, their thoughts and hesitations while there, the driver's breakfast? And how much of these? By reducing this event to a technicality, the technics of explication settle on *a* set of relevant contingencies, crystallizing them in the virtual as the correct, unstupid certainties that made this event "what" it "is." Much like the "potential" Frau Tuzzi, modern societies rely on reducing events to impersonal technicalities in order to satisfy itself with them, regardless of whether it understands (or cares to understand) them. Its citizens and parties are then content to wield, interconnect, and reproduce these explications as the communicable matter of business, society, and culture: the details relevant to those *other* contingencies are irrelevant—or more quickly, stupid. But in clinging to the specific qualities of the reduced, righteous technicality, what *kind* of reality are we left with—and what have we lost?

Musil dedicates numerous moments in his novel to working this out. Chapter 4, titled "If There is a Sense of Reality, There Must Also Be a Sense of Possibility" highlights exactly the implicit framework that makes every sense of reality possible. In opposition to Arnheim's disposable technicalities, the chapter describes a person with the sense of possibility, one who "does not say, for instance: Here this or that has happened, will happen, must happen: but he invents: Here this or that might, could, or ought to happen"; upon being told something "is the way it is" this person "will think: Well, it could probably just as well be otherwise" (2011, 11). Much like the determined-undetermined opening of Musil's novel, the sense of possibility invites invention—it notices reality *as* possibility, not reality as explicated "reality." "Such possibilists," Musil's narrator goes on,

> are said to inhabit a more delicate medium, a hazy medium of mist, fantasy, daydreams, and the subjunctive mood. Children who show this tendency are dealt with firmly and warned that such persons are cranks, dreamers, weaklings, know-it-alls, or troublemakers.
>
> Such fools are called idealists by those who praise them. (2011, 11)

The scope and potential contradictions—or stupidities, from a logical or "real" perspective—taken in by these judgments of the possibilist demonstrate the paradoxes and ambiguities propping up the explicative manipulation of the real, or Sloterdijk's "auto-operative rotation." Its desire to call the possibilist "stupid" even extends to those who praise them—a point where Musil's faithfulness to possibility notably challenges the "real's" insistence on binary distinctions over possibility's messy overlaps—those who see an idealist in "reality's" fool. Rather than remain in this foolishness like the "weak subspecies" of the possibilist, "those who cannot comprehend reality" (2011, 11) and who Musil seemingly derides, the essayistic possibilist *senses* the virtual space of reality but leaves it open, implicit. This kind of strong possibilist resists attention-sapping, immovable judgments: they *act on* possibility—while the idealist merely contemplates it—writing the interminable novel, committing their possibilities to paper, unafraid of potential contradictions—these only add to their possibility's possibility. As Sloterdijk reminds us, "Musil's essayist art imagines itself as an experiment to investigate the difference between an existence that remains trapped and sheltered within valid distinctions, and one in which constitutional differences are abandoned to dissolution" (2011, 456). The possibilist thinks through actions, entertaining their possibilities; he weaves his own tightrope between stupidity and inaction as he walks it, essaying new futures with every step. It is precisely for this reason that for a "reality" too quick to label both as stupid, sensing the difference between these subspecies of possibilist in the form of nameable qualities is a near-impossible task. Musil's strong possibilist, not content with speculative vagaries, essays the virtual realm of possibility sensible, but inexplicable, in the implicit. For this possibilist, stupidity or foolishness is an impossible category—to *know* stupidity is to judge it as such, which means limiting its possibility and thus, acting stupidly. Here, Musil introduces us to the titular problem of the novel—a man without *explicable* qualities appears, on first, "realist" judgment, to be a man without qualities. But much more is possible in thinking through what appears fixed, as Musil's unfinishable novel shows: it is the impossibly written but always *potentially* read story of a possibilist invested in reality.

This "man" is introduced to us as Ulrich, the novel's eponymous protagonist. He both confirms and resists this label, precisely because he is introduced to us as this kind of strong possibilist: for Sloterdijk, "Ulrich, the man without qualities, figures as the living intersection between the discrete and indiscrete forms of being [. . .] the life-practically impossible position on the boundary between pure observation and absolute participation" (2011, 456). This operative boundary could be mistaken for "foolish" idealism, but closer attention reveals the intellectual productivity in such active inclination toward possibility. And precisely to show the idealist heritage of this implicit thinker, Musil has him contemplate the role played by spirit in action, this indivisible remainder that avows (or at least hints toward) the ineradicable possibility *of* possibility, that which cannot be averaged out or explicated.[8] Ulrich frequently essays the qualities of spirit, and in doing so, reflects on this radically elusive yet formative (or "life-practical") force. "But what of 'spirit' standing by itself, a naked noun, bare as a ghost to whom one would like to lend a sheet?" he asks.

> One can read the poets, study the philosophers, buy paintings, hold all-night discussions—does all this bestow spirit on us? If it does, do we then possess it? And even if we should, this spirit is so firmly bound up with the accidental form in which it happens to manifest itself! It passes right through the person who wants to absorb it, leaving only a small tremor behind. (2011, 161)

Ulrich's reflections on spirit describe a force without quality, an implicit essence that exceeds categorization. It is the *possibility* of thought, that which identifies but leaves only the traces of anamnesis that are never quite the same—the "small tremor" of think*ing* that mystifies explicative determination.[9] Ulrich reflects on the power of spirit to keep possibility alive in thinking, especially when it comes to his own identity that, as the beginning of the novel finds him, is purposely held in an undefined space of promise, from whose unpredictable future "every possibility beckoned him, but something stronger kept him from yielding to the attraction" (Musil 2011, 162). This tension raised within possibility, where in the moment one seeks to identify *what* makes it possible one collapses that possibility, is a key element of Musil's reckoning with "spirit"—and its tensile, virtual place between the explicit and implicit. To define the future (as x) is a seemingly stupid gesture but one whose possibility creates space for those futures not being thought—if only as slight variations of the predicted future that cannot come to be because of its finite prediction. But these can only remain (spiritually) possible if that first, retrospectively stupid definition is made in conjunction with these other possibilities, its countertendencies. This is the constituting paradox of temporal experience—the possibility not only of getting the future wrong but the necessity of doing so: only then can there be "a" future. If the future is already definitively mapped out, it is not a future: it has become present. These are the stakes of the explicit/implicit relation—to collapse the necessary temporality of spirit and possibility into a ubiquitous "reality." Ulrich's suspended reality, one "without qualities," is testament to this understanding of possibility as spirit. "Obviously, he said to himself, what was keeping him spellbound in this aloof and nameless way of life was nothing other than the compulsion to that loosening and binding of the world that is known by a word that we do not care to encounter by itself: spirit" (Musil 2011, 162). The loosening of the world that comes with the positing of *a* world invites stagnation, stupidity: but without it there would not be any world to speak of—a proposition yet to be churned through "the real."

This is a central problematic for Ulrich—and indeed, the narrative's motivating force. "It is not immaterial that Ulrich could say to himself that he had accomplished something in his field" (2011, 41): such is the beginning of the chapter that introduces his lack of qualities. The "spiritual" nonimmateriality of Ulrich's accomplishments does, however, only manifest in recognition of a very particular sort.

A thirty-two-year-old mathematics Ph.D., Ulrich's burgeoning work generates the highest kind of recognition in his field for someone of his standing: he acquires the epithet of "promising." Precisely, this is a question of age: as the text points out, no matter how significant a young scholar's achievements, their "promise" can never concretely result in "admiration [. . .] for even in the realm of truth, admiration is reserved for older scholars on whom it depends whether or not one gets that professorship or professorial chair" (Musil 2011, 41). The apparently material manifestation of intelligence is one tied ineluctably to immaterial power structures. Despite his "not immaterial" accomplishments, Ulrich's achievement, and his identity, are bound to an immaterial order—the structuring belief that "he had remained 'promising.'" To *remain* promising is to always remain explicated as such, short-circuited even in the virtual realm where that "promise" might become something (for to err and potentially become something else would risk developing beyond the definitional limits of being "promising," perhaps even refuting them). He could split the atom, solve Hilbert's problems, break world records, but his youth, academic novelty, and relative success means he must remain explicated as promising. But this strange paradox, this misapprehension caused by the desire to explicate even the implicit (of "remaining promising") also means that none of his "not immaterial" accomplishments can be judged as completed creations, and in this respect, Ulrich retains the promise of essayism, the escape from totalized judgment—the freedom to *be* stupid, which might allow him to *become*-other.

THE QUALITIES OF SPORT

This possibilist freedom materializes when Ulrich "stopped wanting to be promising." He wants to contribute to the development of his culture. However, as fortune would have it, his is a time in which "genius" (which one assumes is the culturally sanctioned, *explicated* opposite of stupidity) is being spoken of "on the soccer field or in the boxing ring," attributed to "a halfback or great tennis-court tactician" (Musil 2011, 41). This kind of genius, the eradication of stupidity, mirrors the functions of its burgeoning automatic society: it represents the most explicable, preempted, and known response to the identifiable display of said genius. Ulrich resolves, since "now that genius is attributed to soccer players and horses [. . .] to take a year's leave of absence from his life" (44). To be promising but to never offer any creations is to essay all of its implicit stupidities. Hence, Ulrich realizes, the day he seeks to become more than promising, that such a desire is futile. In reading "the expression 'the racehorse of genius'," he "instantly grasped the fateful connection between his entire career and this genius among racehorses" (41): that "a horse and a boxer have an advantage over a great mind in that their performance can be objectively measured," that is, fed into a repetitive, explicable schema. "This is why sports and strictly objective criteria have deservedly come to the forefront, displacing such obsolete concepts as genius and human greatness" (42).

This is why our defined and *objec*tive culture finds it so paradoxical to relate genius to possibility—because it means to reverse our expectations regarding what is not immaterial: it would mean following every explication outside of itself, and thus attending to a different form of reality to the predominant one. To go on essaying as Ulrich and *Der Mann ohne Eigenschaften* do, writing without end (and therefore, as Ulrich suggests, to be forever creating while also abstaining from finishing any kind of categorical creation) is to defer a final judgment as to what any material fact is. To take leave does not mean to *not* write, think, or produce but rather to resist finalizing them—to not follow the rules of the game, to not reject stupidity, which inevitably means to make the mistakes that only action (and not silence) can produce. Hence, Ulrich's year of absence produces far more possibilities than his promising career ever could because none of them take a completed form. This is exemplified later in the novel when Musil's narrator returns to this problem, asking: "What is actually going on when that agile species man calls a tennis player a genius? Something unstated is at work here. And when they attribute genius to a racehorse? Something more is left unsaid" (494). What goes unsaid is what cannot be said, the implicit thought that makes such a recognition possible. But for Musil, modern culture purposefully discounts the value of such thinking, directing attention only to explicated surfaces. It calls one sportsperson a genius and waits for the next, where such judgment is dictated by an "uncertainty of values, passed over and ignored; it is probably less its idea of genius that makes this era attribute genius to a tennis player of a racehorse than its general distrust for the world of the mind, of the intellect, to which the term rightly belongs" (494). Such a world of the intellect not only knows no limits but is directed toward the unknown (and unknowable) that can be its only motivation—the "objective" stupidity of that which cannot be already know*n*, of what must be called, each time anew, think*ing*.

The sporting analogy employed by Musil here is not only telling but exemplary of the explicative, short-circuiting approach to thinking taken by so much of industrial culture since modernity.[10] Sports are defined by precise rules that institute, emphasize, and commend "exact" repetition. The rules that facilitate the sporting contest do so to limit, or deny, the attentional possibilities implicit within the act itself. In his work on modern sports, Grant Farred has highlighted the link between sports' explication of temporality into "time(s)"—"with the fetishization of counting, statistics, and standardization." Farred points out "that sports historians have traced the rise of sport as we technologically know it to the late-nineteenth-century invention of the stopwatch, the most 'precise' recording of athletic achievement, the technology that enables statisticians to keep 'records' in nanoseconds" (66). The stopwatch, with all of its technical potential to create new moments, to afford attention to the (and every) nanosecond, becomes a disindividuating device in which these newly recordable, miniscule fractions of time are systematized, bound to the symbolic fixtures of vulgar, repeatable time. Sport's reliance on this systematization reifies the pattern of its explicative logic.[11] In this respect, modern industrial sports are auto-operative: their generating systems must be prefigured so as to allow an ephemeral passage by the skilled player through what can be identified or always-already known by the viewer as only slightly removed from the standard—or, in the case of sporting "genius," exemplary of it. Any act too radical—any act of actual genius—disrupts the game. As Musil argues in his essay "Durch die Brille des Sports," in modern sports like tennis or fencing, one must synthesize muscles with nerves and resist any contemplative thinking—"as soon as a ray of thinking falls into the darkness of muscular dominance, then you drop out of the race" (Musil cited in Becker, 156).

Sloterdijk also highlights how the explosive uptake of industrial sports can be tied almost synchronously with hegemony of explicative "reality"—and the way it defines and reproduces conceptions of "genius". Sloterdijk sums all of this up with a unique insight: it is worth citing him at length to gain the full impact of his reading.

> Thus the sports system has developed into a multiverse with hundreds of secondary worlds, in which self-referential motion, useless play, superfluous exertion and simulated fights celebrate their existence somewhat wilfully, in the clearest possible contrast to the utilitarian objectivism of the working world—no matter how often a dull-witted sociology might claim that sport is merely a training camp for the factory and a preparation for the capitalist ideology of competition. One must admit, however, that those parts of the sporting world closest to the 'circus' in the ancient sense, especially in the vicinity of the Olympic industry and in the professional segments of football and cycling, have meanwhile become subject to a result fetishism that absolutely rivals the compulsive product-oriented thinking of the economic sphere. But what does that mean if, on the other hand, statistics show that in those sports there are ten thousand amateurs or more for every professional? (2013, 213)

Much like Musil, Sloterdijk first highlights how the "useless play" of specular industrial sports seems opposed to the dominant objective, utilitarian cultures of explicative modernity. However, the admission that he subsequently grants, about what we can learn from the "result fetishism" of industrial sports' calculative bent, underlines its explicative manipulation of the virtual—the circumference of its auto-operative rotation. "One can only shoulder the whole if one trains as an athlete of impartiality," Sloterdijk argues in *Globes*, "for whoever gets involved in small and medium affairs does not have their hands free for the great ones" (2014b, 67). While thousands of amateurs' psychic lives become patterned according to the explicative figures of the system itself, they form the implicit background of the sporting industry. Its only performative, explicit interest appears to be in the professionals, the athletes of genius, but their very explication is made possible by the "fans" that support them, engendering "an era in which the performative separates from the procedures and aims of the working world, erecting countless stages for completely autonomous presentations" (Sloterdijk 2013, 213). Because these amateurs take on and implicate the sporting industry's calculative metaphysics, its "exhibition of self-referentially practising acts" (213), they are turned out into its finite reality: possibilists become interested in sports only within its very strict, reproducible grammars, ignorant of or unable to shoulder the "whole" that relies on, but can never account for, implicit thinking.

As Sloterdijk's text briskly moves on from this concluding question, I want to linger on it for the course of this essay. My proposal is precisely that the performative aspect of sports Sloterdijk turns around here is instructive, in more surprising ways that the sociology he accosts, and his latently phenomenological position is helpful here. The spheric loop connecting sports' performativity to its results-fetishism, passing through its creation of thousands of amateurs, has something significant to tell us about the implicated results-fetishism of the modern individual, who disavows the "whole" emphasized by possibilists like Musil's. Techniques of self-fashioning, increasingly buttressed by the "quantified self," online avatar and curated profile, seek to draw out identity by piling it up as a plethora of explicable details. We are increasingly defined, and define ourselves, by the external traces and marks we use to anchor our identity: pages visited and "liked," watch and purchase history ("because you liked . . . we [at Amazon, Netflix, Oxfam] think you'll love . . .), faces drawn on ubiquitous sands. The quantification or "statisfaction" of the phenomenal world carves our perception of it into rigidly uniform, infinitesimal, but homogenous grammars, sequestering wonder, possibility, and even *thinking* to always-already calculated logics of a machine that never sleeps. In this light, marketing cultures have so effortlessly married themselves to the contemporary sports system that the latter explodes out of Sloterdijk's conception of it as simply the "'circus' in the vicinity of the Olympic industry and in the professional segments of football and cycling" to become the barometer and intellectual template through which we measure "striving for greatness" and the pursuit of continued success—whatever that hollowed-out paradox (the great as the repetitive) might mean.

This is weighty conversation on the topic of sport. But it is also the implicit basis of the kinds of industrial sports in question here, one increasingly shunted out of their discursive specificity. There is a lot of money to be made in modern sports. Perhaps for this reason, infinitesimally refined and explicated toward an inch of their life, sports are increasingly being turned into something that is inaccessible to the senses. Not only has the ubiquity of replay and slow-motion technologies become indispensable to how we view and make sense of apparent sporting contests (hollowing their "reality" out of the "live," manifest temporality and unpredictability of their contest), but the acceptance of video referees, Hawk-Eye, and coaches' challenges anchor this "reality" as a requisite part of the rules. In doing so, it disfigures the sporting event by draining any remaining *possibility* of the implicit from it. Consider that "racing," in all of its guises—swimming, athletics, horse racing, and so on—has always inclined toward this logic, with its integration of the "photo-finish" (without which, retrospectively, it is difficult for us to imagine how the contest could have even been judged). But now watching the race itself becomes almost irrelevant; one need only tune in for the slow-motion video to judge whose nose or fingernail crosses the finish line first. This can only be accessed through the newly real temporality of the slow-motion shot, one almost recognizable from its jerky frame-by-frame beginnings, and one that is far removed from "real time." As it is provided by interposal graphics and formulae that tell the viewer who in "reality" won the race (regardless of what we saw), it alters the *quality* of the contest, following Sloterdijk's "auto-operative rotation." Here, automatic explication not only provides new ways of seeing the world unknown and imperceptible to human "genius" but *relies* on the maintenance of these methods to go about supplanting sensory reality. "Only after the auto-operative rotation did recent knowledge find itself in the position where things become phenomenal that were in no way intended for the human perceptual apparatus, at least not in its first design," Sloterdijk notes (2016, 78). Becoming phenomenal, exhausting a virtual realm of endless categorization and inscrutable detail, the sporting contest fires itself into an automatic sphere that its actors and athletes perform *for*, not in (consider the now common phenomenon of the athlete watching the big-screen replay during play to see what he in fact did).

Carved up and "analyzed" by explicative technologies that seek to reduce the *temporality* of the sporting contest to a near-atomically calculable quantity of events that, for this reason, lose their evental status, the intent in freezing the sporting "event"—be it the kick, shot, foul (or more interestingly, *error*)—into frames of proof for analysts to "break down" is to explicate its every implicit possibility. Driven by the monetization of the most split, specular second wrought into and around their contests (think of the eye-watering value of a thirty-second Super Bowl commercial, and work backward through the most mundane iterations of a sporting fixture, like the filling in of time when Wimbledon or Lord's is washed out), the sporting event is always-already a nonevent. Its possibilities—drained of time, shorn of implicit spirit—are inscribed within a finite system of explication. What remains is the "genius" racehorse, the stupid play: the readily identifiable, indeed predictable automatism of extracting possibility from the sporting rules—the completed, "set" play, the visualized and perfectly executed race strategy, the "perfect" ten.

What remains implicit in the perfect routine, play, or race is, of course, its apparently unpredictable romance, the kind so celebrated by sports commentators and aficionados. As the techniques and formulae of sporting contests increasingly take place in a virtual realm inaccessible to human senses (the kind developed and cultivated by the error, confusion, and uncertainty that make possibility possible) "genius" can easily be attributed to a soccer player or racehorse. But it is an attribution—indeed, it is a "genius"—that, already explicated by and within the pure presence of the atemporal system that makes it possible, is of a spiritless kind. Without implicit possibilities that cannot be defined, that must remain outside of the system of explication or identification the hypermediated sports market relies on, the auto-operative culture collapses in on itself—it attempts to craft, to forget, indeed to *stupefy* its own possibilities, by making the explicit implicit. "What was shifted to the surface by research had to be 'brought to light' or 'unconcealed' in a form of cognitive mining," Sloterdijk writes. "Modernity offers various names for the origin of these extractions: they come either from the 'unconscious' or from latency, from ignorance, from concealment on the insides of the phenomenal folds or from some other framing of the cognitive not-yet." (2016, 78–79). The explication of this "cognitive not-yet" is the fuzzy, unattainable stupidity that has been the (implicit) focus of our reading here. By explicating or attempting to trap the not-yet in a frame, the infinitely *possible* space of cognition disappears—it escapes the frame and lingers in some other mode of the un- or nonconscious. Importantly, Sloterdijk here notes that "ignorance" is what we might call this disappearance into the "phenomenal folds" of think*ing* (the pristinely phenomenological horizon of implication).

Perhaps this is best represented, and indeed least identifiable, in the sporting moments that it would be unfair to call stupid—the technical error, the gap between desire and execution that no amount of training can bridge. Consider the missed free throw or penalty kick after the final whistle—most would agree that there is nothing "stupid" about such a concentration of understanding intended toward such a specific target—and indeed much to be learned from such misses. Athletes increasingly train for these technico-psychic scenarios, practicing "game awareness" and how to "block out outside noise" and fixate on the goal. But it is precisely in this superabundance of attention that the "human perceptual apparatus" is turned away from, or rather forecloses phenomenal (that is *implicit*) reality, a reality constituted *by* irreducible, contingent, and contradictory possibilities—and the forms of time (pasts, futures, memories, fantasies) they open and close. The "results fetishist" split between a narrow conception of success or failure reduces the event to demonstrable figures. To train foreclosure seems, fairly predictably, to produce the excess "hauntology" of such a shortfall between desire, practice, and perceived reality—that is, fixing only on *one* reality. The haunting reality of failure is the structuring stain in the picture of industrial sports.

Here we meet the kinds of for-itself "stupidity" that seem to typify modern industrial sports. We should not only think of the explicative "genius" of slow-motion or VAR contests that distance the viewer (or even athlete) from the experience of the contest but also the posthuman forms industrial athletes take on, where ignorance or phenomenal folding is expunged by the ubiquitous rules of the game. Every apparent iteration of ignorance or stupidity is already-explicated in sporting contests: error, mistiming, and miscalculation are *present, evident to us* as the athlete's limited intentions. We split apart the psychic potential of the "cognitive not-yet" and flatten it into explicable intentions. It is written on the athlete's face. But rather than follow the potentially valid though well-worn line pursued by the romantics besotted by the explicitly perfect ten, we should remain within the same virtual realm that makes possible Musil's critique of the racehorse of genius. Rather than discuss the "posthumanity" of the admittedly historically unprecedented size and span of the average professional athlete's body—a critique that would remain within the spiritless explicative system (forty-inch quadriceps, twelve-foot wingspan, eighty-five-inch standing jump) of industrial sporting genius—we might here assess the apparent "spirit" of the game. The results fetishist sports machine, in voracious need of explicating what it deems as every last contingency relevant to the sporting event, seeks out accounts of the event from the athletes taking part. Media-trained in reproducibility, these athletes rehearse explicative phrases about the nature of the contests. Interestingly, these are usually framed around their intent and feeling during the contest but made up of reproducible platitudes and clichés. The apparent meaninglessness of this kind of cliché is an uncharitable assessment: these athletes, usually steeped in life experience seldom removed from the sports system (whose days consist in mixing training, promotion, travel, contest, and sleep), truly *feel* this reproducible "reality" for-themselves. But where success is the only *possible* measure of life, there is no "cognitive not-yet," only the categorical, finite success or failure—the genius and his stupidities.

SPORTING GENIUS

The judgment of stupidity, then, is an explication. In doing so, it makes reality into "the real," a quantifiable entity that loses its possibility or spirit. Thanks to explication, we can *know* that the stupid player didn't intend to drop the ball—and they can tell us as much. What we lose, though, is the possibility in the attempt—and, much more significantly, what that player might have made possible had they been stupid enough not to think "within the rules," to leave their intentions open, undefined. Rather than ride the virtual possibility that events make perceptible, bleeding out of any explicative judgment that can never fully account for their richness, we might imagine a sporting contest among possibilists, where dreaming enters the athletic event to disfigure it to the point of misrecognition, or *attention* and *creativity*. It is for this reason that the theme of sporting "genius" plays such an interesting role in Musil's enormous text. Focused attention on it, like the short, two-page chapter 93, allows Musil's narrator to provide a possible account of what he there refers to as the "civilian mind." The chapter begins by outlining what promises to be a discussion between Ulrich and one of the novel's other major characters, General Stumm von Bordwehr, a representative of the military establishment. But instead of providing us with their conversation, it notes how both characters "were absorbed in listening to a conversation going on just in front of them"—a debate between anonymous citizens about the merits of tennis players Beaupré (described by the first speaker as being "positively touched with genius") and Braddock (who, for the second, represents an explicative form of "scientific tennis" over "the intuitive kind"). The first speaker argues that "Beaupré's genius, his dazzling unpredictability, is at its peak where science fails." As the argument goes on, this claim is rebutted twice by a "third voice," who insists that "calling it genius [is] overdoing it a bit [. . . and] going too far" (Musil 2011, 458). This impasse, like Musil's address "On Stupidity," suffers from the difficulty of "knowing" the elusive form(s) of genius. Indeed, stunted in this fabricated, potentially stupid deadlock, opposing "genius" to "science" might allow us to compare Musil's fictional 1913 men's tennis universe to the superlative one I write in the twilight of—the oft-made distinctions between either the artful classicist Roger Federer or the idiosyncratic unicity of Rafael Nadal, against the unfortunate, mechanistic Novak Djokovic, whose metronomic athleticism, constantly returning the ball as if he were a concrete wall, conforms to Musil's "normal laws of tennis" (2011, 458) but in such a way as if to test their iterability. As is the case with Musil's debate, few conclusive answers emerge here: often determining the "better" player is a matter of taste—a foreshortening decision that ignores the broader narrative (one can always be stupid enough to look at the statistics . . .).

But what Musil's debate does offer is a fourth, intervening voice—a musician, for this reason seemingly disinterested in the forms of the discussion (the players themselves) and offering comment only on the abstract terms being contested—namely, the genius-science divide. The musician argues that it is the terms of such a divide that deserve scrutiny. Countering the suggestion that "'genius' is going too far," the musician argues that such a point of view overlooks the "physical thinking involved in sport," that doing so follows the "habit of overvaluing the logical, systematic kind of thinking" (458–59). From this perspective, physical movement is a kind of intentional but *implicit* thinking that takes visible form as it is thought by the body's movements, as with Beaupré's "dazzling unpredictability" that, in its pure and immediate action, seems to exceed even his ability to think it: "You can see the genius in sports without a second's hesitation" (459), the musician notes. In this sense, physical activity (typified by sporting genius) is what appears to us as the evidence of gestures but is made up entirely of the actor's *re*-actions to implicit *aisthesis*: it simply "occurs," spiritually, always-already, before the athlete can *re*flect on intending for it to occur. And insofar as it is unthought—implicit, sensible, *possible*—one could see it as utterly stupid. Yet it is this capacity that, for the musician, lends it a radical genius: he argues that "physical movement in itself is so magical that we can't stand it without some sort of buffer" (459). This buffer (one that industrial sports applies in the form of rules, statistics, roles, and positions) allows us to collapse the attentional implications of physical movement into explicated, binary logics of success-failure. It ratchets down the *implicit* "magic" of physical movement, the very unthought stupidity of the event of physical endeavor—one defined by the growth of its possibility from its potential failure(s)—under a metric of easily, indeed automatically defined and *known* "possibilities" (insofar as their being-already-known opposes them to Musil's "spirit," which is *truly* possible because it remains open). It is in this implicit space—or *reality*, shorn of modernity's scare quotes—that binaries like intent-accident, hit-miss, or smart-stupid dissolve. The physical event remains genius: but the moment we can identify it as such it loses its possible stupidity—its confusing, unknown, and unknowable depths—and collapses.

Sloterdijk emphasizes this possibility within physical movement in one of his most direct accounts of the relation between stupidity and sports. "Even manifest stupidity, incidentally, cannot be taken as a simple datum: it is acquired through long training in learning--avoidance operations," he argues. "Only after a persistent series of self-knockouts by the intelligence can a habitus of reliable mindlessness become stable—and even this can be undone at any time through a relapse into non-stupidity" (2013, 408). A surface or industrial understanding of stupidity can only be identified, or "had," once it is explicated into a binary logic as not-success. But to *train*-through "reliable mindlessness," steadfastly avoiding the "relapse into non-stupidity" or explication, is to open the future to possibility and individuation, the truly scientific attitude that sees the value in experimentation not as a predicted result but the unknown future its event draws onto the horizon. This is perhaps why Musil employs a musician to identify the sticky a-categorization of physical movement. So much of musical training is grounded in technical precision, identifying the exact places to press or sounds to hear over the course of exhaustive rehearsals. But the goal of this training is the "reliable mindlessness" of implicit genius, where the music seems to play itself, the enlightened but always-unknown state of conception that explodes explicative or notational forms into the virtual realm of boundless experimentation. To the uninitiated, musical genius seems moot: Surely there are only so many combinations of those notes, chord progressions, major-minor-major constructions that songs and symphonies must ultimately write themselves? But music's ephemerality—that it can never be *fully* explicated—makes it a space where the possibilities—or the experimentations—of the implicit remain.

Experimentation in sport is perhaps equally desirable but increasingly colonized by rules and the explicative fixity of its clocks, stats, slow-mos, and finite quantifications. Through our close analysis of the realm of the virtual inhabited by Musil's sense of possibility and Sloterdijk's of the implicit, we can see that the value of sports—especially through Sloterdijk's theories of practicing and anthropotechnics—is its implicit "stupidity," where athletic movement emerges as genius through its unthinkable possibility. This virtual space of possibility is epitomized in a discussion between Ulrich and his twin sister, Agathe, who describes herself as "stupid" because she doesn't "assimilate what [she] understands" (2011, 763). Upon replying in the negative to Ulrich's inquiry as to whether she has "any idea [. . .] what a categorical syllogism is, or a verification," Agathe responds that this kind of formal knowledge is largely meaningless: "Things lie in my mind because I don't know what to do with them—so much for my good memory. Because I'm stupid, I have a terrific memory!" (764). Agathe attends to, and is rich in, the implicit in her sensations: she has a terrific memory that *remains steeped in that memory,* one not transformed, constricted by explication. She appears stupid, perhaps; however, it is precisely because of this that her mind can entertain unfixed, exploratory, potentially genius performances. She is not bound to statistical homogeny; instead, things lie in her mind, implicit, and burst into reality at the opportune moment of never-complete possibility. Musil returns to the athletic performance of tennis to essay the possibilities consisting within Agathe's attitude, where she describes how her physical performance purposely unwinds the fixed grammar of tennis.

> When, in learning to play tennis, I deliberately for the first time place my racket in a certain position in order to give a specific new direction to the ball, which up to that point had been following the precise course I intended, then I intervene in the flow of phenomena: I am experimenting! (765)

Agathe's game style is essayistic. It identifies the possibilities that are implied in and as physical movement and pays attention to them, whether performed in the intended manner or in error. On the other side of the net, Agathe's husband, Hagauer, aims for a markedly different approach. An academic who has graduated beyond "being promising," Hagauer is precise in his actions but makes sure that these remain within the bounds of identifiable acceptability and recognition. When Ulrich contends that Hagauer's work cites diverse sources in a way that is "positively revolutionary for a schoolmaster" ("he quotes not merely academic sources but even aircraft designers, political figures, and artists of today"), Agathe counters,

> "What he does," Agatha [*sic*] added, "with music, for instance is to go recklessly as far as Richard Strauss, or with painting as far as Picasso, but he will never, even if only to illustrate something that's wrong, cite a name that hasn't become more or less established currency in the newspapers, even if it's only treated negatively" (740).

In Musil's eyes, Hagauer's "positively revolutionary" genius is of the industrial sporting kind. It consigns itself to established currencies instead of splitting them open and allowing spirit to *imply* new futures. Hagauer's tennis style follows what he, later in the novel, describes as "the buttons method":

> It consists in taking a systematic approach to one's problems, even problems that cause great agitation, on the same principle on which a man has buttons sewn on his clothes to save the time that would be lost if he acted on the assumption that he could get out of his clothes faster without buttons. (1030)

Or, one might advance, it explicates the same principle that a machine-learned application will decide for each of us what we like best—the next clip, article, insurance policy—on the basis of our "tastes," or the rules we follow. Like Braddock, Hagauer interprets the terms of the game and the problems it poses and devises a system *within its system* to respond to it. It actuates perennial, horizontal existence, disavowing the depth of what is "explicitly" stupid that, from Hagauer's systematic perspective, only need be incorporated into an expansive enough system to have their problem solved. Unfortunately, the only identifiable feature of this implicit think*ing* is that it can never be systematized and that it must *remain possible*, unactuated, and thus always exceed such a system as Hagauer's. This is the fundamental, ineluctable flaw of datafied consciousness and automatic society: in assuming that every event exists as an event to be systematized, explicated as predictable circuits, it disavows the spirit of possibility. Agathe, who never stops experimenting (even during a match), responds to Ulrich's question as to whether Hagauer is "a good tennis player," with the simplicity of the explicit scoreboard. "I beat him six-love" (765).

CONCLUSION

Petty point scoring such as this doesn't exactly serve my argument here. Indeed, the most vulgar act in sports—one far from the *spirit of the game*—is to gesture to the scoreboard when one (or one's team) is leading. One wonders at first why this is such an offensive act. Seemingly because, in explicating the contest while it is unfolding, its spirit, which is only possible if the contest itself remains in some kind of contact to an implicit past, is sapped. The immanence of the game loses its possibility; to be explicated in such a brute fashion, to be reminded, or to have one's attention drawn to the always-explicit "reality" of the game defeats the purpose of "playing"—experimentation, possibility. Without these the ruse is loose; the pretense of sporting endeavor vanishes. Agathe's game style is successful, scoreboard or not, precisely because it values "experimenting"—possibility, spirit, the event *in-itself* or implicit within itself—over explicating what that event *should* mean. Its spirit essays through the virtual realm, attentive only to the possibilities it can superimpose and perhaps even "stupidly" inhere. The spirit of the game precedes and exceeds the ineffectual, forgettable scoreboard, and it is only by forgetting the latter *before* and *during* the contest that the former becomes sensible.

This is implied later in the novel, when its antagonist Arnheim is discussing myriad subjects with Stumm, who is still eager to learn the mysteries of physical culture. He settles on the theme of spirit and its cultural iterations, arguing that German spirit can only be saved from its rationalism by looking back to the past of "original intuitiveness," typified by the slightly backward Austrian culture, where "things have not yet gone so far." Indeed, Arnheim notes that "the difference between Germany and Austria always reminds [him] of billiards, [where] everything goes wrong if you try to do it all by calculation instead of with feeling" (621). This is a fairly straightforward, if predictable analogy, typical of Arnheim's elitist attitude. But as it develops, he illuminates similar conceits to those of Ulrich and, one might believe, Musil himself.[12] Arnheim admits that he never plays billiards but nonetheless proceeds to list the possible ways to do so. One can hit the ball from different angles or with different degrees of force, via other balls and buffers, seemingly endlessly: "If you imagine each of these elements with all their inherent gradations, you have an almost infinite number of possible combinations" (622). Not to mention, as Arnheim does—but only theoretically, thus making them lie implicit, as subjunctive but unexplicated possibilities within the novel—"the laws of mathematics and statics, the mechanics of solids, plus the laws of elasticity" and many other technical factors. These are ways of describing, of attempting to form or classify, what is implicit within a possible performance as it is foreshortened into an event. But all of these implicit events have themselves seemingly infinite relations that cannot be realized, or even identified, as their links of contingency not only extend but loop over and back into each other. Static or linear temporality is only one implicit element of contingency. "You must be enough of a mathematician to see that it would take a lifetime to plan a single carom shot in that fashion," Arnheim argues. Indeed, it *takes lifetimes*, and everything implicit and unnamed within them (the fact that they have been) that render the world *as this world*, that such an event as the carom shot can ever come into existence—that it can become an event. It is as and through lifetime(s) that Arnheim can then note the paradox of calculation. "And yet I step up to the table with a cigarette between my lips, a tune in my ear, and my hat on, as it were, and hardly bothering to look over the board, I take my cue to the ball and the problem is solved!" (622).

But is the problem solved? What would it mean to solve a problem in billiards—(how) would the solution consist? The fixity of the game's laws suggests that the problem can never *remain* solved: points can be scored, matches can be won, competitors can be vanquished. But what remains implicit within the game itself—its unpredictable possibility for error, doubt, failure, stupidity (even by the best players)—looms over the solution and underwrites the seemingly miraculous execution of the carom shot. A contest can never be totally or completely won. However, sporting genius, per Beaupré versus Braddock, isn't necessarily the solving of the problem but rather the bringing to light of new problems, stimulating the imaginative capacity that may or not be present in the execution of the shot—the event shadowed by its possibilities, the seeping out of its own evental status through the possibilities that it recognized (that consist *because of it*), but are never, definitively, presented. "The event exists," Farred argues in his reconceptualization of a particular sporting event, "(solely) to generate its own supplementarity, inveterately transforming the 'event' from the colloquial to the philosophical, from historic to epistemological" (60). The event exists so as to motivate (its own) implicit senses, and in doing so, to draw out supplementary meanings, consequences, and possibilities from them—the incessant training we come to call culture, or even more drastically, feeling. The event is impossibly possible. Physical movement and sporting feats are demonstrative of this status: they exist, forever *pars pro toto*, always symbolizing far more than the instrumental act that they are thought to perform. This endless, never fully explicit supplementarity that the event cannot become without is "that precise but difficult-to-name-exactly moment in which the event-derived 'something other' becomes, through excess, symbolism, and cultural memory, the figurative thing itself" (Farred, 60). The sporting event emerges through these sensible but absent excesses that generate a "plethora of contested meanings and relentless rhetorical activity" (Farred, 60)—this is the infinite possibility that emerges as an explicable event becomes "eventful." It is precisely in this overflowing, excessive status that the event bleeds outside of how it can be named, identified, or scored, and becomes the nameless sense of a culture that can never be predicted. The number in the points or wins column always remains; even the "buttons method," given adequate attention, has the potential to exceed its immediate explication.

It is for this reason that sport's "genius" is of as much interest to Musil as it is to Sloterdijk—its "evental," or implicit, possibility. "Man's greatness is rooted in the irrational" (Musil 2011, 622), Arnheim notes, capping off his exposition. This root is always implicit, the frames of stupidity, doubt, and possibility that make any identifiably great act possible. The apparently intentional apparatus of sport, with its clear boundaries between actuated genius and ignoble stupidity, is always rooted in the irrationality of performance. Performing explodes intention and context, where the event of the act is always undetectable from what runs implicit within and outside of it—undetectable *as* the event but arranging the context and framework that make the event possible as such. This has interesting consequences for philosophies of intentionality, but Musil's contribution here aligns with his overall thesis on possibility, the unfinished nature of thought, essayism, and, indeed, his novel as a "whole." "The truth is not a crystal that can be slipped into one's pocket, but an endless current into which one falls headlong" (582), his narrator argues. This comment comes after a discussion of citations: what remains, even after trying to shear down an event to its causes, is still a network of other endlessly signifying currents, marks that link to and imply infinitely other events. Despite our best efforts through practices of symbolization and organization, this "endless current" flows past and through us, and speaks to the endless supplementarity implicit in every event.

Ulrich asks us to take even the simplest concept, one most culturally manifest and self-evident,

> and think how it keeps wavering among its many possible variants. It's like a breath that changes shape at every exhalation, with nothing to hold on to, no firm impression, no logic. So when we simply leave out in art whatever doesn't suit us and our conceptions, we're merely going back to the original condition of life itself. (626–27)

Art, literary reading, and "sports" consist in paying attention to what is left out of explicit forms. In trying to imagine what is "there" in an artwork, novel, or sporting contest, we rely on what we can conceive, on what is implicit in what we "simply leave out." For Musil the "original condition of life itself" aroused by such attention is what gives the possibility of a future, but only insofar as it can never be known. "Think of great writers," he asserts on this point, "they have given so solid a form to what once moved them that it confronts us like pressed metal even between the lines." Every novel fixes these myriad, elusive concepts to some kind of inscribed form, but these rely on being read, that is, taken up so that they may lie implicit within the reading mind, immersed in a culture of equally innumerable supplements that *remain* implicit. The novelist knows this and, indeed, seeks to inscribe it: the novel stands as an event where existence, despite its fixity, its confronting us like "pressed metal," remains shrouded in its shifting, implicit contexts that make any meaning possible. The great writer is trapped under their words, always becoming-other—like the athlete, always *becoming* the event of their contest, but never able to claim, hold on to, or possess it (outside of the increasingly arbitrary trophies and statistics that do even less to capture the implicit thrall of the event itself). "But what have they actually said?" Ulrich asks. "Nobody knows. They themselves never knew all of it at the time." A novel, in this respect, always remaining the way it was found but never to be read the same way again, forever retains its supplementarity. The great writers cannot, perhaps never could, control their work's future. As forged and explicit as it might be, it remains without qualities. "Their thoughts and feelings show all the gradations between truth and even error, as can be demonstrated if necessary, and changeable natures that come close to us at will and then elude us when we try to observe them closely" (626).

It may seem contestable, idealist, or overly possibilist to compare the great writers Ulrich describes here to the athletes and athletics so often critiqued in Musil's work—the categories of "genius" are vastly different. But insofar as how we discern genius, be it that of a composer, a technician, or a croquettist, is implicit in shifting cultural sands, the futures we hope to report them into are unpredictable. As Sloterdijk points out, "In a culture of research that, like our modern one, is opened up by ongoing explication, learning means participating in processes of constant pattern revision" (2016, 285). This relativist conception of learning is what we are left with after modernity has explicated everything—an Anthropocene imaginary speculating on distant futures where no sense, history, or meaning from our present have remained to illuminate these all-too-human marks that used to imply our having-been. But the possibilist response, to retain the implicit in the realm of the virtual and attend to its spirit (at the risk of missing the immediate point and being judged "stupid") implies another solution. If the future is not simply not-yet but only *possible*, it is up to us to imagine it. And by attending to as many gradations of the seemingly fixed, and explicated, as possible—especially those *between* "truth and even error"—we can go on extending the elusion, bringing forth ever new futures through their implication.

James Dutton teaches at the University of New South Wales, Sydney. His essays have appeared in journals such as *SubStance*, *Cultural Politics*, *Angelaki* and *Paragraph*, and his book *Proust Between Deleuze and Derrida: The Remains of Literature* was published in 2022.

Notes

1. See special issues in 2014 of *The Monist* (97, no. 1, "Robert Musil's Philosophy") and 2013 of the *Germanic Review* (88, no. 1) covering diverse topics regarding Musil's philosophical and cultural outlook, as well as Perloff, 71–100; Mehigan; Freed 2011; Ronell provides a relevant analysis of stupidity in Musil's thought, though avoids applying this to *Der Mann ohne Eigenschaften*.

2. Bersani briefly mentions Sloterdijk's productive interest in Musil's essayism (99), though this makes no mention of explication, while Isenberg takes up a sociological position, limiting reference to Sloterdijk to a footnote.

3. As Zivin notes, "The concept 'error'—and in a sense *every* concept—can be thought *only* at the point of mutual exposure, or encounter, between discourses, disciplines, fields" (16).

4. Freed provides a detailed analysis of this essayism, arguing that it is "a discursive strategy [. . .] that derives from his appropriation of the essay as a discursive *space* between science on the one hand and art and life on the other" (2013, 90). It is "a 'doing' as opposed to a 'knowing'," that incorporates, as Freed's discussion claims, technicity and its inherent expropriation as part of this "doing" process (95). Much has been written about Musil's essayism: see also Erwin, Nübel, and Harrison.

5. For more detail on his position here, see Sloterdijk 2007.

6. Sloterdijk admits that here he owes much to Foucault, 241–42.

7. Rees makes some interesting observations on this point. "The body now a text," Rees notes, makes for an experience of having it "submitted to the rigours of close reading, as the unassuming surface of experience is peeled back to reveal an ever-richer array of sensations and stigmata" (297).

8. For Genno, the novel expresses Ulrich's "desire for a Utopia of essayism where nothing is labeled true or false, rational or irrational, real or imaginary"—uniting commonly opposed senses like "precision and passion, reality and phantasy" (118).

9. Mulligan describes this as Musil's preference for "Living In" rather than living *for* something (76).

10. Interestingly, the roughly agreed timespan attributed to the beginning of modernism almost exactly coincides with the emergence of professional sports. I would suggest that this is in fact not coincidental, but contingent, for reasons of explication mentioned above. For more context on this point, see Dyreson or Sloterdijk 2013, 88–94; for its aesthetic currents, see Vere.

11. Of course, given the complex subjective forms, desires, and possibilities sport intersects with, it should be noted that this essay interprets sport in its relation to industrial explication as a departure point, not as a comprehensive account of the limits of this multiverse.

12. Nanay makes the interesting point that while Arnheim is "one of the least likeable characters in [Musil's] book," his and Ulrich's "general outlook is very similar in many respects." This isn't due to some unconscious polemical overlap on Musil's part but a calculated effort to resist "taking the human mind to be fully and entirely rational and [to] emphasize the nonrational elements in human behavior and life"—where Musil shows "us two examples that have so much overlap that we immediately focus on the differences and the reasons for these differences" (4). Musil's novel folds back on itself, resisting fixed categories, characters, contingencies: its formal or logical "stupidity" opens its possibilities.

Works Cited

Becker, Frank. 1995. "Sportsmen in the Machine World, Models for Modernization in Weimar Germany." *International Journal of the History of Sport* 12, no. 1:153–168.

Berardi, Franco. 2017. *Futurability: The Age of Impotence and the Horizon of Possibility*. London and New York: Verso.

Bersani, Leo. 2018. *Receptive Bodies*. Chicago: University of Chicago Press.

Dyreson, Mark. 2003. "Globalizing the Nation-Making Process: Modern Sport in World History." *International Journal of the History of Sport* 20, no.1:91–106.

Erwin, Andrew F. 2013. "Musil's Novelistic Essayism: *Der Mann ohne Eigenschaften* and the History of Its Genre." *Journal of Austrian Studies* 46, no. 3:77–107.

Farred, Grant. 2007. "The Event of the Black Body at Rest: Mêlee in Motown." *Cultural Critique* 66:58–77.

Foucault, Michel. 2003. *The Birth of the Clinic: An Archaeology of Medical Perception*. Translated by A. M. Sheridan. London: Routledge.

Freed, Mark. 2011. *Robert Musil and the NonModern*. London and New York: Continuum.

———. 2013. "Robert Musil and the *techne* of Rewriting Modernity." *Germanic Review* 88, no. 1:83–96.

Gailus, Andreas. 2013. "How Literature Thinks: Robert Musil and the Writing of Modernity." *Germanic Review* 88:1–5.

Genno, Charles N. 1983. "Observations on Love and Death in Musil." *Neophilologus* 67, no. 1:118–125.

Graff Zivin, Erin. 2020. *Anarchaeologies: Reading as Misreading*. New York: Fordham University Press.

Groys, Boris. 2014. *On the New*. Translated by G. M. Goshgarian. New York: Verso.

Harrison, Thomas. 1992. *Essayism: Conrad, Musil and Pirandello*. Baltimore: Johns Hopkins University Press.

Isenberg, Bo. 2018. "A Modern Calamity—Robert Musil on Stupidity." *Journal of Classical Sociology* 18, no. 1:55–75.

Mehigan, Tim. 2020. *Robert Musil and the Question of Science: Ethics, Aesthetics, and the Problem of Two Cultures*. Rochester, NY: Camden House.

Mulligan, Kevin. 2014. "Foolishness, Stupidity, and Cognitive Values." *Monist* 97, no. 1:66–85.

Musil, Robert. 1990. *Precision and Soul: Essays and Addresses*. Edited and translated by Burton Pike and David S. Luft. Chicago: University of Chicago Press.

———. 2011. *The Man Without Qualities*. Translated by Sophie Wilkins and Burton Pike. London: Picador.

Nanay, Bence. 2014. "The Dethroning of Ideocracy: Robert Musil as a Philosopher." *The Monist* 97, no. 1:3–11.

Nübel, Birgit. 2006. *Essayismus als Selbstreflexion der Moderne*. Berlin: De Gruyter.

Perloff, Marjorie. 2016. *Edge of Irony: Modernism in the Shadow of the Habsburg Empire*. Chicago: University of Chicago Press.

Rees, Will. 2021. "Hypochondriacal Reading: Phantom Illness and Literature." *Oxford Literary Review* 43, no. 2:290–315.

Ronell, Avital. 2002. *Stupidity*. Urbana and Chicago: University of Illinois Press.

Sloterdijk, Peter. 1987. *Critique of Cynical Reason*. Translated by Michael Eldred. Minneapolis: University of Minnesota Press.

———. 2007. "What Happened in the Twentieth Century? En Route to a Critique of Extremist Reason." *Cultural Politics* 3, no. 3:327–356.

———. 2011. *Spheres, Volume 1: Bubbles: Microspherology*. Translated by Wieland Hoban. Los Angeles: Semiotext(e).

———. 2013. *You Must Change Your Life: On Anthropotechnics*. Translated by Wieland Hoban. Cambridge: Polity Press.

———. 2014a. *In the World Interior of Capital*. Translated by Wieland Hoban. Cambridge: Polity Press.

———. 2014b. *Spheres, Volume 2: Globes: Macrospherology*. Translated by Wieland Hoban. Los Angeles: Semiotext(e).

———. 2016. *Spheres, Volume 3: Foams: Plural Spherology*. Translated by Wieland Hoban. Los Angeles: Semiotext(e).

Vere, Bernard. 2018. *Sport and Modernism in the Visual Arts in Europe, c. 1909–39*. Manchester: Manchester University Press.

Wallen, James Ramsey. 2015. "What is an Unfinished Work?" *New Literary History* 46, no. 1:125–142.

A POLITICAL THEOLOGY OF INTERPELLATION

ON SUBJECTION, INDIVIDUATION, AND BECOMING NOTHING

Alex Dubilet

A POLITICAL THEOLOGY OF INTERPELLATION

Of all the primal scenes that account for the genesis of the subject, it is perhaps the most well known.[1] A call rings out—"Hey, you there!"—and with the resulting recognition and physical conversion, the subject becomes what it is. Louis Althusser's classic staging of interpellation offers a condensed explanation of how subjects come to function without external coercion, "all by themselves," how subjects come into being as subjects while feeling themselves free (Althusser 2014, 269).[2] The subject is something constituted—and that constitution is what is narrativized in the scene of the police hail—yet, in a more fundamental way, it is always already there, functioning: the subject is always already subject, always already turned in on itself, working in obedience and submission. And the subject is not only the one who works, and works all by itself, but the one who recognizes itself as unique and irreplaceable, with a proper name, a proper task, and a proper place in the world: all assured and rendered obvious through the quotidian rituals of ideological recognition in which the subject continuously partakes.

The "little theoretical theatre" of the police hail and the ensuing encounter with the law is meant to stage the general structure of ideology, which functions by constituting or hailing "concrete individuals as concrete subjects" (264). Though purportedly staging the general structure of ideology, it is nevertheless deemed insufficient on its own, at least insofar as to more fully illustrate its logic Althusser provides an additional example, under the heading "Christian religious ideology." No special status is claimed for this example. "As the formal structure of all ideology is always the same," Althusser writes, "I shall restrict my analysis to a single example" (266). When this example has been taken up in subsequent analysis, it has become an object of critique and symptomatic reading.[3] Althusser's example has been read as attesting to a sanctification of religious authority, an unwitting reproduction of Catholicism in the realm of theory—uncritically embodying and naturalizing the perspective of ideology that he is staging. It has been interpreted, in other words, from a secularist perspective that in broad terms understands the theological and the religious as defects to be remedied by a more fully secular theoretical approach.

Is there a different way of questioning the significance of this example, one that would probe the possibility of it being more than merely an example but without making it an object of a secular or secularizing critical gaze? Althusser's turn to Christianity as an example, I want to suggest, may be neither a theoretical shortcoming nor merely contingent, didactic, or explanatory. Rather, the presence of the "Christian religious ideology," centered on the subjecting effects found "not only in its two Testaments, its theologians, its sermons, but also its practices, its rituals, its ceremonies, and its sacraments" (266), has decisive political-theological ramifications. After all, a key thread of political theology has focused on the critical exploration of conceptual transfers, processes of secularization, and rigorous conceptual analogies between the political and the theological domains. By diagnosing the theological elements operating within secular modernity and tracing the general transference of theological concepts into political ones, political theology has undermined the triumphalist ways that secular modernity has narrated its own essence and development. In its insistence that political modernity is imbricated irrevocably with theology, political theology has called into question the self-congratulatory attempts of the secular to disburden itself of Christianity.[4]

As a critical trajectory, political theology should not be conflated with the religious legitimation of political authority.[5] Instead, it presents a site for questioning the operations of justification and legitimation that span across the Christian and the secular in dissimulated ways, dissimulated precisely by the insistence on the structuring primacy of that binary. Rather than a conservative project of restoring something lost, political theology becomes a space for making visible the collusive lie that Christianity and secularity partake in when they situate themselves as enemies—a space where both sides of the opposition may become targets of delegitimation. This has generated a variety of distinct claims, including that both Christianity and secular modernity enact structures of temporal deferral or the not-yet via an overcoming of the Gnostic tendency of world refusal; or, building on the insights of early Marx, that secular modernity is itself the political realization of Christianity; or, more succinctly, that secularism might be the name by which Christianity forgave and forgot itself.[6] Althusser's theorization of interpellation offers a valuable addition to this critical trajectory of political theology. His deployment of Christianity as an example (and as the sole example) suggests, as will be fully developed below, that all the elements that comprise the political-theological *dispositif* of the subject—specular (self-)recognition and enclosure, subjection and agency, temporal distension and topological emplacement, naming and the guarantee about the coherence of the future—are to be seen as shared across the Christian/secular divide, rather than being the exclusive property of one of the poles. The subject is not just the resident of the secular domain, as is often assumed, but is a fundamental element, a complex *dispositif* that anchors both the secular and the Christian: it is a site of imputation and responsibility in which and through which legitimation takes place.

The subject is constituted as at once free and subjected, as free in its subjection, in relation to an interpellating transcendence. It is so constituted in the moment when it recognizes itself as the one addressed in the call of the transcendent voice. This logic occurs not only in the "little theoretical theatre" of the police hail but also no less in the scene of the divine hail that stands at the heart of Althusser's religious example. God calls out to Moses, and Moses recognizes himself as the one called, responding in self-recognition, *C'est (bien) moi!—It is (really) me.* It is in this recognition of being really the one called that one becomes a subject, "a subject subjected to God, a subject through the Subject and subjected to the Subject" (267)—and proof of this is found in the obedience that follows. Althusser schematically renames God as the Subject (with a capital S) to denote its status as the Subject par excellence, a judgment arising out of the declaration of divine self-adequation (in Exodus 3:14) "*I am that I am.*" The theoretical presence of this self-identical Subject is a "strange phenomenon" that may be seen as casting doubt on whether indeed "the formal structure of all ideology is the same" (267). It may be thought that it is precisely here that the difference between the theological and the secular becomes visible—namely, in the assumption of a divine, self-identical transcendent Subject, an assumption made by only one of the sides. The theological, on this account, would be the domain for the articulation and defense of "a Unique, Absolute, *Other Subject* i.e. God" (267) as a kind of sovereign transcendence that subjects. Yet the effect of drawing the parallel between the logics and effects of the two encounters points in exactly the opposite direction, that it is less important to ascertain whether one assumes the existence of God—"this new and remarkable Subject" (267)—than to diagnose the shared logic and mechanism of the subject, in which one recognizes oneself in relation to a transcendent subjecting call, which bestows a proper name, a place in the world, and freedom in obedience.

The two scenes suggest that the subjecting effects of transcendence occur neither exclusively in the theological domain nor exclusively in the secular one. Offered alongside one another, they make visible a shared structure: the subject as agency in subjection, whose identity and "entrance into the language of self-ascription" (Butler, 107)—the declarative *Here I am* of (self-)recognition—are established in specular relation to transcendence. It suggests a political-theological convergence in the correlation of transcendent interpellation (interpellation from beyond) and subjection, in the constitution of the subject freely obeying authority. Both scenes probe "the whole mystery" of subjects "working by themselves [*marchent tout seuls*]," which resides in "the ambiguity of the term *subject*": at once autonomous or free subjectivity and a subjected being "who submits to a higher authority, and is therefore stripped of all freedom except that of freely accepting his submission" (269). What defines subjects is that they work—they go along, function, and remain operative. And the structure of ideological capture and subjection is fundamentally a way of legitimating and normalizing the concomitant field of operativity.

In contrast to any clean opposition between autonomy and heteronomy, in which the former would stand for the secular (and modern) and the latter for the theological (and nonmodern), the logic of the subject always entails an irreducible entwinement of the two. The subject is the site and form in which heteronomy is appropriated as autonomy, and autonomy retains within it a heteronomous relation: the two remain irreducibly entwined. The subject is a knot in which there is no freedom that does not entail submission and no submission without it being taken up and enacted as a form of freedom. One may discern a difference in emphasis, such that in one case, this subjective knot might be seen as a (freedom-in-)submission and in the other as freedom(-in-submission), but what is contested is the theoretical gesture that would polemically oppose the autonomy of secular modernity to the heteronomy of theological imaginaries. Rather than contrasting the egoic or self-possessing modern subject to the subject structured (as open, affected, or wounded) in relation to the transcendent Other, Althusser's diagnosis downplays the seemingly insurmountable difference, intimating that the *dispositif* of the subject always functions as an individuated freedom-in-subjection through specular interplays with subjecting transcendence. This is made clear in Althusser's summary statement: "The individual is interpellated as a (free) subject in order that he shall submit freely to the commandment of the Subject, i.e. in order that he shall (freely) accept his subjection, i.e. in order that he shall make the gestures and actions of his subjection 'all by himself.' There are no subjects except by and for their subjection" (269).

If such a structure is shared across both the Christian and the secular domains, a distinctly different theoretical endeavor than merely defending one side of the polemical opposition becomes necessary: to think otherwise than through the subject and to experiment within an anteontological priority to the specular enclosure effected by subjecting transcendence. Rather than asserting the full, achieved autonomy of the subject or reconstructing the subject in relation to the address of the Other by means of a theological—or psychoanalytic—wounding of the subject's heroic and secular pretensions, this entails exploring the occlusions enacted in the imposition of the subject form and thus inhabiting the refusal of subjection and naming, of work and individuation. This task, undertaken in the final section of the essay, will move outside of the delimited site of Althusser's text, even as it remains guided throughout by its theoretical parameters. By reconstructing the conceptual morphology of becoming nothing in the mystical thought of the fourteenth-century figure Eckhart von Hochheim, commonly known as Meister Eckhart, I will articulate *a logic of deinterpellation.* Turning to Eckhart in the final section for this theorization is intended not only to produce a certain defamiliarization in regard to strictly secular readings of Althusser but also, and more importantly, to make visible that neither interpellation nor articulations of its subversion are exclusive properties of the secular. More significant than maintaining a clear demarcation and opposition between secular and religious discourses and domains will be ascertaining whether, in any given discourse or domain, the conceptual matrix in which the subject is constituted in relation to an interpellative transcendence is upheld and legitimated or, by contrast, diagnosed and refused. Before proceeding with this, however, it is necessary to further elaborate the constitutive elements of the *dispositif* of the subject established by the Althusserian problematic, beginning with the role of individuation, whose primacy will likewise be unsettled in subsequent sections through an exploration of dispossession-in-common.

THE CALL OF INDIVIDUATION

Althusser identifies what is interpellated into subjecthood as the individual. In fact, that is his central thesis: "All ideology hails or interpellates concrete individuals as [*en*] concrete subjects" (264). Even though "individuals are always-already subjects" (265) and subjection through transcendence has always already occurred, the analytical distinction between individuals and subjects needs to be made in order to retain the idea that the subject is something *produced.* Althusser continues to rely on the distinction between individuals and subjects despite the fact that individuals as such, independent of their positions as subjects, do not exist, and does so "because of the contrasting effect it produces" (266). Althusser's recourse to the individual, as Judith Butler insightfully suggests, satisfies the "grammatically induced 'need to know' *who* undergoes this submission in order to become a subject" (117). One might further add that even though, on Althusser's insistence, ideology functions through recruiting *concrete* individuals and transforming them into *concrete* subjects, individuals themselves outside of their standing as subjects are, according to his own logic, merely abstractions.

To designate what precedes the always-already subjected state as the individual occludes, I would suggest, the fundamental fact that interpellation not only subjects but also individuates. After all, a central effect of interpellation is the confirmation "that we are indeed concrete, individual, distinguishable and (naturally) irreplaceable subjects" (263). That we are, that is, only what is proper to each one of us and nothing more: discrete, delimited, differentiated, and determined. Subjects are inscribed into a symbolic field of recognition, into an intersubjective space of the world, through their self-recognition as subjects—self-identical and named, unique and irreplaceable. The subject becomes singularly what it is when it hears itself as the one being addressed in the "you," when it recognizes itself as the one "really" addressed in the call. This means that the interpellative call politically and theologically individuates rather than merely recruiting or conscripting individuals already available. The question of individuation is elided in the statement that individuals are interpellated as subject (or, following the French original *en*, not only *as* but also *into*, i.e., individuals are interpellated *into* their status as subjects) because, grammatically, individuals are presumed to be there for conscription and address. It is, then, insufficient to say that any reference to the individual is abstract because the individual only exists in the form of the subject; it is also necessary to add that individuation itself (which generates the individual as discrete, delimited, self-identical, as a reference *tout court*) is the result and effect of subjection. Subjection essentially entails the recognition that it is indeed *I* who is called and subjected, a recognition that is always a misrecognition insofar as it isolates and confirms the subjected self as the unsurpassable horizon for life and thought.[7]

As Étienne Balibar, among others, has argued, the peculiarity of the modern conception of the subject lies in the fact that it unites the political dimension with the ontological dimension. It ties the achievement of agential freedom in subjection to grammatical and ontological individuation (Balibar, Cassin, and de Libera; Balibar). To see in interpellation a mechanism of individuation—and thus as constituting, rather than presupposing, individuals—is to avow both of these fundamental elements constitutive of the etymological field of the modern subject. To subject (through recognition and naming) is to individuate: the form of the subject is individuated, but it is also what individuates. All of this is established, as will be explored in greater detail below, materially through actions, inserted into practices, governed by rituals, and partaking in apparatuses—which is also a way of saying that the temporal schema is always already in place and occurring "without succession." For now, let me just underscore that these "rituals of ideological recognition" (263) entail the recognition of oneself as individuated, as a unique subject distinct from others.

The individuating proclamation of self-recognition (before God), "Here I am," anchors another classic theoretical investigation. This response, uttered by the figure of Abraham, is for Jacques Derrida "the first and only possible response to the call by the other." That response, which proclaims the self in a concrete place—"Here I am"—"is the only self-presentation presumed by every form of responsibility" (Derrida, 71). Derrida's theoretical concern is to illuminate the unavoidable ethical aporias and the dispossessive responsibility toward the other that the call produces—and, as such, is quite distinct from Althusser's critical delineation of the subject as a site of freedom-in-subjection. In both, however, the transcendent call provokes a response that renders the subject literally responsible, but in both as well—and this is what I would like to emphasize—it is a mechanism of individuation occurring through (self-)recognition. In recognizing oneself as the one called and responding to that call, the subject asserts or claims its singular being: *Here—I—am.* Even if one stresses, as Derrida does, an ethics of infinite debt or the aporetic sacrifice of ethical universality that takes place in response to the call of the other (68), seen from the perspective outlined up to this point, such ethics seem to only extend, now with deconstructive subtlety, the ruse of interpellative transcendence. The obedience and submission arising from Moses's self-recognition (in Althusser's example) might be said to be only aporetically infinitized in the responsibility arising from Abraham's response (in Derrida's example).

In Althusser's delineation of the "Christian religious ideology," interpellation carries the connotations of summoning before the law (or to responsibility), but it also draws on a longer tradition in Christianity going back to Paul's elaboration of the call (in the form of Greek *kaleo* and Latin *voco*).[8] It is through a return to this conceptual history that Max Weber earlier elaborated the knot tying Christianity and modernity together. In Weber's account, the theoretical constellation of the call intimately entwines the logics of operativity, individuation, and productivity. Weber shows the way that a transcendent call produces a solitary quest for salvation, which in turn manifests an inner-worldly asceticism. The desire for personal salvation necessitates discipline, generating an endless productivity and the absolute refusal of idleness (Weber, 106). It is here that Weber located the genesis of the diligent fulfillment of one's duty that, in a secularized form, becomes the core of the modern subject. Just as significantly, the call generated a calling, a *Beruf*, "in the sense of one's station in life or defined area of work," (28) and determined an individuated vocation, a place in the world with a worldly activity structured by submission and productivity. This directly converges with Althusser's elaboration of (self-)recognition as entailing self-determination (this is who I am), a proper task (this is what I must do), and an assigned place.

As Weber notes, it was only in the wake of the Peasants' War that "the *objective* historical order into which the individual had been placed by God became," for Luther (who acts as the lynchpin in the secularization of the Pauline call into a calling or vocation), "more and more the direct outflow of the divine will" (32). In other words, the modern justification of the proper place and proper task—the calling "was a (or rather the) divinely appointed *task*" (32)—arises out of the final repression of the heretical, socialist, and apocalyptic tendencies of the late medieval period that affirmed that all should be in common. It was also in the aftermath of this repression that capitalist modernity might be said to emerge as a counter-revolution (Federici, 21–59). The resulting productive drive at the heart of modernity (and of the modern subject) is installed at the outset of the epoch of New World colonization, primitive accumulation, the transatlantic slave trade, and the enclosure of the commons (see Marx, 873–940; Linebaugh and Rediker). These developments form the violent and coercive history (one that continues to this day) that is necessary to produce subjects working "all by themselves." In a myriad of sites and in a myriad of ways, there is an extermination of idleness, of what does not work, is not properly disciplined, or escapes the logic of operativity; and, simultaneously, there is an enforcement of a morality that divides those who work and work freely (i.e., in subjection and submission) and those who don't or won't. In other words, the interpellative matrix of the subject constituted in relation to the transcendent call works as a sorting and enforcement mechanism, a mechanism that segregates those who cohere as individuals and as subjects and those who do not: a moral distribution (which is also a theological, political, and legal one) between the proper (self-possessed) subjects and all that is improperly (dis)individuated.

These reflections on individuation allow for a reconsideration of the pessimistic political anthropology that undergirds Carl Schmitt's political theology. Schmitt insists on the centrality of "theological dogmas of sin" but also "the evilness [*Sündhaftigkeit,* or sinfulness] of the world and man" for all genuine political and theological thinking (1996, 64–65). Original sin does not only entail a moral culpability, a foundational guilt, which necessitates and justifies the need for salvation and thus for authority—it also, in that very gesture, poses full individuation as its presupposition. Nowhere is this link between atomistic unity (or full individuation) and external authority to which it is bound in obedience more foundationally instantiated in political modernity than in Thomas Hobbes. No less fundamental than the question of guilt before the law or the subject's original sin is whether one accedes to and remains enthralled by the fantasy of the individuated (and thus discrete, delimited, and unique) subject. The fundamental decision, contra Schmitt, is not whether "man" is taken to be good or evil, but whether we are always already and exclusively individuated or whether this is a secondary and specular effect of transcendent interpellation. Perhaps obedience as submission to authority is proved by the fact that subjects work all by themselves, but it is also established by the fact that they are individuated—or function under this form. If authority requires a structure of individuation, then to be without desire for authority is not to assert the fundamental goodness of "man" (as Schmitt diagnosed in anarchism) but to give up on the desire for coherence, identity, and (self-)possession—to not seek to inhabit what might be called *the transcendent positionality of the subject* (as what comes into being in relation to transcendence and therewith partakes in its promise of identity and coherence).

The subject is the site for mediation and work, for the reproduction of the world, but it is also a boundary dividing and separating out what is properly individuated—what can be inserted into the hierarchy of being, be held responsible theologically, morally, legally—and what is not: too idle and inoperative, too undifferentiated and, to introduce a phrase out of mystical lexicon to which we will return, "without a why." This imposition of the individuated subject as the unsurpassable horizon and ontological frame—and the transformation of everything improperly individuated and subjected into an aberration or at best an exception to be overcome—is shared, as this essay has argued, across the Christian/secular political-theological divide, even if one of the poles might prioritize submission and the other freedom. For the apparatus of subjecting transcendence, which is always indelibly imbricated with sovereignty, the useless and idle must be converted into what is proper and appropriated, into what can work all by itself; or, it must be rendered illegible (or legible *as* illegible) to the point of extermination. In this schema, what appears more fundamental than the question of saving the subject (of being saved and protected) is salvation itself taking the form of the subject. The subject becomes a normative imposition—not the bearer of norms but the inescapable violent norm of political ontology as such—with the price of subjective coherence being abjection externalized elsewhere.

What, in the last instance, is the subject a cover for? What does it conceal or suppress? What is the world, or power, foreclosing and rendering invisible through the process of subjection? Gil Anidjar has posed a version of these questions when he sought "to determine what it is that we—and power itself, in its dissimulation—appear to want to escape, to emancipate ourselves from, by ways of acts, action, formation, production, labor, praxis and work" (2003, 11). What does action and operativity obscure? The answer that Anidjar proposes is absolute submission: the sovereign subjection of pure passivity. I would suggest a slightly different, though not wholly opposed, answer. The distribution of concepts formed by the distinctions between praxis and subjection, freedom and obedience, autonomy and heteronomy cover over idleness shared in dispossession. Modernity's violence repeatedly targets the idle and excessively in common as a problem, to be restructured into proper (self-)possession and the subject form when not dominated into submission or eliminated outright.[9] The subject who freely acts in submission is a mechanism of imposition that renders unthinkable what is below its ontological threshold—what is too idle and useless, too improper and improperly undifferentiated. Rather than detecting an absolute submission under the specular and spectral autonomy of the subject, what must be avowed is an anteontological dispossession-in-common: in lieu of the subject as destiny, there are, in the words of Fred Moten, "the ones who disavow possession, the ones who, in having been possessed of the spirit of dispossession, disrupt themselves" (188). In common (because having forsaken the lures of individuation and appropriation) and in perpetual evasion of the theater of action into which subjects are interpellated by theopolitical calls, they index an (atopic and anonymous) inoperativity, an idleness refusing the productive drive lodged within subjects.[10]

At this point, the role of naming in Althusser's constellation becomes significant. To have or be called a proper name is to be "recognized as a unique subject" (263), as Moses was when he recognized himself as the one "interpellated-called by his name" (267). Being named registers the subject as unique, embedded within a symbolic field, fully individuated and capable of being recognized as a concrete subject. The proper name fixes an individuated identity and inscribes it into the apparatus of the world, into the exclusionary ties of kinship and the nation. But naming forecloses namelessness. It overwrites anonymity by constituting the subject and installing it within the field of individuated intersubjectivity, within the spatiotemporal coherence of the world. One way to understand what is at stake is to recall Saidiya Hartman's claim that "'Stranger' [that is, the disinherited and dispossessed, the one indelibly marked by slavery] is the X that stands in for the proper name" (8).[11] This statement is a reminder about the delimited ambit, the violent function, and the exclusionary distribution inherent in the proper name. It acts as the groundless ground for Hartman's appeal to give up the name and to inhabit the field of the commoners, the stateless and the slaves, those without masters—outside of the mediational grids that establish the violent field of kinship's proper namings. To embrace namelessness as a potentiality (which is rendered unintelligible by the installation of the subject as the ontological site and horizon of intelligibility) would be to inhabit as and with the unsaved and the unsavable, rather than seeking to achieve salvation, regardless of whether the latter follows a religious or a secular logic. Namelessness is linked with the fugitive dreams of the maroons and the commoners against the sovereignty of states, which always upholds order, the order of the world, which is also to say the distribution of proper places and proper names. If sovereignty upholds the order of the world (against all anomic threats), it also overlays and overwrites the nameless by foreclosing what does not fit within and abide by the imaginary distribution of fully individuated subjects. It is against the sovereignty of states and subjects that the dreams of fugitivity of unsovereign, nameless strangers take hold.[12]

PRACTICE, REPRODUCTION, GUARANTEE

A central dimension of Althusser's overall argument is that ideology is material. It arises not out of the machinations of deceitful religious authorities or alienated imaginations, but out of acts, practices, and rituals that, in their reiteration, (re-)produce the subject and its distorted, imaginary relation to the world. The subject who possesses a proper interiority, endowed with a consciousness and a capacity for belief and ascent, is the ultimate "ideological 'conceptual' device [*dispositif*]" (259), produced in its imaginary freedom through the repeated performance of practices, ritualized within "the material existence of an ideological apparatus" (260).[13] Adapting and translating Pascal's famous dictum, Althusser renders the status of belief and agency secondary to the very practical constitution of the subject possessed of an interiority capable of belief and agency. In other words, the ideological element par excellence is not a set of ideas or beliefs but the subject itself (after all, "the category of the subject . . . is the constitutive category of all ideology" 262) constituted and recognized as individuated, determined, named. What Althusser proposes is an inversion of the idealist circuit that presumes the preexistence of the subject (to be filled with beliefs and ideas) into a materialist one that sees the subject as arising out of a perpetual double movement of subjectivation and subjection—of agency and obedience in submission—that takes place in acts, practices, and rituals inscribed in apparatuses. And this vision of the reiterative constitution of the subject is offered as the full theoretical elaboration of the original temporal staging of the subject's coming into being.

Prioritizing practices over beliefs may be read as a Catholic retort to a Protestant modernity—and, of course, much has been made of Althusser's Catholicism (see Hamza). Althusser, however, is not merely offering a proleptic recapitulation of the logic recently articulated in the critiques of the secular (e.g., Mahmood; Keane, 1–82) that target the liberal Protestant subject by bringing to the front the mediational power of material practices (in constituting the subject and its form of life). To the theoretical affirmation of the significance of practices for the constitution and cultivation of the subject (e.g., Foucault 2001), Althusser adds the substantial caveat that the subject constituted through practices is the very way that reproduction takes place. Indeed, it is the subject as a complex *dispositif* that becomes the answer to the question of how reproduction (of social relations and capitalism but also of the enclosure that may be termed the world) takes place. The subject maintains its consistency through practices, and its actions not only enact its freedom-in-subjection but also become the site of mediation through which the reproduction of the world takes place. By elaborating the subject as the individuated and agential site for reproduction, Althusser's thought surprisingly exceeds the neo-Foucauldian turn because it carries within itself the specter of reproduction's interruption. This remains implicit as Althusser asserts the eternity of the material structure of ideology. This assertion, however, hardly amounts to a valorization of practices. Not only is the reproduced world one of violence and domination, but the process of reproduction also repeatedly forecloses everything that it renders illegible within the framework of the interpellated subject. Impeding reproduction necessitates a different theoretical task (to be taken up in the next section): no longer to apprehend the subject as essential site and unsurpassable destiny but instead to avow that there is nothing but the subject *except for an unmoored, dislocated nothingness, a dispossession-in-common of what is unsubjected, nameless, and not one.* Working against the collusive interplay of Christianity and the secular, this theoretical task is a delegitimating experiment with what both sides of the opposition seek to overwrite and dissimulate through the imposition of the subject form.

What is reproduction except persistence across time, the way the now is made to work for and be converted into a future? Insofar as it takes itself to be free and individuated, the subject can act and act all by itself—but only, of course, in obedience and subjection and via practices imbedded in apparatuses; and it is through the activity of the subject, which has to be constantly (re-)enacted, within the place assigned to it in the world (or its subject position), that reproduction takes place. It becomes, in this way, the very site for the conversion of the now into a future.[14] In working for a projected future, it repeatedly actualizes the possible, suturing and guaranteeing the coherence of historical time and the reproduction of the world as it is. One could suggest that the projected horizon of futurity (of future possibilities) is the last form of transcendence that the secular world can affirm, a temporal transcendence seemingly independent of all theological remainders. Rather than emphasizing such a distinction between the theological and temporal modalities of transcendence, however, what needs to be brought to the front is the political-theological diagnosis of the logic of deferral, of temporal distension and the not-yet, that produces the subordination of the now to the future, for which the subject as freedom-in-subjection must work.[15]

The subject's freedom-in-subjection, which is at the heart of reproduction, is assured through what Althusser calls the guarantee: "the absolute guarantee that everything really is so, and that on condition that the subjects recognize what they are and behave accordingly, everything will be all right: Amen—'*So be it*'" (269). The ultimate theological form of the guarantee is the assurance of salvation, a sufficient recompense for obedience and appropriate action *in via*. More broadly, the guarantee is what assures the meaningfulness of action and justifies obedience; it is the assurance that allows for work to take place, for reproduction to occur through the mediation of a projected future with the operative present. The declaration *Here I am* (a claim amalgamating a place, an individuated subject, and an ontological affirmation) enacts the availability and the responsibility of the subject. This (self-)recognition of being hailed does not only individuate, it also inserts the subject into a theater of action: without the resulting specular enclosure, there is no partaking in practice and thereby no participating in reproduction. In its bestowal of assurance, the guarantee is the part of the conceptual *dispositif* of the subject that is most directly tied to justification and legitimation. If, as I have argued above, political-theological reflection as a critical trajectory calls into question the operations of legitimation and justification, then one of its primary targets must be the subject as the individuated, named, self-possessed site for assured action since it is the very site through which the legitimation and reproduction of the world take place. Unworking justification necessitates abandoning the process of futural projection and historical suturing by inhabiting the idleness of the unconvertable (non-)time of the now. This confronts the impossibility of salvation, be it secular or theological, of the unjustified, the anonymous, and the never properly individuated.[16]

IV. DEINTERPELLATION AND BECOMING NOTHING

The subject, let us recall, comes into being through the formative experience of conversion, of turning around in response to the call. By "this mere 180-degree physical conversion he becomes a subject" (264). This movement of recognition and submission is a turning toward authority but also a turning in on the self: it registers and arises out of an attachment to the coherence of identity. Moreover, insofar as the subject is always already subject, it finds itself always already turned around, twisted upon itself, susceptible to the voice of authority, and recognizing itself as individuated. And this permanent state of having-been-turned-around, a kind of inversion or even introversion, becomes the site for operativity and practice, for the legitimation and justification of authority and thereby of the world across the span of its temporal reproduction.

Is there any refusal of or exodus from the imposition of the *dispositif* of the subject? If the transcendent call not only induces the conversion that brings the subject into being but also entails a preceding "readiness or anticipatory desire" or a "founding submission" that accounts for the turning—and forms "the non-narrativizable prehistory of the subject"—then the subject is destiny even before its destiny comes to be narrated (Butler, 111–112, 107). But what might it mean to not have been exhaustively captured and determined by the strictures of conversion—or to think otherwise than through the destiny of the subject turned in on itself? How would one delineate a path that would refuse conversion, an anticonversion (or even an anteconversion) that would be less an operation than a kind of inoperativity that would unsettle conversion's constitution of the subject in relation to the transcendent call? What might index the obverse occluded by the subject that is always already subjected, individuated, named, and working all by itself?

There is no unified or coherent tradition to turn to for such questions, but there are fragments to be found in various discursive sites and archives—the literary, the mystical, the fugitive, the insurrectionary—fragments that register the impossible lived force occluded by the subject. They experiment with the perpetually concealed truth that individuation in obedience and submission is not the only destiny. To delineate one path through these questions, what follows turns to a surprising source: the fourteenth-century figure Eckhart von Hochheim, commonly known as Meister Eckhart, whose mystic speech elaborates a logic of what I would term *deinterpellation.* In a mystical-theological idiom, Eckhart's sermons acknowledge the fact that the subject is constituted through a relation of interpellating transcendence—that the subject is, in Althusser's parlance, "a subject through the Subject and subjected to the Subject" (267)—and at the same time formulate the exigency of challenging the exhaustiveness of the resulting enclosure's reach. One can distill from the sermons a project of inverting each of the constitutive elements that comprise the *dispositif* of the subject, suggesting that just like the logic of subjection through interpellative transcendence, deinterpellation is not the exclusive property of any one domain, secular or religious, but acts as a delegitimating force against the interplays of transcendence and subjection wherever they are found. The inversion operates via the logic of becoming nothing, which takes on a diversity of conceptual formulations in Eckhart, among them to have become nothing, to be equal to nothing, to be as you were when you were not, *abegescheidenheit* (detachment), and *gelâzenheit* (rendered variously as releasement, abandonment, and giving up). Becoming nothing fundamentally inverts the logic of the call and its imbrication with hearing and obedience no less than with individuation and subjection.[17] Rather than establishing the good or true call in contrast to the false or deceiving one, or rejecting subjection in and of the world by means of a nonworldly call,[18] it forms an undertow of an uncreated anteontological radical immanence of those who are equal to nothing.

If conversion as a turning around produces subjection and individuation, Eckhart's formulations of becoming nothing or detachment should be understood as forms of anticonversion or, perhaps, as deformations of conversion. In abandoning the self as proper and property, they assert an impossible (within the grammar of the subject) yet real antecedence of a disappropriated and dispossessed nothingness without qualities (*âne eigenschaft*) to the enclosure of interpellative transcendence. If interpellation confirmed "that we are indeed concrete, individual, distinguishable and (naturally) irreplaceable subjects" (263), Eckhart's becoming nothing suggests an abyssal kernel at the heart of all determination, an anteontological insistence of what is without properties, determinations, or qualities. In Eckhart's most radical sermons, we are not (and never have been) individuated and self-possessed: more intimately than any possession, we are "wholly empty and free"[19] (2:34, EE 180), a dispossession-in-common without properties, lived as real immanence against all interpellating calls of transcendence.

Rather than opening the self—in responsiveness and responsibility—to a (divine) call, becoming nothing dislocates the entire specular matrix of interpellative transcendence and the subject. It discloses "a strange and desert place [that] is rather nameless than possessed of a name" (28:322, CW 131). Taking on various figurations as the spark, the little something in the soul, the innermost, this (groundless) ground "is remote and alien [*verre und vremde*] from all createdness," and in it the soul and God are "one and not just united" (12:146, TP 269). The nameless ground is the abyss in which the subject and interpellating transcendence (creature and creator) collapse in indifference and indistinguishability. Whereas in the classic paradigm of negative theology established in Christianity by Pseudo-Dionysius the Areopagite, uncreatedness and namelessness are exclusively ascribed to divine transcendence, to be humbly exalted as the ineffable beyond by the creature, in Eckhart's distinct mutation, the uncreated and the nameless are ascribed to the (abyssal) ground that suspends (the difference between) the soul and God. With no hierarchical difference remaining, the soul is uncreated and annihilated, nameless and without qualities, and as such in antecedence to the entire field of creation, determination, and naming, in antecedence to the ontological field that delimits, subjugates, and hierarchizes. The antecedence of the unsubjected to subjection, theologically articulated as the antecedence of the uncreated to the created, suggests that prior (with an impossible-yet-real priority) to being and being a subject in the world, one is uncreated—without what is one's own and without the self as proper and property—in an improper, empty living, which is, to turn to one of Eckhart's formulations with the richest theoretical afterlife, "without a why" (*âne warumbe*), untethered and unmoored. The subject is always already subject, but only so within the time of the enclosure (within the realm of the created), while Eckhart's deinterpellative assertion of the uncreated ground claims an impossible-yet-real antecedence that delimits and subverts the subjecting hold of transcendent interpellation.[20]

Whereas the subject is the locus of mediation that reproduces itself and the world through material acts, practices, and rituals in which it partakes, becoming nothing does nothing but insist on a certain indifference to works and practices. It is not an action or a practice that mediates and reproduces the subject and the world but a detachment from what is one's own without a medium (*âne mittel*)—an erosion of the subject form and its imperatives to work, to mediate, to be saved. This is one way to understand Eckhart's critique of works and ways: whereas practice subjects by necessitating the mediation of (the not-yet of) transcendence, becoming nothing discloses the collapse of mediation, "without ways [*âne wîse*]" (5b:70, EE 183–84). If the guarantee and salvation to come render action coherent by endowing it with futurity, Eckhart's abyssal without ways and qualities is without deferral, in opposition to the structure of the not-yet enacted by Christianity and the secular alike. Becoming nothing is a nonaction or an inaction that discloses the inexhaustive reach of the logic of transcendent interpellation and the structures of mediation and reproduction that it perpetuates. It is, to borrow from François Laruelle's (2018) lexicon, the nonaction of unilateralization that affirms a mystical core of indifference to the world. It radically decenters and deabsolutizes—without refuting—Althusser's claim that there "is no practice except by and in an ideology" (261) or, in other words, that the subject expresses its freedom in delimited action within a determined mediational field of material apparatuses.

Eckhart's deinterpellative speech makes available a freedom of the "uncreated and uncreatable [*ungeschaffen und ungeschepfelich*]" (12:146, TP 269)—the unsubjected and the unsubjectable, if translated out of the theological idiom—a freedom that is intimately dispossessive of what is one's own, an annihilating disowning of the proper.[21] Not the freedom-in-subjection of the unique and individuated subject enacted in actions within mediating practices but a freedom of what is without name and quality, an inhabitation of "the most intimate poverty [*næhste armuot*]" (52:558, EE 202) that indexes an ante- and anoriginal refusal of all subjection and obedience. "Those who are equal to nothing, they alone are equal to God [*Die nihte glîch sint, die sint aleine gote glîch*]" (6:82, EE 187), because no hierarchical difference remains when the apparatus of transcendent interpellation is undone in the groundless ground. Those who are equal to nothing are not *under* but *with* God: "not . . . servants but friends" (6:84, EE 188). As Eckhart underscores, "the highest poverty" of those who are equal to nothing entails that one "lives so that he may be free both of his own will and of God's will, as he was when he was not" (52:558, EE 201). The spiritual poverty of becoming nothing entails thus not the negation of the self to produce a site for the work of the Other, but the collapse of the very difference between self and Other: "So long as you have a will to fulfill God's will, and a longing for God and for eternity, then you are not poor" (52:554, EE 200). Rather than affirming the heteronomic kernel of the Other as structuring the subject, as proposed by certain psychoanalytic and theological perspectives,[22] Eckhart's becoming nothing or the spiritual poverty of the poor in spirit who "wants nothing, and knows nothing, and has nothing" (52:550, EE 199) articulates a total refusal of hierarchical external relationality—between Other and self, between transcendence and the subject.

Eckhart states: "The just man serves neither God nor creatures" (28:320, CW, 130). The just, another figure for those who are equal to nothing, do not require justification: they are just without justification, detached from the imposition of the matrix of obedience and salvation.[23] To be created and named, to be unique and irreplaceable, is to be inserted into a moral-soteriological horizon in which obedience is exchanged for salvation. By contrast, the heretical thrust of Eckhart's deinterpellation affirms those equal to nothing as radically indifferent to all quests and guarantees of salvation. In anteriority to "everything created" or the field of creation, these annihilated ones inhabit an unruly, nameless, and uncreated freedom in common (in common as it abdicates both individuation and the proper). This uncreated freedom of namelessness remains furtive and underground, in unintelligible detachment from the theopolitical calls that compel it to appear as either guilty or responsible but always amid the dialectical ruses of action and subjection. This detachment from the theater of action is a claim of immanent refusal: to never have been interpellated into the ontological field of the named, individuated, and subjected, and thus to remain invisible, anonymous, and sustaining a destituent potential to the created order of things.

In making available an uncreated freedom of those who are equal to nothing, Eckhart articulates, in a mystical register, an underdetermination of the nexus of freedom in subjection constitutive of the *dispositif* of the subject. Not a freedom through the law but a freedom in antecedence to the law for which the attachment to identity and coherence is but one more ruse of the law itself. As such, it does not abide by the guilt or original sin that would necessitate redemption and thereby justify theological and political authorities—but instead inhabits a dispossession-in-common that abjures attachment to coherence and identity, possession and the proper. A deregulation of the subject form by means of a freedom too undifferentiated and in common, irreducible to the individuated site of accusation and subjection. "There are no subjects except by and for their subjection" (269)—Eckhart understands this Althusserian truth, but with an inversion: no subjects except for their subjection and, therefore, an exigency of an ante- and anoriginal refusal of interpellative transcendence and the conversion it elicits. Becoming nothing declares you are not one, you are none, "all creatures are a pure nothing" (4:52, TP 250): an undertow of the groundless ground that renders those who are equal to nothing unavailable for subjection. Repudiating the submission to the law as destiny, deinterpellative becoming nothing indexes an unsubjected freedom of dispossession-in-common that is not only antinomian, but also, more profoundly, antenomian, in antecedence to and in anoriginary refusal of the imperative imposition of the law (and the desire for coherence, identity, and possession that it induces).[24] This intimation of the antenomian casts a different light on the aforementioned mutually beneficial polemics between autonomy (as moral or political ideal) and heteronomy. Each, in its orthodoxy, forecloses the real—but undeclared—shared enemy: the antenomian refusal of the law and its subjecting imperatives in unruly disobedience and general antagonism.[25] Whereas the subject is always already subject, in submission to the law, becoming nothing discloses the nameless and whyless nothing that never was and yet remains as real in antecedence to all individuated subjection: as you were when you were not, uncreated, in abyssal detachment from action, mediation, and reproduction.

CODA: THE ATOPIA OF IMMANENCE

To conclude, let us return to a final effect of interpellation in the Althusserian matrix: "This is your place in the world! This is what you must do!" The subject is emplaced. It is assigned its proper place, in which it will enact its proper task. The subject recognizes this in the initial moment: that the subject really is a subject, that it really does occupy the place designated for it in the world and "this fixed residence . . . obtains from [the subject] the recognition of a destination" (266–67). A place and a position, with a set of material imperatives, a calling uniquely theirs that installs subjects into the order of possibility to be actualized. All of this is taken to be legitimate: a place in the world, a destination, and the necessity of action, work, and mediation to achieve it. This topographical emplacement of the subject (the assignment of its proper place) is corroded by Eckhart's groundless ground, that "lowest place" of annihilation that is fundamentally atopic. To cling "to place [*stat*]" is to cling "to distinction [*underscheit*]" but the poor in spirit or the annihilated ones "should not be or have any place in which God could work" (52:560, EE 202). The inhabitation of this atopic dislocated freedom "without a why" is as indifferent to *topos* as to its imperatives of action. Revealed in deinterpellative becoming nothing, this atopic freedom does nothing—but undo the proper place and its injunction to the proper task. Hence "without a why," a conceptual formulation that directly inverses the imperative of the proper task assigned to the subject, whose every activity only reproduces the world as it is.

The transcendent call has the worldly effect of topographically overlaying radical immanence.[26] This is not the ersatz immanence of the specular enclosure of the subject-in-the-world but rather what retains an anteontological primacy of the real vis-à-vis that enclosure. Radical immanence is one way to indicate what is foreclosed by the *dispositif* of the subject imposed by both the Christian and the secular, which, unable to bear it, set up subjection and deferral in its place (and as the proper place). Against this overlaying and occlusion, radical immanence persists as a kind of incoherence that refuses the assigned place and the general distribution of proper places. Radical immanence indexes an atopic or utopic dimension, foreclosed and rendered impossible by the grammar of the world. It might be said to be "an irreducibly material immanence, of that which lies below" (Moten, 113) that troubles the spatiotemporal coordinates of the world. It registers the general disturbance of the topographical and temporal coherence of the world and, as such, aligns with the deinterpellated and unsovereign, against the unitary reproduction of the world (through the subject) and its exceptional reconstitution (through sovereignty).

Here, a final dimension of the antenomian becomes evident: the assertion of uncreated freedom not only in anoriginary antecedence to and refusal of guilt and obedience, individuation and identity, but also in anoriginary antecedence to and refusal of *nomos* as enacting appropriation, division, and production (Schmitt 2003). In this unceasing movement against nomic distributions of the proper, which arise out of the logic of the segregated universal, a universal imposed through division, it also aligns with the earth as what is in common and unbounded.[27] If the subject is the site of legitimation and justification, antenomian deinterpellation in its inhabitation of the "utopic commonunderground of this dystopia" (Harney and Moten, 51) is an insurgency of the delegitimation and even the destitution of *nomos*. It reveals a radical immanence, whose utopian indifference—without appeal to mediation, operativity, or practice—carries a force capable of ungrounding the world and disorganizing the time of its reproduction.

Alex Dubilet is assistant professor of English at Vanderbilt University. He works across contemporary continental philosophy, critical theory, philosophy of religion, political theology, and the critical study of secularity and secularism. He is the author of *The Self-Emptying Subject: Kenosis and Immanence, Medieval to Modern* (2018). He is also the coeditor (with Kirill Chepurin) of *Nothing Absolute: German Idealism and the Question of Political Theology* (2021).

Notes

1. I would like to thank Joe Albernaz, Kirill Chepurin, Aaron Eldridge, Jessie Hock, Ross Lerner, Jacob Liming, Milad Odabaei, and the anonymous reader at *Cultural Critique*. Their thoughtful engagements with this essay were invaluable.

2. All subsequent citations to this text appear as parentheticals. I have silently removed italics from the original wherever necessary. For the French, see Althusser (1995).

3. In an influential theorization of interpellation, Judith Butler reads the presence of the theological and the religious in Althusser symptomatically. "To what extent is the persistence of the theological model a symptom," Butler asks, "one that compels a symptomatic reading?" (113).

4. For a convergent mapping and theorization of political theology, see Dubilet (2021b) and Chepurin and Dubilet.

5. For a sophisticated engagement with political theology that understands it in this way, see Kahn.

6. For the first, see Albernaz and Chepurin; for the second, see Dubilet (2021b); for the third, see Anidjar (2006).

7. One reader who perspicaciously stresses the primacy of individuation in the logic of interpellation is Jodi Dean. Dean is right to see that through interpellation "what was a crowd becomes so many separable individuals" (79) and to conclude as well that the individual is "a form of capture" (76). Her insistence on the interpellation as a theory of individuation is carried out, however, to recover a different conception of the subject, psychoanalytically inspired and decoupled from the individual, whereas what follows seeks to critically articulate the entwinement of subjection and individuation rather than attempting to decouple them.

8. Montag (2017) makes this point in a nuanced rereading of interpellation.

9. That idleness is fundamentally slated for extermination in modernity is attested to in Frank B. Wilderson III's theoretical recounting of the colonial encounter with the KhoiSan: "Without those textual categories of Dress, Diet, Medicine, Crafts, Physical Appearance, *and most importantly, Work,* the KhoiSan stood in refusal of the invitation to become Anthropological Man. S/he was the void in Discourse which could only be designated as 'idleness.' *And idleness had been (a) counterposed to work and (b) criminalised and designated with the status of sin, long before the Europeans reached the Cape*" (235; emphasis added). The example of the KhoiSan shows how idleness must eliminated (if it cannot be converted into productivity) for the colonial world and subject form to take hold. Importantly, Wilderson emphasizes the importance of constructing a postrevolutionary vision centered on idleness rather than on the valorization of work or productivity, which for him requires affirming the figure of the slave rather the figure of the worker: "The worker calls into question the legitimacy of productive practices, the slave calls into question the legitimacy of productivity itself" (231).

10. Idleness was targeted for elimination not only by the matrix of capitalism and colonialism but also eventually by both Nazi Germany and the Soviet Union—a fact that demonstrates the extent to which productivity dominates the spectrum of political modernity. For this point and reflections on the figure of "the workshy," see Gordon.

11. The rest of this paragraph engages with the final chapter of Hartman.

12. For the unsovereign, see Chandler.

13. In calling the subject an "absolutely ideological 'conceptual' *dispositif*," Althusser might be distinguished from Giorgio Agamben, who formulates the subject as the site of mediation between living beings and the *dispositif*. Expanding

Foucault's conception, Agamben defines a *dispositif* as "literally anything that has in some way the capacity to capture, orient, determine, intercept, model, control, or secure the gestures, behaviors, opinions, or discourse of living beings." By contrast, he defines the subject as "that which results from the relation, and so to speak, from the relentless fight between living beings and apparatuses" (14). Of course, throughout Althusser's essay what is standardly rendered as apparatus (as in "an ideological apparatus") is not *dispositif* but *appareil.*

14. For conversion and the now, see Barber.

15. The diagnosis is a political-theological one because the structure of temporal deferral or the not-yet is an element shared by Christianity and the secular. For a classic version of this claim, see Löwith; see also Dubilet (2021a).

16. This line of thinking can be read against the background of Frantz Fanon's claim that individualism is "the atheist's form of salvation" (12).

17. Mladen Dolar reminds us that the link between hearing and obedience is not only conceptual ("listening is 'always-already' incipient obedience; the moment one listens one has already started to obey, in an embryonic way one always listens to one's master's voice, no matter how much one opposes it afterward") but also etymological across a number of languages (2006, 75–76).

18. Even those calls that are not of the world remain enmeshed in structures of transcendence and permutate a set of constitutive elements, including subjection and individuation, striving and mediation. The laboring that the subject undertakes may be either in the world or out of it, or even against it, but insofar as the subject is in place and working, it remains constitutively bound to transcendence. Not even a call from elsewhere, an alien call, sufficiently problematizes this conceptual matrix.

19. For ease of access, the German is taken from Eckhart (1993a and 1993b). For English translations, I use Eckhart (1981; 1986; 2009). The in-text citation will be first, when necessary, by sermon number (Quint numbering), then by page number in German editions, and then by page number in English editions (which are referred to in text as EE (1981), TP (1986), and CW (2009), respectively). I have modified the available translations silently whenever necessary.

20. In a way, a convergent relation between groundlessness and the subject was already established by Althusser himself in "Three Notes on the Theory of Discourses," an earlier text exploring interpellation and ideology, written in 1966 but published posthumously. There, Althusser critiques Lacan's theory of the split subject and writes, "There is no *divided* or *split* subject, but something else entirely; alongside the *Ich,* there is a *Spaltung,* that is, literally, an *abyss,* a precipice, an absence, a lack. This abyss is not a subject, but that which opens up *alongside a subject . . .*" (2003 77–78). This passage contains the kernel of a retort to Lacanian critiques of Althusser's interpellation, which assert "that there is already an uncanny subject that precedes the gesture of subjectivization" (Žižek, 64). For important discussions of "Three Notes," see Ípola (53–63) and Montag (2013, 131–40).

21. Deinterpellation may be productively contrasted to what James Martel recently theorized as misinterpellation. With the concept of misinterpellation,

Martel explores the disjuncture between the system of power and its reception or, to put it otherwise, the situations when subjects show up for calls not intended for them or show up for calls wrongly, in manners and modalities that subversively call the whole staging of authority into question. Misinterpellation produces the recognition of the subject "as having always been anarchist, decentralized, and multiple;" and generates the question, "What kind of subject emerges from the breakdown of interpellation?" (Martel, 7–8). Sympathetic to refusing the interpellative powers of authority, I seek to theoretically explore the potentiality that no subject form at all remains on the obverse side of the immanent refusal of the subject's conversion to authority. In other words, refusing transcendent interpellation may also necessitate refusing the grammar of individuation and subjection; this renders articulations of becoming nothing much closer to Harney and Moten's experiments with the undercommons than to alternative, pluralized visions of the subject.

22. For Dolar, psychoanalysis (in opposition to theology) suggests a heteronomic origin of the subject and the necessity of a "fidelity to the "foreign kernel" of the voice which cannot be appropriated by the self . . . following precisely the heteronomic break in which one cannot recognize oneself" (2006, 122–23). Dolar (1993) defended such a position, as a critique of Althusserian interpellation, when he insisted on the presence of an irreducible alien kernel at the heart of the subject, which makes that subject haunted by lack and constitutively related to the Other. A convergent position that articulates the role of the Other in the structure of the subject, but which positions psychoanalysis, theology, and mystical archives in a productive constellation (rather than in polemical opposition), is elaborated by Pandolfo.

23. For a full articulation of Eckhart's figure of the just and how it transforms the parameters of political theology, see Dubilet (2022).

24. It is possible to constellate a dispersed lineage, a kind of nontradition that fails to cohere, around the antenomian. In Eckhart's vicinity, there was Marguerite Porete and her errant joy but also the nameless wild ones (conjured by Henry Suso's disciplining gaze), and the free spirits (see Vaneigem). Moving outside of the medieval frame, one might think of the Quietists and mystics of pure love whose idleness was deemed as impermissible to the authorities as the fanaticism of excessive activity and, beside them, the radical materialists in the Spinoza lineage—who likewise abdicate all claims to (self-)possession and to the subject as site of theological, political, and moral imputation—(see Coleman), no less than Gerrard Winstanley and the Diggers who asserted the earth in common anterior to all hierarchical subjections of the proper. Refusing the subject as the site for accusation and accountability always brought on the condemnation of the authorities, which saw only licentious disorder of moral dissoluteness therein. This enumeration is meant only as an initial indication of dispersive elements, which take on mystical, aesthetic, exilic, insurgent, fugitive, abolitionist—and not only—idioms. Indeed, traces of such an anoriginary antenomian refusal in modernity can be found across a range of forms in excess of the mystical, in those of marronage and of rebellions against the incessant imposition of nomos in modernity, in those

of the general strikes of pure means and divine violence destituent of law, no less than across the undercommon socialities in antagonistic subtraction from the imperatives of government and regulation.

25. Another figure who refuses to grant primacy or legitimacy to the law is George Jackson, whose proclamation that "it was *the thing in the street that was real*" and whose elaboration of the line of escape in the statement "I may run, but all the time that I am, I'll be looking for a stick!" can productively be contrasted, as Michelle Koerner has shown, to Althusser's theoretical theater. For Jackson, the confrontation with the police in the street does not engender an obedient conversion of the always-already subjected but rather a running away, a fugitive escape from subordination. What is significant, as Koerner underscores, is that what may appear as reactive is, in fact, anterior to capture: running "is not finally reducible to an escape from capture; instead, it names an autonomous force that precedes capture" (168). Such an assertion of antecedence that refuses the law as violent destiny might however be understood as forever deviating from all (self-)correcting logics of autonomy and thus as a marker of the antenomian.

26. In using this term, I mean to evoke Laruelle's theorization of radical immanence as something that under-determines the world and contains a kernel of mystical indifference to the world's pragmatics. I do not think, in contrast to Laruelle, that radical immanence should be associated with the individuated figure of "Man-in-Person" or ordinary man, because I understand individuation to be fundamentally a worldly operation and thus align radical immanence with the nonindividuated, the impersonal, the nameless, and the improper. For a fuller articulation of this point, see Dubilet (2017; 2021a; 2015).

27. For a theoretically rich exploration of the earth's relation to nomos, see Albernaz.

Works Cited

Agamben, Giorgio. 2009. *What is an Apparatus? And Other Essays.* Translated by David Kishik and Stefan Pedatella. Stanford: Stanford University Press.

Albernaz, Joseph. 2021. "Earth Unbounded: Division and Inseparability in Friedrich Hölderlin and Karoline von Günderrode." In *Nothing Absolute: German Idealism and the Question of Political Theology*, edited by Kirill Chepurin and Alex Dubilet, 124–43. New York: Fordham University Press.

Albernaz, Joseph, and Kirill Chepurin. 2020. "The Sovereignty of the World: Towards a Political Theology of Modernity (After Blumenberg)." In *Interrogating Modernity: Debates with Hans Blumenberg*, edited by Agata Bielik-Robson and Daniel Whistler, 83–107. New York: Palgrave Macmillan.

Althusser, Louis. 1995. *Sur la reproduction.* Paris: Presses Universitaires de France.

———. 2003. "Three Notes on the Theory of Discourses." In *The Humanist Controversy and Other Writings*, edited by François Matheron, 33–84. Translated by G. M. Goshgarian. London: Verso.

———. 2014. *On the Reproduction of Capitalism: Ideology and Ideological State Apparatuses.* Translated by G. Goshgarian. London: Verso.

Anidjar, Gil. 2003. *The Jew, the Arab: A History of the Enemy.* Stanford: Stanford University Press.

———. 2005. "Secularism." *Critical Inquiry* 33, no. 1: 52–77.

Balibar, Étienne. 2017. *Citizen Subject: Foundations for Philosophical Anthropology.* Translated by Steven Miller. New York: Fordham University Press.

Balibar, Étienne, and Barbara Cassin, and Alain de Libera. 2014. "Subject." In *Dictionary of Untranslatables: A Philosophical Lexicon,* edited by Barbara Cassin, 1069–1091. Translated by Emily Apter, Jacques Lezra, and Michel Wood. Princeton: Princeton University Press.

Barber, Daniel Colucciello. 2014. "The Immanent Refusal of Conversion." *Journal of Cultural and Religious Theory* 13, no.1: 142–50.

Butler, Judith. 1997. *The Psychic Life of Power: Theories in Subjection.* Stanford: Stanford University Press.

Chandler, Nahum. 2014. *X—The Problem of the Negro as a Problem for Thought.* New York: Fordham University Press.

Chepurin, Kirill, and Alex Dubilet. 2021. "Introduction: Immanence, Genealogy, Delegitimation." In *Nothing Absolute: German Idealism and the Question of Political Theology,* edited by Kirill Chepurin and Alex Dubilet, 1–34. New York: Fordham University Press.

Coleman, Charly. 2014. *The Virtues of Abandon: An Anti-Individualist History of the French Enlightenment.* Stanford: Stanford University Press.

Dean, Jodi. 2016. *Crowds and Party.* London: Verso.

Derrida, Jacques. 1995. *The Gift of Death.* Translated by David Willis. Chicago: Chicago University Press.

Dolar, Mladen. 1993. "Beyond Interpellation." *Qui Parle* 6, no. 2: 75–96.

———. 2006. *A Voice and Nothing More.* Cambridge, Mass.: MIT Press.

Dubilet, Alex. 2015. "'Neither God, nor World': On the One Foreclosed to Transcendence." *Palgrave Communications.* http://doi.org/10.1057/palcomms.2015.27.

———. 2017. "(Non-)human Identity and Radical Immanence: On Man-in-Person in François Laruelle's Non-philosophy." In *Superpositions: Laruelle and the Humanities,* edited by Julius Greve and Rocco Gangle, 31–45. London: Rowman & Littlefield.

———. 2021a. "An Immanence without the World: On Dispossession, Nothingness, and Secularity." *Qui Parle* 30, no.1: 51–86.

———. 2021b. "On the General Secular Contradiction: Secularization, Christianity, and Political Theology." In *Nothing Absolute: German Idealism and the Question of Political Theology,* edited by Kirill Chepurin and Alex Dubilet, 240–55. New York: Fordham University Press.

———. 2022. "The Just without Justification: On Meister Eckhart and Political Theology." *postmedieval: a journal of medieval cultural studies* 13, no.1–2: 5–28.

Eckhart, Meister. 1981. *Meister Eckhart: The Essential Sermons, Commentaries, Treatises, and Defense.* Translated by Edmund College and Bernard McGinn. Mahwah, NJ: Paulist Press.

———. 1986. *Meister Eckhart: Teacher and Preacher.* Edited and translated by Bernard McGinn. Mahwah, NJ: Paulist Press.

———. 1993a. *Werke I.* Edited by Niklaus Largier. Translated by Josef Quint. Frankfurt am Main: Deutscher Klassiker Verlag.

———. 1993b. *Werke II.* Edited by Niklaus Largier. Translated by Josef Quint et al. Frankfurt am Main: Deutscher Klassiker Verlag.

———. 2009. *The Complete Mystical Works of Meister Eckhart.* Translated by Maurice O'C Walshe. New York: Crossroad.

Fanon, Frantz. 2004. *The Wretched of the Earth.* Translated by Richard Philcox. New York: Grove Press.

Federici, Silvia. 2004. *Caliban and the Witch: Women, The Body and Primitive Accumulation.* Brooklyn: Autonomedia.

Foucault, Michel. 2001. *The Hermeneutics of the Subject: Lectures at the College de France, 1981–82.* Translated by Graham Burchell. New York: Palgrave Macmillan.

Gordon, Avery. 2018. *The Hawthorn Archive: Letters from the Utopian Margins.* New York: Fordham University Press.

Hamza, Agon, ed. 2016. *Althusser and Theology: Religion, Politics and Philosophy.* Leiden: Brill.

Harney, Stefano, and Fred Moten. 2013. *The Undercommons: Fugitive Planning and Black Study.* Brooklyn: Autonomedia.

Hartman, Saidiya. 2007. *Lose Your Mother: A Journey Along the Atlantic Slave Route.* New York: Farrar, Straus, and Giroux.

Ípola, Emilio de. 2018. *Althusser, The Infinite Farewell.* Translated by Gavin Arnall. Durham: Duke University Press.

Kahn, Victoria. 2014. *The Future of Illusion: Political Theology and Early Modern Texts.* Chicago: University of Chicago Press.

Keane, Webb. 2007. *Christian Moderns: Freedom and Fetish in the Mission Encounter.* Berkeley: University of California Press.

Koerner, Michelle. 2011. "Line of Escape: Gilles Deleuze's Encounter with George Jackson." *Genre* 44, no. 2: 157–80.

Laruelle, François. 2018. *A Biography of Ordinary Man: On Authorities and Minorities.* Translated by Jessie Hock and Alex Dubilet. Cambridge: Polity Press.

Linebaugh, Peter, and Marcus Rediker. 2000. *The Many-Headed Hydra: Sailors, Slaves, Commoners, and the Hidden History of the Revolutionary Atlantic.* Boston: Beacon Press.

Löwith, Karl. 1949. *Meaning in History.* Chicago: University of Chicago Press.

Mahmood, Saba. 2005. *Politics of Piety: The Islamic Revival and the Feminist Subject.* Princeton: Princeton University Press.

Marx, Karl. 1982. *Capital: Volume 1.* Translated by Ben Fowkes. London: Penguin.

Martel, James. 2017. *The Misinterpellated Subject.* Durham: Duke University Press.

Montag, Warren. 2013. *Althusser and His Contemporaries: Philosophy's Perpetual War.* Durham: Duke University Press.

———. 2017. "Althusser's Empty Signifier: What Is the Meaning of the Word "Interpellation"? *Mediations* 30 no. 2: 63–68.

Moten, Fred. 2018. *Stolen Life.* Durham: Duke University Press.

Pandolfo, Stefania. 2018. *Knot of the Soul: Madness, Psychoanalysis, Islam.* Chicago: University of Chicago Press.

Schmitt, Carl. 1996. *The Concept of the Political.* Translated by George Schwab. Chicago: University of Chicago Press.

———. 2003. *The Nomos of the Earth in the International Law of the Jus Publicum Europaeum.* Translated by G. L. Ulmen. Candor: Telos Press.

Vaneigem, Raoul. 1998. *The Movement of the Free Spirit.* Translated by Randall Cherry and Ian Patterson. New York: Zone Books.

Weber, Max. 2002. *The Protestant Ethic and the "Spirit" of Capitalism and Other Writings.* Edited and translated by Peter Baehr and Gordon C. Wells. New York: Penguin.

Wilderson, Frank B., III. 2003. "Gramsci's Black Marx: Whither the Slave in Civil Society?" *Social Identities: Journal for the Study of Race, Nation and Culture* 9, no. 2: 225–40.

Žižek, Slavoj. 2014. *Absolute Recoil: Towards a New Foundation of Dialectical Materialism.* London: Verso.

THE HAUNTING IMAGE OF THE FROZEN JEW (IN CHRISTIAN SELF-UNDERSTANDING), THE SELF-DETERMINING UNIVERSALITY OF HUMAN REASON, AND ANTICIPATING THE SECULAR-NATION-STATE

FROM HOBBES TO KANT AND BEYOND

Rahul Govind

Religion remains very much alive in the world today and not merely as a matter of private belief involving public consequences.[1] Even in ostensibly secular states its status is far from settled in jurisprudence.[2] Systematic thinking on its global forms and political articulations remain contentious and controversial. In the academic world a dominant paradigm traces to the seventeenth and eighteenth centuries the beginning of the straightforward unmooring of political principles from religion.[3] On the other hand, in recent times, theoreticians such as Giorgio Agamben, drawing on the work of Carl Schmitt, have argued for the foundational and persistent significance of theological concepts in seemingly politico-secular norms. While this essay argues for the persistence of the theological in the political, in doing so it simultaneously essays a reinterpretation and rearticulation of both terms, which will serve ultimately as a critique of the line of Agamben and Schmitt, as much as the paradigm of scholarship for whom political modernity is defined in terms of its mere liberation from the religious and the theological.

More concretely, this thesis claims that central to understanding the now repressed foundation of modern political categories such as the nation and the ("secular") state, as well as the formative relations between the two, requires an attentive turn toward the bifocaled lens adopted in the philosophical arguments of Thomas Hobbes and Immanuel Kant. This bifocaled lens in both philosophers articulates two interrelated forms of universality. One consisted in the (historical and pre-Christian) image of Judaic law and the Jewish people in the self-understanding of what claimed to be a universalizing (moral) Christianity. The other consisted in a concept of reason that articulated and expressed human morality as a characteristic faculty of freedom that constituted political society and its laws. In the following essay, the common matrix and specific distinctions between Hobbes and Kant are plotted on the terrain of biblical interpretation and history as much as morality and reason. In anticipation, one might say that while for both Hobbes and Kant the moral faculty is universally human, by simultaneously arguing for the "particularity" of Judaic law / the Jewish people, there emerges an unmistakable divergence in an evaluation of what is imagined as universality indexed by the figure of Jesus. This differentiation from within a shared ground will be seen to have important implications for understanding the ways in which the relationship between the universal and the particular as much as history and moral-political subjectivity are envisioned.

In the frozen image of pre-Christian Judaic law and the "Jewish people" within Christian self-understanding, one can speculatively trace, historico-conceptually, the normative foundations of both the nation as *a* human collectivity (in its proclaimed uniqueness and sovereignty with respect to the rest of humanity) as well as a terrestrially rooted polity (that in itself determines the distinction between "religion" and "law," the "sacred" and the "temporal" in its [self]governance). The contemporary dominance of national sovereignty as an ideal does not detract from the fact that nationalism even today finds it difficult to normatively justify itself without turning (in)to assertions of race superiority.[4] And yet even if, paradoxically, such assertions are no longer formally deployed, the only normative justifiable way in which "the nation" and the "secular" state could be grounded, we argue, would be to trace it historically and conceptually to the "Jewish nation" as a "chosen people" precariously imaged by Christian self-understanding. The paradox of characterizing the modern state, which carries within itself the right to distinguish between the secular and the religious (and therefore determine them), lies in these very historico-conceptual origins.

Paradoxical, because if the state were to call itself secular, it's mode of defining the religious would amount to a secular determination of the religious, therein voiding the latter as an independent category by enfolding it *within* its "secularity."[5] It is this status of being neither religious nor secular exclusively but determining both and beyond both, that characterized the image of (pre-Christian) Judaic law in its Christian conceptualization; an image that haunts the contemporary conundrum of distinguishing the religious from the secular. Underlying the crucial historico-conceptual role of Judaism has been the attempt to build on recent work all the same, arguing for a deepening of its role in coming to terms with the categories of the secular, the political, and the nation: the encircling sphinxes of our times.[6]

The above specific narrative on the place of (historical) Judaic law needs to be contextualized within the idea of reason as a moral faculty universally characterizing humans and grounding humanity as much as the diversity of laws. Even so, the biblical narrative and the value of the historical Hebraic constitution (and the "Jewish nation") remain crucial for normatively justifying the existence of a political constitution in *this*—"secular"—world. The emphasis on reason, as interwoven with the question of God as much as the (historical) Hebraic constitution, is undertaken so as to critique not merely a dominant paradigm of studying the birth of politics as a secular activity simply liberated from religion and bereft of theological concepts. It is also to question the arguments of commentators such as Agamben and Schmitt, who have not sufficiently attended to either the problematic of universality (as a figure of the common moral faculty operating in political constitution and History) or the "Jewish nation" in its specific figuration. Before the turn to the detailed analysis of Hobbes and Kant, some engagement along these lines is undertaken.

Deeply relevant, in one sense, to the present investigation is Agamben's argument that contemporary politics necessarily refers to theology and "the very secularization of the world becomes the mark that identifies it as belonging to a *divine* oikonomia" (Agamben 2007, 6). This provides an entry point for his detailed and subtle treatment in *The Kingdom and the Glory* of the debates around the Trinitarian doctrine that is to have enabled Christianity to engage with the government of the world through the distinction and dynamic between theology (sovereignty) and *oikonomia* (economy). This problematic is itself traced back to debates and discussions around the nature of God and Christ and (then), kingdom and government, sovereignty and administration (through "angels"[7]), being and acting.[8] Agamben is clear that his intervention in theorizing the Trinitarian doctrine and its reiterations across history is, contra Schmitt, a way to scrutinize the importance of the "divine economy" in making sense of the emergence of politics in its theological "signature" (66). And this intervention works as a critique of what is perceived to be the "unsaid" underlying the debate between Carl Schmitt and Erik Peterson. While Schmitt affirms a (Christian) political-theology by theorizing politics as a muzzled space, the *Katechon* preventing the end, Peterson denies the very possibility of a Christian political-theology by affirming a Christian politics that participates in a cosmological order through liturgy; the end is only prevented by the nonconversion of the Jews (15–16) (Schmitt 2008, 87).

By embedding both Schmitt and Peterson within an eschatology, despite their divergence, Agamben does not in his own work on the divine economy confront an early critique made by Hannah Arendt and Hans Blumenberg on the then prevalent theses propounding the Christian foundation for secularism and historical progress. Arendt[9] and Blumenberg had argued that Christian theology cannot be made the basis, or even the reference point, of the "modern," whether in science, politics or history, because the former is constituted by an eschatology while the latter was not.[10] This latter secular-this-worldly modern reveals its distinctiveness as a form of knowledge working out its own "infinity" through a method that is not validated, or made meaningful, by reference to eschatology. In this lies the inherent difference between an infinite progress—Arendt theorizes this as "process"—and an eschatology defined by a "discontinuous" (divine) break that consummates the end. From such a critical perspective, Agamben's detailed parsing of the Trinitarian doctrines and their reiterations does not account for the "modern" and its characteristic features—at least from the seventeenth century onward—because the Agambenian excavation of the theological remains structured by the singularity of the incarnation[11] as much as an "other-wordly" expectation of the end (i.e., eschatology). This leaves the modern untouched.

By building on Arendt's and Blumenberg's (anticipative) critique of the position according to which the pre-seventeenth-century theological world laid the basis for what comes to be constituted as the secular political, this essay argues that the eschatological is deducted in the works of Hobbes and Kant to make way for an autonomous space of politics. As will be shown below, this is accomplished in wholly distinctive ways by theorizing a this-worldly secular politics.[12] In Hobbes, this eschatological "deduction" takes the form of a "history" (a past biblical incident of God ruling the Jewish people in the [secular] world is "paradigmatic"), which is explicitly divorced from an eschatology (the return of Christ is banished from having any determining force in the present); even as "natural" reason constitutes a political present that is explicitly rendered independent of Christian belief. While in Kant, history as world-history, is embedded in a teleology such that the meaning of "Christian" is severely opened to determination—even in relationship to the Judaic—so as to enable a specific "infinitizing" formulation of worldly secular politics and virtue. Both Hobbes and Kant thereby employ arguments of a theologically rooted "natural right" to constitute the logic of a world and history independent of Christian eschatology, interweaving their interpretations of scripture with the historical and paradigmatic place of the Jews.

In this way the possibility of a secular this-worldly politics emerges, one that would otherwise be impossible in a Christian theological idiom that was either indifferent to a politics of this world (Peterson), or saw this world as but a moment plotted in a grander teleology (Schmitt). Such embedding implies that neither Peterson nor Schmitt could formulate or account for the crucial importance of natural reason as a divine-human moral common faculty for the constitution of politics. Nor could they take into account the rule of God over the Jewish people as narrated in the Old Testament as having paradigmatic force. Their anti-Semitism was at one with their inability to recognize the historical and theoretical role that a particular episode of scripture played in the constitution of a modern-secular politics, as it took shape in Hobbes and Kant. The same could be said of the Trinitarian discussions curated by Agamben since it was impossible within this Christian idiom to ground such an autonomous this-worldly domain of either the state or the nation bereft of (Christian) eschatological concerns.

On the other hand, as will be argued below, the constitution of such worldly autonomy through "natural reason" and the Old Testament Jewish episode, enable the theoretical constitution of both state (as coercive secular rule independent of eschatological expectations) and nation (as unique collective secular sovereignty unstructured by these very eschatological expectations). In arguing for the importance of the novel and bifocaled envisioning of theological concepts (such as "natural reason") and biblical hermeneutics (the valorization of a specific episode of the Old Testament), this essay also departs in crucial ways from the arguments of Arendt and Blumenberg as much as the dominant perspective according to which the modern simply emerges whole out of—and without—a trace of its theological context.[13] This arc of arguments is substantiated below through the following schema. First, the moral and the Judaic are interpreted in a reading of Hobbes's *Leviathan.* The problematic will then be rearticulated through a reading of Kant's shorter works on history and cosmopolitanism as well as his *Religion within the Boundaries of Reason.* The concluding section returns to the implications of such an interpretation for contemporary theorizing of the state and nation, secular rule and universal right, to work toward a broader philosophical ethics that is sensitive to the miscegenated lineage and historical weight of concepts.

HOBBES: "NATURAL REASON" AND THE PRESENT (UNFOLDING THE JUDAIC PAST AND THE CHRISTIAN FUTURE)

That Kingdom of God

In a way hitherto perhaps unrecognized, the English philosopher Thomas Hobbes was the most radical secularist imaginable—almost impossibly so. Not because he found a science of politics that was independent of God, as might the contemporary secularist. Hobbes went a step further, not only arguing that politics—if understood as the system of laws having authority and coercive powers—was of *this world* (i.e., temporal) but that even the Kingdom of God was a historical episode that took place here on Earth and would be repeated right here again. This is not the standard secularist analysis of seeing God as a sign or symptom of another set of material or psychological forces. But rather it is the literal ascription of the Kingdom of God in history and in a future that will also take place here on earth. While the Kingdom of God was historically defined, the Kingdom of Christ, when he returns as king, will also be an everlasting kingdom of this world on this Earth. Between these two Kingdoms of God, the definitively past and the irredeemable future, Hobbes says, that all one can say for now is that "there is, therefore, no other government in this life, neither of state nor religion, but temporal" (Hobbes, 316).

The Kingdom of God was the special rule of God as king over the Jews as a "peculiar people" beginning with God's covenant with Abraham; but really taking shape with the renewal of the covenant by Moses,[14] until the deposition of God as king by the Jews when they demanded a human king like other nations (323). This was granted to them. The first coming of Jesus was to redeem through his death the sin inaugurated by Adam. But Christ's kingdom was not of this world; it was not of this time. His kingdom would only be realized when he chooses to return as king, and between his first coming and his second coming, his doctrines are merely meant to prepare and persuade Jew and Gentile for his second coming as king (326–27).[15] Until then, existing sovereigns could legitimately determine the meaning of scripture and law. This power of the sovereign extended back to Abraham and before. Hobbes makes it clear that God's covenant with Abraham, which Abraham entered into voluntarily, recognized Abraham's sovereignty over his family and progeny. God's power was thus enforced on family and progeny through Abraham (317–18). By contrast, at the time of Moses renewing the contract with God—which is the Kingdom of God proper as it were— Moses's power was derived from the people's consent to recognize him as the one who carried God's word (318–19). The importance of consent in the constitution of the Kingdom of God is only further underwritten by their power to depose their king who was God. In the Kingdom of God, the lieutenants of God—from Moses through to the priests and the kings until Saul—exercised univocal sovereignty over both civil as well as religious power over a people who were by themselves holy, a "holy nation," special in being ruled by God through consent and not might, as was the case with other nations.

Two points may be underlined from the above narrative before moving on to the ontological dimension, which provides a context for the historical narrative given above. Firstly, the religious and the civil are necessarily united and determined by sovereign power in this temporal world in the Kingdom of God. Secondly, this kingdom involves a "holy nation," a collectivity of people, which are seen as of special concern to God, where consent is constitutive in relation to God, his lieutenants (from Moses onward), *as much as each other.*[16] This provides a powerful normative foundation not only for the unity of sovereignty and the nation but also incorporates the critical element of consent as constitutive of the structure. This normative argument and structure will have a long afterlife torn when shorn of its originating context.

Ever This Natural Reason

The ontological (and/as epistemological) is to be taken in the sense that the "what" of reason can itself only be determined by reason: that is, that which is to be known cannot be delinked by the manner or faculty through which it is known. God-given-natural-reason simultaneously occupies and unfurls both. This dimension allows for a radical intrahuman political subjectivity but also provides a context for the historical dimension, including the historical episode of that which was the Kingdom of God. This dimension is a "declaration" of God, that is, His "rational" word that humans listen to and receive through their own "right reason." A "natural law," this is the *word* of God—it is not for nothing that Hobbes often uses the phrase "*dictate* of reason"—that is rational, as distinguished from the narrative above, which is rendered as the prophetic (i.e., the word of God given to and heard by particular individuals). That natural laws and natural reason, as specifically human, are contexts for prophetic episodes, is clarified by God when he repeatedly argues that these laws exist alongside the prophetic. So, for example, Abraham already had "natural reason" and a moral faculty before he undertakes his covenant with God. Existing with the prophetic, natural reason is in no sense diminished since it, too is the word of God.

By emphasizing this ontological-epistemological dimension, not only is the normative emphasized, but this normative is routed through a notion of God that is assumed by—even as it cannot be discerned without—reasoning. In this sense we build on recent Hobbesian scholarship that emphasizes normativity in contrast to the self-interested instrumentality of a more familiar and long-standing tradition. But by binding it to God, we depart both from this literature as well as the literature that recognizes the role of the divine but sees it only as a command, bereft of the ineluctability of reason.[17] In chapter 15 of the *Leviathan,* Hobbes writes that "the true and only *moral* philosophy is the *science* of the laws of nature" (100). The moral is a science, a form of reasoning that is able to guide our actions in the form of the laws of nature.

The question of universality is robustly pitched at the level of a human nature, one that allows for a natural law that is itself understood as the moral and the reasonable. As divine laws, they ground human society and the making of laws that will be the characteristic feature of sovereignty.[18] On the one hand, Hobbes's morals or the "dictates of reason" are to be distinguished from laws since the latter indicate an obligation. On the hand, the dictates of reason as commandments by God are universal (obligations) and therein ground all laws. While calling them divine, Hobbes, following a long tradition, argues that we cannot know *what* God is even while we are certain *that* God is (239). The dictates of (human) nature as natural reason and natural law therein become ciphers for universality. Hobbes specifically distinguishes the universality of natural law from the particularity of the prophetic in its "divine positive command." It is from such universality that the institutions and acts of sovereignty are rendered intelligible.

This grounding of sovereignty in natural law ensures that such powers are never wholly abdicated. As a "dictate of reason" natural law allows for the human being to defend against any power *including* that of the (historically and temporally) established sovereign. This is so important that it is perhaps the only natural law that is repeated in chapter 14 in sections 8 and 29. Hobbes writes that the characteristic of the "voluntary act" is done with the intention of some good being achieved by an actor. And so a voluntary transfer of rights by its very nature cannot exclude the right of resisting him who assaults by force; with the same being said of "wounds, and chains and imprisonment." The good entailed in the voluntary transfer of right is not merely security but the "means of so preserving life as not to be weary of it" (82). The parameters are thus fairly wide and allow the political subject through his distinctive characteristic of natural reason to determine when a natural law is being violated and undertake commensurate action.[19] Thus the moral as a specifically human faculty is the source as well as key to what comes to be the legal. The legal in its various specific guises can itself only be understood in the constellation of universal concepts that are natural law, dictates of reason, moral philosophy, and divine command. To reiterate, the divine is a figure of the universal; the common that binds. This importance of the reasoning individual in constituting the moral, and therein the legal, has not been sufficiently attended to in the extant scholarship.

It is thus possible to articulate a theory of human politics and reason with reference to God that is not necessarily limited to specific reference to biblical laws or specific revelations. However, the *Leviathan* is imbued with the biblical idiom, even though Hobbes also offers a general theory of religion that he relates to both curiosity about cause and fear. While Christianity is granted a special sort of revelation that he does not seem to find in others, the theoretical grounding of politics is largely done so through reference to the Old Testament and not the Gospel.

For This and Never That: Natural Reason and the Kingdom(s) of God

Arguing that there exist no clear criteria on deciding the meaning of scripture, its rendering into law is established by the existing sovereign. This might be seen to lie in tension with the argument about "natural reason" and the ultimate right of resistance. For example, in the course of legitimizing sovereign authority Hobbes resorts to analogies from the Old Testament, in light of which he interprets the significance of Christ.[20] The covenant was made with Abraham who was *already* sovereign, thereby legitimizing the argument that no miracles or prophecy could be used to undermine existing laws (317–18). It is in this literal, historical context that Hobbes interprets the meaning of holy as that which is either public or the king's. Holy and the public is thus to be understood—by analogy with the Kingdom of God—as either "the person of the commonwealth itself or something that is so the commonwealth's as no private person can claim any propriety therein" (277). However, it is important to note that Hobbes adds a crucial clause, arguing that holy (and therein the public) taken properly "signified propriety, gotten by *consent*" (277; emphasis mine).

It is the Jewish people who were a "holy people" and the entire earth will be ruled by Jesus Christ on his return. By historically limiting the Kingdom of God as an existence in a specific past and ascertaining the definite return of Christ in an indefinite future, Hobbes undercuts any possible historical or prophetic appeal in the name of which political change is sought to be effected.[21] The obvious object of Hobbes's critique is the entire range of "Puritans" and the entire tradition on which they built their "religious politics" (249–50). In a "depoliticizing" act, the figure of Jesus Christ, Hobbes argues, is to be understood as the savior, teacher, and future King. The future "Kingdom of Christ" is stated as a certain prediction but is to have no bearing on the political present.[22] Christ's denying that his kingdom was of this world, is interpreted to mean that the 'present' was freed from Christ's sovereignty, which would only be actualized in a specific future time. His first coming and sacrifice, as well as his role as a redeemer, were of persuasion and preparation for his second coming. As both the scape and escape goat, he was both sacrificed and set free (to return as king). Even his return, like the historical Kingdom of God, would take place in this world, on earth, the "footstool of God" (313).

However, perhaps the strongest argument delinking the role of Christ as political savior, in his first coming, with existing sovereigns and their divine sanction, is articulated by Hobbes's point that even in a case where a king or sovereign forbade one from believing in Christ, one may believe in one's heart but one must obey one's sovereign and the law of the country. Our speech is external, and so we may accept such a command even as we inwardly hold steadfast to our beliefs. This is once again justified with reference to the episode from the Old Testament regarding the Prophet Elisha and Naaman the Syrian. We thus see a theorization of political power and consent beyond what we conventionally understand as Christianity. Hobbes recognizes the temporal—and therein is implied the sacerdotal—authority of non-Christians. In the wake of the controversies surrounding the precise status of non-Christians,[23] Hobbes's recognition of non-Christian sovereignties has to be underlined. It is this perception of non-Christian sovereignties that can also allow for the absolutism of a sovereignty that even in Christian republics can decide on the nature of the Christian canon and determine the import of its holy books.[24] All of which is done through the simultaneous recognition of existing, literal, historical sovereign powers, as well as the universal natural grounding of such power through the "dictates of reason" (i.e., the moral).

Following from this, one can cite many specific instances where Hobbes underlines the fact that non-Christians have natural laws, which are the word of God.

How is one to coordinate "natural reason" if one were to imply that the human had the moral faculty to reasonably resist, with the specific historical narrative of the Kingdom of God? There is no doubt that the latter supports the former if we remember the crucial importance of consent that characterized the latter. The initial covenant with Abraham is characterized by consent because the specific status that Jews had in relation to God was based on consent, in contrast to his rule of other nations through might. Secondly, both the more formal beginning and ending of the "Kingdom of God" is characterized by consent, not only in connection with God but also in connection with each other. Moses's authority, according to Hobbes, is not only derived from consent, but such consent is the grounding power of the authority of princes of other nations. In Hobbes's words, "His authority therefore *as the authority of all other princes,* must be grounded on the consent of the people and their promise to obey him" (319; emphasis mine). God's might over other peoples—as opposed to his covenant with Abraham—thus did not mean that their kings were not chosen by consent. Moreover, it is this very consent through which God is deposed since the Israelites wished to have a king like other nations.

There seems little doubt that the historical narrative converges with the ontological principle of natural reason, allowing for both the constitution and dissolution of sovereigns. The latter is well supported by further arguments such as the Hobbesian recognition of both institutional and acquisitive forms of sovereignty, as well as the argument that not only did sovereigns live in a state of nature in relationship to each other but also the deeper kinship between war and rebellion: "Rebellion is but war continued" (208). The distinction between the state of nature and sovereignty is therein not amenable to any a priori law denuded of the subject. On the other hand, the formality of reason is substantiated with a substantial good (i.e., peace and life which is not wearying) (82).[25] By underlying natural reason as a constituent of humanity and human community it is clear that Hobbes cannot be accused of indulging in an individualist notion of self-interest since such self-interest is intelligible only as a universal human feature in the forming of human society (i.e., in the act of coming together to achieve peace). To misunderstand this would be analogous to arguing that Socrates reduced reason to self-assertion and self-interest when he declared famously in the *Gorgias* that he could disagree with the entire world but could not disagree with himself.

Notwithstanding the human faculty of reason and human society, the exemplary exception lay in the "holy nation" of the Jews, in the Kingdom of God. But the historical deposition of God and the coming of Jesus Christ had left one now in a situation where there was no collectivity that could claim any special status. And yet, the characterization of the pre-Christian Jewish people and the Old Testament provides for the norm of a sovereign people—a secular this-worldly nation as well as a politics outside an explicitly Christian ambit—as we might understand it. And yet in its passing its example is retained while the indefinite passage toward the return of Christ redeems the secular-temporal in new ways. How was Hobbes to know that a few centuries from his time the "holy nation" as a model would haunt modernity, becoming a paradigmatic form searching (in vain) for normative foundations in the form of ideologies such as nationalism and race?

Yet we have jumped ahead of ourselves. Hobbes's use of the biblical narrative—and its critique by locating the "Kingdom of God" as a past episode and the "Kingdom of Christ" as a future episode—leaves the present to itself in its sovereign self-determination (i.e., natural reason). It is no wonder that in his "review and conclusion" Hobbes writes that if age were to be revered, then "the present is the oldest" (496). In this present between the Kingdom of God and the Kingdom of Christ, natural reason would have to be taken as the touchstone: something repeated in this very "review and conclusion." Any interest Hobbes has in history is thus linked with sovereignty and therein with natural reason as a sustaining element. While Hobbes is clear on natural reason and the constitution of sovereignty as a moral human faculty, and therein an implied right of resistance, as we will see below, Kant makes this connection less clear since the moral is famously "noumenal," even while he salvages humanity in and through history as much as universal experience in his later shorter works. In this endeavor—along with his *Religion within the Boundaries of Reason*—he organizes the figure of the "Jewish people" as one of extreme ambivalence. They are both origin of as much as obstacle to (Christian) universalization. Unlike Hobbes, we will see that the emphasis on history is the simultaneous emphasis on a future orientation. Meant to reveal and guide, this emphasis is not reducible to Hobbesian sovereignty.

IMMANUEL KANT: UNIVERSAL HISTORY, MORAL FREEDOM AND THE JUDAIC SPECTER HAUNTING CHRISTIANITY

The difficulty of conceptualizing moral action, in so far as the moral is essentially noumenal (while action takes place in time), has been much discussed in Kantian scholarship.[26] This problem, which we explore below, is amplified in Kant's writings on world history (where the species being of the human is "the subject") and religion (where the moral is signified through an argument about the relationship between Judaism and Christianity and the role of the Jesus). This could be taken either in the sense of a world history, without direct reference to the Bible, or a more recognizable "Christian" universalizing history based on a reading of Scripture, which is caught in a dialectic with its origin that it images as the "particularistic Jew." As we will see below, though Kant also traces the promise of a unified sovereignty from Judaic law and the Jewish nation, in conceptualizing the inauguration of the moral promise of a universal "Christianizing" history through the figure of Christ, he ends up being simultaneously critical of Judaic law as much as the record of "Christian history."[27] This religious narrative captures and exhibits his fundamental political critique, in the writings on world history, of contemporaneous (Christian) states in their rapaciousness. Far from superseding the "primitive," such states intensify "savagery" in their peculiarly modern tone.

As much recent scholarship has shown, there is an intersubjective content to Kantian autonomy in his writings on world history and religion.[28] In the writings on religion there is a slow move away from the more individual-centric deontological arguments of the *Groundwork* just as there is a more concrete fleshing out of the "Kingdom of Ends" argument of the *Critique of Practical Reason*, that is, greater content is given to the notion of the "Highest Good" in the context of an intersubjective community that is given a historical and moral orientation. Yet less attention has been paid to how the writings on religion address the problem of history (in the interrelations between Christianity and Judaism historically) as well as the radical contingency and moral freedom that Kant diagnoses *as* historical movement in his writings on world history. It is to the latter that we first turn.

Moral Freedom and Indeterminacy in the Heart of History

Kant speaks of humanity and human history as the ultimate end of physical nature[29] and yet nature is that which brings about a law-governed society though antagonism, drawing humankind out of his "primitive" contentment (31–32).[30] All the same, human nature is marked by the ability to "produce everything by himself," from physical needs to all other human needs. This is justified with reference to the Old Testament where the arising of reason is plotted in the biblical Adam. This is the beyond of instinct, in the forms of greedIness, refusal, and the expectation of the future (51).[31] The argument about the human species and human morality-reason, its history as much as its destiny, requires a conceptualization of the human in terms of principles that are not reducible to objects of theoretical knowledge.[32]

It is from such an understanding of human knowing and freedom that Kant in his shorter essays on world history conceptualizes (human) history in terms of the contingent imbrication of pasts and futures. This allows for a speculative analogy of movement in history: the move from the savage to the civil constitution is comparable to the move from the civil constitution to a global federation. All the same, the fundamental moral indeterminacy / freedom is the present pivot that enfolds past and future. This is forcefully articulated: "Before this last step (the federation of nations) can be taken—and it is not more than halfway in mankind's formation—human nature must endure the harshest of evils, which pass in disguise as well-being; and as long as we have not reached this last state to which our species has still to climb Rousseau was not so far from right in *preferring* the state of savages"[33] (emphasis mine). This same indeterminacy / freedom of / from the content of historical sequence of the human species only amplifies Kant's earlier arguments in the first Critique about time as inner sense: that is, as both that which itself reveals no shape but acquires and requires spatial analogies to be understood as well as that which allows for the representation of things as simultaneous and successive and therein permitting contradictory predicates of the same object. This problematic relating to content and tense is maintained in Kant's sustained work *Religion within the Bounds of Mere Reason,* where the Jewish question takes on a particular salience.

The Limits of the Jewish Nation and its Secular Laws and the Universality of the Jesus

In *Religion within the Bounds of Mere Reason,* both religion and morality are ascribed a specifically human freedom that is simultaneously historical and purposive. In this "universal history" based on scripture, Kant, much like Hobbes, names the Jewish theocracy as the *exemplary political-secular* constitution concerned with visible and coercive laws (Kant 2001, 118).[34] In this reading of scripture, after the biblical fall, the "good principle" retained a hold on earth only through the establishment of the Jewish theocracy. As a union of a number of individuals, it did not distinguish between religious ceremonies and law, and external compulsion was primarily civil. God was a *secular* regent, and the laws were merely concerned with external actions and observances indifferent to morals or the conscience, with secular rewards and punishments (119, 154–55). The Jewish polity, according to Kant, could not be considered genuinely religious because in its (secular) focus on the here and now, there was no conception of a future. Yet according to Kant it was a conception that provided an orientation, a direction for moral action that was characteristic of the genuinely religious. Insistently secular-political, the Jews could not be "ethical." In reiterating a stock argument from the tradition, far from establishing the church universal, they excluded the rest of the human race from communion according to Kant. (Allegedly) hostile to others, they were (allegedly) treated hostilely by them.

This reading of scripture persists in arguing that notwithstanding the existence of the germs of morality because of individual Jews and the influence of the Greeks, the supremacy of the moral was clearly established only by the birth of Jesus as the archetype of a mankind above temptation. Subject to suffering by the law because of the possibility of revolt in a foreign dominion, "his story was not in vain." This was because in his death he remained a moral exemplar, leading to a "religious transformation that quietly spread *everywhere*" (120) (emphasis mine). While the "physical result" showed the good principle to have failed, it was in the realm of freedom—not nature—that the death was a "manifestation of the good principle, that is, of humanity in it moral perfection, as example for everyone to follow" (121). This was a kind of universality achieved through "teaching" and "example"[35] that was necessarily denied to the particularity of the Jewish theocracy and its external laws that were localized in the Jewish "stock." Since humans could not form a concept of "moral disposition," this was exemplified in Christ, the very disposition as represented in (scriptural) narrative.

Going against the weight of canonical doctrine, almost veering toward the Marcionite heresy, Kant further argues that Christianity originally was a total abandonment of the Judaism from which it originated. It grounded an entirely new principle, effectuating a total revolution in doctrines of faith (155).[36] And while prophesies (referring to the Jewish past) and miracles might have been required for the historical faith, these were not required for genuine religion and morality. Yet, to not require prophesies and miracles was not to deny them. Since denial assumed that it could be known that such miracles were not possible, and this statement was itself impossible to establish rationally.

Christian History and Amplifying the Haunting Persistence of "The Judaic"

In fact, Kant argues, contemporaneous learned witnesses to Jesus did not make reference to miracles. Only when Christianity had its own learned public did it abandon its own moral dimension. The universality of the moral exemplar was, however, poisonously corroded in the history that unfolded in its name. Thus, Christian history recorded nothing but the mystical enthusiasm of monks and the celibate, alleged miracles, blind superstition, impositions of hierarchy upon free human beings, and violence and war, fragmenting the Christian world into warring opinions and parties.[37] It was a strife that remained in Kant's own time, since in it lay dormant in the "fundamental principle of ecclesiastical faith and its despotic tendencies" (143).[38] Kant's indictment of Christian history was so powerful as to suggest that whatever passed on as Christianity was in fact an amplification of the defects of Judaism made into the foundation of a universal world religion. "Whereas all that turmoil which has wrecked the human race, still tears it apart, stems from this alone: because of a bad propensity in human nature, what should have long served at the beginning to introduce this pure faith—i.e. to win over the new faith, through its own prejudices, the nation which was accustomed to its old historical faith [Judaism]—this was subsequently made the foundation of a universal world-religion [Christianity]" (143).[39] Expressed here is simultaneously the critique of the contemporary political-civilizational rapaciousness in his writings on "world history."

The violence of this legacy was such that for Kant, of all the ages of "Christian" history, it was the *present* that was the best. One might well ask in such a context what was to be made of the "historical" event of universal import that was to have constituted a complete break in the birth of Jesus. Yet the deepening of the present was a way to argue that there always remained, here and now, the chance and opportunity to approximate to that true church, ever uniting human beings, which constituted the visible representation (schema) of the invisible Kingdom of God on earth. Only pure religious faith was rationally communicable across the world and universal, whereas historical faith was morbidly local, being derived from facts. The true universal church would sacrifice the most important mark of its truth (universality) when it based itself upon a historical faith that was "dead, being alone" (i.e., of itself), containing no universal moral import reaching down to the here and now, as Christian history seemed to have done (143).

The Moral, the Invisible Church: the Present Turn to the Future, the Kingdom of God is Coming

In such a context, how was one to conceptualize the future? Particularly, since morality as practical, as the action and the demand for action, was seen to be essentially concerned with genuine religion, the very religion denied to the Jews. In his reading of sacred history, Kant interprets the "Kingdom of Heaven" as that which is not only "coming nearer" but is also "being ushered in as well" (163). This is further interpreted as a "symbolic representation" aimed at stimulating greater hope and courage for its own realization in conjunction with the prophecy that such a "Kingdom of God" would be visible on earth. The importance of the "earth" is reiterated—both like and unlike Hobbes—with the argument that it was in Christ that the "Kingdom of God" was manifested, even as the significance of such manifestation lay in the assurance of the possibility and merit in becoming "citizens of the divine state" through morality (165). Being ready for it meant truly the (self) recognition that humans were "chosen citizens of a divine (ethical) state" (165). The future is thus once again neither to be quarantined from the present nor to be deduced *ab extra* from any present investigation or thought.

Rather, it is only in such a context that the urgency and significance of the true Church and the universality of the Christian exemplar could be extracted. The urgency and significance lay in the challenge of radical evil at the level of the subjective will, as much as the evil produced in the society of humans; both of which speak to the universality of the human in its species being. The only way to prevent such evil would be to establish a union and work toward a society according to the laws of virtues, which would have to be incumbent on the entire human race. Such a state would be the ethical state, united under the noncoercive laws of virtues alone. A state that exists in the midst of a political community while simultaneously organizing it as its figurative polestar. In contrast to a political society, the duties of virtue would concern the entire human race and therefore refer to the ideal of the "totality of human beings." Designed to promote the morality of actions, such morality could not be visible in the manner of the legality of actions, which were visible and coercive.[40] In speaking and thinking about the ethical, the argument is made that the supreme lawgiver of such a universal ethical community was necessarily the "concept" of God, as a "moral ruler of the world" (134).

Such an ethical community was called a "Church," and while it was impossible to have an adequate intuition of the Invisible Church, it could work as a practical regulative principle with an objective reality that one could work toward and whose end was the pure religion of reason. Like Hobbes, Kant argues that rather than an "assertoric" knowledge of the existence of God, only the idea of God as *a moral imperative* was required and possible. Moreover, he argues that although questionable, it was not reprehensive to say that every human makes a god for himself, and must make one according to moral concepts to honor in himself the one who made him on the basis of revelation alone: but without the concept of morality previously laid down as touchstone, religion, and all such reverence would have nothing to distinguish itself from idolatry (189). Analogously, if something is represented as commanded by God, and is yet is in direct conflict with morality, it could not be a divine miracle despite every appearance of being one.

A Future (Christian) Universality Making Moral Demands on the (Jewish) Ruins of a Historical Present

On such principles, the move toward an ethical community, a "community of insight" was possible even in the midst of visible churches and states with their civil and external laws (179–84). Christianity as a moral religion found it necessary to intertwine itself with Judaism to best propagate itself when it (historically) arose. Yet these *means* were soon codified as "articles of faith," "acquiring legal force." Christianity in its historical record thus became a "statutory faith" and as such was a "delusion of religion" rather than the moral religion that Jesus Christ inaugurated (188). The distinction between the Church as the moral community and the statutory laws of a civil constitution, however, appears as deeply fraught. While Kant specifically states that statutory laws as legitimate were "divine," on the other hand, he also states that when human beings commanded "something evil in itself (directly opposed to the ethical law) we may not, and ought not, to obey them" (134 note). If the divinity of the civil laws couldn't help but narratively be traced to the Jewish theocracy, it's supersession through morality is simultaneously affirmed through the universal Christian narrative. And all the same, in concrete terms, Kant strongly indicts contemporary kingdoms and their expansionary agendas in terms we might conceptualize as a double perversion of the original Jewish theocracy and Christian morality, a universalism in ruins that never succeeded in liberating itself from the mark of its origin.

The above narrative is sustained by a whole set of subarguments on the nature of the human subject as moral and free, with implications for human history as much as teleology. While clear that interest cannot be an end, Kant argues that there is a natural need in humans for justifying moral actions (where formal and unconditional duty is united with the highest good as the end of action). This unity is postulated as God and therein the argument that morality inevitably leads to religion.[41] Freedom as characterizing man implies not merely the opposition to nature as pathological and mechanical but also the possibility of an evil maxim antecedent to experience (81–82).[42]

Evil is therefore a sign not only of subjective freedom as "radical evil" but also justified through its equal distribution across time and space from the "state of nature" (constant wars between American Indians), to "civilization and culture" (secret falsity and hatred, war and aggrandizement) (80–81). As radical it has its origin not in time but in reason. This condition is rendered as a narrative in scripture allowing for a universal understanding essentially concerned with moral improvement. Evil insidiously lay in the will and not in the openly visible inclinations as argued by the Stoics (81–89). Here the challenge to morality lies within the social or the intersubjective milieu since envy, addiction to power, avarice, and malignant inclinations arise in society. Departing from his earlier picture of the "Acadian shepherd"[43] or the work of reason even in a "race of devils" in his shorter works, Kant raises the stakes on the importance of the social dimension by arguing that the dominion of the good principle can only be attained by setting up and diffusing a society in accordance with and for the sake of laws of virtue that is demanded of the entire human race in the form of a true Church.

Religion within the Bounds of Reason was written in 1793 during the French Revolution, and one cannot help but be struck by the revolutionary language that Kant uses when he speaks of Christ and the "New Man."[44] The moral decision can only be conceived as revolutionary, as noumenal, since Kant argues that it is only from the ought that man realizes that he can. All the same, he writes, "We cannot comprehend how freely chosen actions as occurrences have their determining grounds in antecedent time (and is not in our control) whereas according to freedom the action (as well as its contrary) must be in the control of the subject at the moment of its happening" (94). This philosophical argument captures the philosophical-historical problematic of the attempted abandonment of the Jewish past, by "Christian morality," a past that is antecedent in time—and therein an origin—but also demanded to be completely annulled in a manner that is literally beyond comprehension and never realizable historically (in time).

Thus, the ghost of the Jewish past "secular" polity is the paradoxical deepening of a present being rendered redundant by its bond to the past even while it is (allegedly) only in reason and morality through Jesus that orientation and hope may take place in the institutional form of the (invisible) Church and moral autonomy.

CONCLUSION

While Hobbes allowed for a conceptualization of natural right inscribed in the very nature of the human being through "natural reason," Kant refashions this by linking rationality and publicity through which natural right, civil right, and cosmopolitan right mutually reenforce each other, accelerating in a gradient subject to (free) reversal at any moment. The conceptualization of an "ethical community" is in direct contrast to Hobbes's understanding of sovereigns being in a state of nature in relation to one another, leaving no (Kantian) scope for the ethical demand (Church) of a mutual building toward a cosmopolitanism. This latter takes the form of time and history, where the Hebraic constitution expressed the "good principle" as the origin of a this-worldly state as much as Jesus the archetype breaking through as universal morality, even if Christian history in its record of disputation and blood lies in its remaining bound and bonded—just as it universally expands—to Judaism as exemplary of an "ecclesiastical faith" with "despotic tendencies." Whereas in Hobbes the enduring value of history is seen in the past (in the form of the Kingdom of God as the Hebraic Constitution) as much in the future (Christ who will return as King in the Kingdom of God). The "this worldliness" of the Hebraic Kingdom as much as a "secular politics" cut off from the definite return of Christ enables the abandonment of Christian practice in the face of a non-Christian sovereign; this is justified through reference to the "Old Testament." No riper conceptualization of the secular may be found, even as "natural reason"—rather than the later "legal positivism" of a state fetish—becomes the ultimate constitutive and regulating ideal of the political. And yet in both Hobbes and Kant the universality and freedom of a moral subjectivity is inscribed in the intensive valorization of "the present" despite the pressing and inexhaustible burden of past and future.

The dialectic of the universal and the particular harbors the impending ruin of history. When Hobbes and Kant attempt to both critique and salvage certain Christian forms of political action, they find it impossible to do so without recourse to characterizing Judaic state law and the Jewish nation as persistent and insistent origin. That any justification of the temporal politics of the times required constant references to the "Old Testament" without immediately being subsumed by the Gospel points to the need to scrutinize the specificity of the variegated "Christian" understandings as being ineluctably bound to their "Judaic" origins. Notwithstanding which, one cannot ignore the conditions in which Jews—as much as other persecuted sects—lived in the seventeenth and eighteenth centuries where such identity was a fundamental criterion in the enforcement of a discriminating and violent legal order. To do justice to this vicious relation between discourse and discursivity is beyond the scope of this article, even if it attempts to exhibit how one is never completely alienable from the latter. For in howsoever attenuated and camouflaged a form, the Jewish presence remained as the preeminent sign of the political and as the "secular" without which it appears impossible to do justice to the historical and conceptual emergence of our modern political categories—whether secularity or nation or state—as much as the institutions and rhetoric in which they labor. In other words, the modern political necessarily emerges with an intensive engagement with the "Judaic" in the form of the "Old Testament," which gives it dimension and form, and this will mark subsequent and renewed attempts to purge these very elements in the name of a pure Christian belief.[45] The engagement by Hobbes and Kant with "the Jewish question" heightens to an intense pitch the question of universality in its violent and redemptive possibilities. It cannot but be seen as ironical that the object of critique as much as fantasy—the cryogenic image of a "chosen" people consumed within the this-worldly (divine) secular—is painfully unmoored to become the paradigmatic and regulating ideal of our times (i.e., the nation-state as *a* people secular and sui generis sovereign). Needless to say, this can scarcely be found in Christian eschatological concerns in its historical and philosophical iterations.

As mentioned in the introductory section, influential works narrating the theological, largely Christian, foundations of modern politics from Carl Schmitt to Giorgio Agamben[46] seem to have little attention for this central nervure within the philosophical tradition that is being traced here and analyzed. Eliding the demand for universality and "natural reason" in moral subjectivity as much as political constitution—as found in figures from the tradition such as Hobbes and Kant—all authority appears to be reduced to the abstract question of a unilateral determination of the exception (and power). This is doubled in the "repression" of the "Jewish question" without which even the attempt at formulating the secular-political, as it unfolded in history and the history of European thought, becomes obscure. From the above, the implicit critique of Schmitt's interpretation of Hobbes as one for whom the "state" was a self-evident category[47]—thereby doing away with both "natural reason" as much as the revelatory paradigmatic "judaic nation"—becomes evident. Schmitt never took the question of "natural right," as the specific ground on which politics was embedded, seriously enough since to do so would undermine his axiomatization of the (political) state and any possible derivation or analogy with the Christian theologic of politics. On the other hand, his more general argument that "theological concepts" were "secular*ized*" ignores the intimately inhering dialectic between the "secular" and the "transcendental," which often took shape with reference to the "Judaic" and the "Christian" *within* Christian consciousness that has been traced here:[48] the so-called particular and the so-called universal.[49] It is this inhering dialectic—its passage and its ruin—that is also purged in Agamben's discussion of the "divine economy" as a Trinitarian articulation of "governance" and/as the "world," which as we suggested at the outset, cannot account for either the state or the nation as an autonomous this-worldly space with its own distinctive teleology. It is in the investigation of the latter that Hobbes and Kant were analyzed.

Finally, in relation to contemporary theorization of the subject, the index of such "forgetting," pertaining to the "Judaic" as much as natural-common reason, might be the retrieval of Paul as an originary moment for thinking modernity. Alain Badiou's work appears to renew a historical tendency within Christianity that traces to him a theory of universality beyond the (imputed) Judaic and the Greek, and other (such) particularities.[50] No doubt in doing so he theorizes universality by speaking of it as an "*indifference that tolerates differences*" rather than a common predication (99). Agamben is both persuasive and unpersuasive in his critique of such a position. On the one hand, the Pauline reference in Badiou certainly does not function as a common predication to be "found" in the "depths" of differentiating differences as Agamben (2005) claims in his criticism.[51] And on the other hand, Badiou opens himself to such a critique when he describes "indifference to difference" precisely as such a predicable, having qualities such as "tolerance" and "benevolence." If Badiou, therefore, uncritically reiterates a self-interpretation of Christianity as "indifferently tolerating" the particular ("Jew" and "Greek"), laying a "foundation" for universalism, Agamben in *The Kingdom and Glory* also traces to Paul the "divine economy" in which he finds the theoretical clue to the problematic of governance, all the way down to modernity. Moreover, Agamben turns to Schmitt's recognition of the importance of "acclamation" in the constitution of a public, a "public opinion"—interlinking democratic and authoritarian-fascistic traditions—as the "sphere" of "glory": glory that had once indexed what Paul had described as "the eschatological situation of the just" (Agamben 2007, 248).

But neither the "state" nor "nation" in their distinctive modern imprint is therein accounted for in either their autonomy or their logic, in the way sketched out in the above sections. It is in fact the "freezing" of the image of the Jew as historical—and therein a paradigm—in conjunction with "natural reason" that supply the model for both the secularized autonomy of the state (as an after-image of the historical rule of the Jewish people) as well as nation (the after-image of the Jewish people as once having collectively ruled by God *in this world* and therein possessing sovereignty). This set of problems that animated Hobbes and Kant, which index the difficulties of negotiating the universal in history (in its violent record), scripture (with the obdurate ambiguities of the "Judaic" origin), and political constitution (a universal and "natural reason") appear to have vanished in much contemporary political-theology.

Natural reason as a universal and common moral faculty, conceived of as essential to the constitution of a state and nation, has animated a whole range of politics within and beyond Europe since the seventeenth century. At the same time, religion was given the force of law in the regulation of several communities within and across empires well into the twentieth century.[52] Once bereft of the context of a universal, shared, and common humanity and its logic, the splintered image of the (Jewish) nation-state, ironically, determined the modern nation-state as a final and finalizing form. To remain was a devastating and indefinitely ambitious political particularism, with little to offer in terms of self-rationalization. Contemporary theories of nationalism as manifested in the inexorability of state-bureaucratized institutional logic also offer little in this regard, where thin lines divide culture, nation, and race; the paradigmatic force of the "Jewish" template is repressed, only to take form in the horror of genocide. To spot the hidden lines between the two is to see race as much as nation, the devouring particularity of our times, find rhythm in the continuing catastrophe of modern war, inward and outward, basing itself as it does on the all-consuming idea of an impenetrable encrustation of a chosen people immobilized in a state of territory.

Rahul Govind has been teaching History at the University of Delhi since 2009 and has held fellowships at Columbia University (for doctoral studies), the Centre for the Study of Developing Societies, Delhi, The Indian Institute of Advanced Study, Shimla, and the University of Cambridge. Apart from his book *Infinite Double* (2015) and his forthcoming *The King's Plunder, The King's Bodies,* he has published several journal articles on themes ranging from political economy and philosophy to imperialism and jurisprudence.

Notes

1. Acknowledgments: This paper draws on a presentation given at Smith College, Northampton, Massachusetts, in April 2019 at the invitation of Jay Garfield. I thank Jay for the kind invitation and the audience for the discussion that ensued. I also wish to thank Jay Garfield, James Martel, and David Nirenberg for their generous and encouraging comments on an earlier draft of this article. I thank the anonymous referee for insisting that I expand on my engagement with contemporary theory.

2. Many court cases from very different settings in contemporary times reveal that the relationship between the state and religion is anything but settled even in democratic regimes. *Lautsi vs. Italy* (in Italy and later the EU, involving the issue of whether the presence of a crucifix in a public school constituted a violation of the principle of secularism), *Warner vs. Boca Raton* (in the United States of America, where the issue was on the possibility of having monuments and / or memorials

inspired by religious belief on the Boca Raton cemetery) and the *Indian Young Lawyers Association vs State of Kerala* (in India, where the issue was whether a temple could disallow women of menstruating age as part of the freedom to practice religion or whether this violated the fundamental rights of women).

3. In recent times, this narrative is perhaps best captured by Lilla; Israel; Habermas 1992; and Rawls.

4. While there have been many important works historicizing and contextualizing nationalism, there has been less effort toward exploring the genealogy of the normative justification of the nation as a category in the same way one might justify categories like the state or justice. For a perceptive discussion on nationalism as it develops in Europe see Hont. For an insightful argument that requires us to revisit and critique a tacit consensus on the relationship between modernity, nationalism, and secularism as embodied in the works of theorists such as Charles Taylor and Benedict Anderson, see Asad, 1–21, 181–205.

5. As we will see, in the description of the "Hebrew Commonwealth" under God, the univocal nature of power makes it impossible to have a clear-cut distinction between temporal (secular) and religious (spiritual); and not only because the two couldn't be seen as discrete. So one sees in Hobbes and Kant the peculiar situation of speaking of this commonwealth ruled by God as in fact being secular. It is this univocity that is sometimes contested today by the argument that since secular courts implicitly determine religious practice, this in effect makes the religious subject to the secular.

6. See, for instance, Nelson and Nirenberg as well as my previous essay in Govind 2013. While Nelson makes the important case that arguments regarding toleration ought to be traced to discussions around the "Hebraic Commonwealth," he does not link arguments around this to "natural reason" and "natural right" (and consent) as the constituent bases of sovereignty, as we try and establish. Nirenberg's magisterial history of "Anti-Judaism," successfully demonstrates the importance of this element in the entire arc of Western thought, while the attempt here is to more directly address the relationship between the figure of the Jew and the bases of sovereignty.

7. One of the most intriguing of components of Agamben's argument, in Agamben 2007, 144–56, is the discussion of angels and bureaucracy. However, notwithstanding several references to Kantorowicz, the latter's argument on the angelic time as a matrix for thinking the King and Kingdom is left fallow; this aspect has an enduring relevance even in seemingly far-removed contexts such as the juristic personality of Hindu temples in India today, as can be seen in Govind 2021.

8. One specific line of argument employed by Agamben is that of the well-known Christian-theological distinction between the "first" and "second" causes, which is related to the "bipartite system" of Kingdom/Government and ontology/*oikonomia;* 133–34. This distinction is to have anticipated the modern distinctions between the legislative/sovereign power and the executive/governmental. Such a distinction between general and particular wills is reiterated in the concluding discussion by Malebranche, which is to have anticipated Rousseau, 262–

74. However, from the perspective of Arendt, Blumenberg, Koselleck, and this essay, the question of the ontological bases and natural-right, the relationship between eschatology and teleology, remain unaddressed in Agamben. For an alternative genealogy of the modern economy (and law)—in its conceptual and institutional articulation—as a function of a deontologization and imperialism see Govind 2015.

9. Arendt writes, "A great deal of evidence has been cited in support of the thesis that modern historical consciousness has a Christian religious origin and came into being through a secularization of originally theological categories"; see Arendt, 65. This is a position she consistently resists in much of her work, and is put forcefully in her argument for the distinctiveness of the modern conception of history and politics in the seventeenth and eighteenth centuries. While on the question of history she writes, "The decisive thing in our system is not that the birth of Christ now appears as a turning point of world history, for it has been recognized as such with greater force many centuries without any similar effect upon our chronology but rather that now for the first time, the history of mankind reaches back into an infinite past to which we can add at will and into which we can inquire further as it stretches ahead into an infinite future. This two-fold infinity of past and future eliminates all notions of beginning and end, establishing mankind in a potential earthly immortality. What at first glance looks like a Christianisation of world history in fact eliminates all religious speculations from secular history. So far as secular history is concerned we live in a process which knows no beginning and end and which thus does not permit us to entertain eschatological expectations. Nothing could be more alien to Christian thought than this concept of an earthly immorality of mankind" (68). And elsewhere on the distinctiveness of modern politics, in opposition to Christianity, Arendt writes, "Thus the political theorists of the seventeenth century accomplished secularization by separating political thinking from theology, and by insisting that the rules of natural law provided a basis for the body politic even if God did not exist . . . the point was not to deny the existence of God but to discover in the secular realm an independent, immanent meaning which even God could not alter" (70). An examination of Arendt's critique of what she diagnoses as "world alienation" and "process," is beyond the scope of the present essay. However, for a critique of her damning diagnosis of "process" (in which she includes Marxism), by way of Lukacs and Benjamin, that ironically points to her own unreflected debt to revolutionary Marxism see Govind 2023.

10. As Blumenberg asks, "What signs are there that even suggest a likelihood that theological eschatology, with its idea of 'consummation' of history by its discontinuance, could have provided the model for an idea of forward movement of history according to which it was supposed for the first time to gain stability and reliability through its consummation or its approach to its consummation?" And later, "Regarding the dependence of the idea of progress on Christian eschatology, there are differences that would block any transposition of the one into the other. It is a formal. But for that very reason, a manifest difference that an

eschatology speaks of an event breaking into history, an event that transcends and is heterogeneous to it, while the idea of progress extrapolates from a structure present in every moment to a future that is immanent in history" (see Blumenberg, 30). In the detailed argumentation Blumenberg shows the implications and distinctiveness of sixteenth- and seventeenth-century science in speaking of the infinity of nature, and the earth as but a stellar object. There is also a specific critique of Schmitt, where Blumenberg makes the argument that Schmitt is unclear whether the secular is genetically derived from the theological or merely structurally analogous to it, to which Schmitt replies; a debate one cannot discuss fully here. In this minimal sense of the distinctiveness of the modern and the relationship between science, politics, and time consciousness, is something that Koselleck's work also converges with.

11. As Hannah Arendt argues, in "Concept of History," that it is precisely because of the singularity of Christ's birth in this world that it cannot be taken as an anticipation of secularization or modern historical consciousness with its valuation of secular events, which from a Christian perspective sees other secular events as without value and necessarily refers to creation and redemption. Relevant here is also Blumenberg's argument that the heretical nature of Bruno's infinite worlds lay in the fact that such infinity necessarily undervalued this earth and therein Christ's birth in it. Hence, the undeniable value of the "geocentric" perspective.

12. Schmitt's thesis is perhaps the most resonant, influential, and powerful one in recent years on the relationship between theology and modern politics. He had written the following: "All significant concepts of the modem theory of the state are secularized theological concepts not only because of their historical development-in which they were transferred from theology to the theory of the state, whereby, for example, the omnipotent God became the omnipotent lawgiver-but also because of their systematic structure, the recognition of which is necessary for a sociological consideration of these concepts" (see Schmitt 1985, 36).

13. As will be clear in the substantial sections of the essay, its arguments regarding "natural reason" and the import of certain forms of biblical hermeneutics were not undertaken by Arendt or Blumenberg.

14. Hobbes sometimes suggests that the "Kingdom of God" began with Abraham but occasionally claims that it began "properly" only with Moses (until Saul) (see Hobbes, 272, 276).

15. Hobbes, 326–27. J. G. A. Pocock was perhaps one of the first scholars to draw attention to books three and four of the *Leviathan.* See also Schwartz and Martel. Even more recently, Nelson notes that for Hobbes, the "Kingdom of God" referred to the historical episode of the commonwealth of the Hebrews. Hobbes's "Hebraic Erastianism" (122), according to Nelson, was thus an important source of modern notions of "toleration" even while it might have been born of Hobbes's religious convictions (see Nelson, 122–28).

16. "It is therefore manifest enough by this one place that by the kingdom of God is properly meant a commonwealth instituted (by the consent of those which

were subject thereto) for their civil government and the regulating of their behaviour, not only towards God their king but also towards one another in point of justice; and towards other nations both in peace and war; which properly was a kingdom wherein God was king, and the high priest was to be (after the death of Moses) his sole viceroy or lieutenant" (see Hobbes 1994, 274). This dimension has not been emphasized enough in the literature that has otherwise been attentive to these sections of the *Leviathan.*

17. Both Lloyd and Zagorin have powerfully and effectively argued for the importance of a normative framework linking morality and the law of nature in Hobbes against instrumentalist-cum-individualist argumenta about self-interest. As will be clear from the essay, we depart from Llyod's contention that Hobbes's defense of sovereignty is ultimately indistinguishable from the later positivist conception, even if such a position were a "self-effacing natural law theory" (see Lyod, 263–65). We also depart from Zagorin in our emphasis on the relationship between the law of nature, reason, and the possibilities of resistance as much as our argument of the inextricable interrelation between the law of nature and the divine. There is a tension between Zagorin's emphasis on the absolute powers of the sovereign and the possibilities of natural laws that is never resolved, and the latter possibilities are never linked with the divine, as I have tried to establish (see Zagorin, 53–75). For a fine and subtle reading of the covenant and promise see Martel where God and the eschatological framework allow for "such a reading [which] keeps our promises at least potentially open-ended and contingent" (136). However, in diverging from Martel we do not distinguish in a fundamentally significant way the "secular covenant described in parts 1 and 2" (140), from those described in part 3; by interpreting and underlining the onto-epistemological function of 'natural reason' and 'exemplary' history the distinction is itself ultimately one that is seen to be staged .

18. See the link between the divine, natural law, and the moral further explained/reiterated in chap. 26 (37, 41). As Hobbes later explains, natural laws are derived from the rational "word" of God to be distinguished from the "prophetic," which was directed to the Jews (235). We thus argue in contrast to the position taken by Curely, 316; 324–26. On the other hand, we diverge from A. P. Martinich, notwithstanding the important analytical emphasis on religion, where his argument for the importance of God is delinked from the "dictates from reason" from God. From this differentiation emerges a theory of the absolute divine irresistibility of sovereignty that we here contest (see Martinich, 97–98, 120).

19. Thus, while Tom Sorel appears to recognize that "the agreement to form the commonwealth seems to have escape clauses that make it unclear when the agreement has been kept and when it has been broken" (142), he seems to conclude by saying, "In terms of compliance, Hobbes's theory of the rights and duties reduces the sources of law and practical guidance to one, the sovereign, and backs this up with all the coercion the sovereign can summon" (146). Moreover, by denying that they were constituted by "divine commands" (146), he does not sufficiently take into cognizance the "powers" of natural reason and right.

20. For a convincing argument about Hobbes's challenge to orthodox Trinitarian doctrine in his characterization of Christ see Lessay.

21. In a brief but important discussion of Hobbes, Nirenberg argues that Hobbes also assigned to the Jews and their history a "role that was simultaneously exemplary and exceptional, paradigmatic and peculiar." We build on this to include the more general reflections on the nature of political constitution in Hobbes. For instance, Nirenberg notes that the importance of Moses lay not in the prophetic but in a contract, while we add to this the fact that the contract is not only with Moses but in relationship to each other, too, and the radical implications of rebelling against God as King on questions of political subjectivity (see Nirenberg, 316).

22. This is where we diverge from the interpretation put forward by Schwartz.

23. For instance, the Council of Constance did not resolve the clash of perspectives on the precise status of "infidels" in the law of nations. And in English Common Law, including that of the seventeenth century, infidels and/as Jews were still perceived as sui generis "aliens"; often "alien enemies" except when given special protection by the king. All this had canonical precedent. For a fine analysis of the figure of the Jew as "Cain," the "included-excluded," in Augustine see Nirenberg, 129–34.

24. See Hobbes, "But the question is not of obedience to God but of when and what God hath said; which to subjects that have no supernatural revelation cannot be known but by that natural reason, which guided them for the obtaining of peace and justice, to obey the author of their several commonwealths (that is to say, of their lawful sovereigns)" (250). The caution with which this point is expressed, almost as an aside, points to its radical nature. Of course historically, Hobbes had argued in *Behemoth* that indeed in Christian history sovereigns had determined right (religious) doctrine, beginning from Constantine.

25. The argument about the substantial good involved has been made forcefully in Maternich and Lloyd.

26. For a succinct discussion of the problem see Stern.

27. In underlining the critique of 'Christian' history we diverge from some of the extant literature such as is to be found in Nirenberg, 387–423, and Susan Meld Shell, 306–34. This literature rightly emphasizes the "anti-Judaism" present in Kant, but by bringing in what we argue to be a critique of "Christian history," we hope a more complete and complex picture can be drawn.

28. See Michalson; Wood; and Habermas 2008, 209–29.

29. See Kant 1983a, 39. "For what use is it to laud and recommend observing the majesty and wisdom of creation in the non-rational realm of nature, if that part of the great theatre of supreme wisdom that contains the purpose of all the rest—the history of the human race—should remain an endless reproach to it" (39).

30. See Kant 1983a, 31–32.

31. See Kant 1983b.

32. See Kant 1983c, 61.

33. See Kant 1983a, 36. Kant describes the continuing present of international politics as being characterized by the pursuit of "violent and vain" design. This characterization is reiterated in the much later essay, Kant 1983d, 116, where Kant speaks of contemporary Europeans, too, as savages much like the American tribes, the only difference being that while the latter were "completely eaten by their enemies" the latter "know how to make better use of those they have conquered than to consume them: they increase the number of their subjects and also the quantity of instruments they have to wage even more extensive wars." This is reiterated by an unflattering comparison between contemporary Europeans and other peoples; Kant says of the "civilized nations," that the "injustice that they display towards foreign lands and peoples (which is the same as conquering them) is terrifying." Describing trade, he writes, was in fact "the subjection of the natives, incitement of various nations to widespread ward among themselves, famine, rebellion, treachery, and the entire litany of evils that can afflict the human race" (119). Later on Kant argues that is it imperative to write a philosophical history—neither a priori nor empirical—that would serve as an example for a future people to look back and continue to inspire national leaders to strive toward a cosmopolitanism.

34. No doubt this is restrained, particularly if one views Kant's fulsome praise of the Judaism in the *Critique of Judgment* as has been noted by Susan Meld Shell. Shell also gives an argument for the historical specificity of this change (see Shell, 306–34).

35. This is an amplification of the notion of "example" that Kant had underlined in the *Critique of Judgement.*

36. In claiming universality and in discarding specific laws such as circumcision, Christianity revealed itself as not political.

37. A long passage moans the violence of Christian states, a passage that begins in the following way: "At any rate from the time that Christianity itself became a learned public, or became part of the universal one, its history so far as the beneficial effect which we rightly expect from a moral religion is concerned, has nothing in any way to recommend it." And this passage from a criticism of monks, celibates, miracles in the East, while in the West "the spiritual leader thus just mentioned ruled over kings and chastised them like children by means of the magic wand of his threat of excommunication, and incited them to foreign wars (the crusades) which would depopulate another portion of the world, and to feuds among themselves; and the subjects to rebellion against those in authority over them and to bloodthirsty hatred against their otherwise—minded confreres in one and the same so called universal Christianity; how the root of this strife, which even now is kept from violent outbreaks only through political interest, lies hidden in the fundamental principle of an ecclesiastical faith which rules despotically and still occasions apprehension over the replaying of similar scenes" (see Kant 2001, 159).

38. Stephen R. Palmquist by taking it as axiomatic the distinction between Christian and Jew, argues that the passage where Kant is critical of Church—but

it is not just Church—history has to be taken as "ideal types" rather than historical descriptions (Palmquist, 220). By contrast, our argument is that this passage, among others, points to the theoretical problem of distinguishing "Christian" from "Jew," amplifying the deeply moral problematic expressing Jesus as the revolutionary not really in time, while having an "origin" (and possibly Judaic) in time.

39. It is this dimension of the critique of Christian (world) history, and the way in which it is the double of a critique of the Judaic, that is not found in the otherwise important analyses of Nirenberg and Shell.

40. Even if the emphasis of such distinctions between the ethical and the civil-political seems to lie in tension with Kant's comments elsewhere on the nature of "public right." See Kant 1983c. One must of course remember that the *Metaphysics of Morals* is divided into the doctrine of rights and the doctrine of virtue.

41. "Morality thus inevitably leads to religion, and through religion it extends itself to the idea of a mighty moral lawgiver outside the human being, in whose will the final end (of creation of the world) is who can and at the same time ought to be the final human end" (see Kant 2001, 59–60).

42. As has been noted in this text on religion, Kant moves beyond the arguments of the *Groundwork* and *The Critique of Practical Reason.*

43. See Kant 1983a.

44. One might argue that this provides the context for Kant's discussion of the "event" of the French Revolution (and the sympathetic spectator) in his *Conflict of Faculties* that has been the subject of much rich commentary from Arendt to Lyotard to Foucault. Here we can no more than underscore the fact that the argument in his work on religion is an important context to the one made later in the *Conflict of Faculties.* Whether the French Revolution was in a sense a superseding secularizing substitute for Jesus—without the Judaic origins—is a question whose investigation is beyond the scope of this particular article but one that I am working on separately.

45. It might be remembered that the acute attention to the "Old Testament" to formulate an idiom of politics was not confined to Hobbes. While there has been much discussion of Spinoza, one should also enlist Grotius, whose debt to this question was not merely confined to broader questions of this worldly politics but also the granular specificity of the laws of war such as prize and plunder. In this context it is not irrelevant to mention that Benjamin in his study of the baroque remarks that the seventeenth century derived much of its political idiom from the Old Testament.

46. See Schmitt 1985, 36; Schmitt 2007; and Schmitt 2008. In Schmitt 2008 there is a response to Peterson's argument that "political-theology" was Judaic or Pagan, but Schmitt does not take up the challenge of investigating the Judaic element within Christian history and self-conception (and neither does Agamben 2007 or Agamben 2005).

47. This critique of Schmitt's reading of Hobbes is an issue that I have pursued elsewhere, most recently in Govind 2021a. Several decades ago Blumenberg

had pointed to the lack of clarity regarding Schmitt's articulation of the relationship between theology and the political-secular (i.e., was it one of [structural] analogy or [historical] derivation?).

48. Schmitt defends his thesis of a legitimate Christian political-theology against Peterson by pointing to the importance of the "earthly" in the context of Christian history (Schmitt 2008). However, this importance is still measured by an eschatology—and the incarnation—and therefore cannot sufficiently characterize the autonomous worldly and the deployment of theological concepts like "natural right," as sketched out in Hobbes and Kant and as interpreted in this essay.

49. Marx's early work was perhaps the most insightful and forceful deployment of the "Jewish Question" in the context of popular sovereignty and "modern" right, where the concepts of state and civil society (political-economy) were scrutinized, notwithstanding legitimate concerns of anti-Semitism in his prose and categorization.

50. Badiou reiterates a historical tendency when he writes, "Paul himself is entirely of Jewish culture and cites the Old Testament far more frequently than the putative words of the living Christ. But although the event depends on its site in its being it must be independent of it in its truth effects. Thus, it is not that communitarian marking (circumcision, rites, the meticulous observance of the Law) is indefensible or erroneous. It is that the postevental imperative of truth renders the latter indifferent (which is worse). It has no significance positive or negative" (23). This is precisely the problematic of the Christ-event in Kant; however, Kant, unlike Badiou, recognizes the aporia in actually distinguishing one from the other as is clearly delineated in the Jewish-Christian history he narrates and therefore attempts a negotiation that takes the form that we had analyzed.

51. Agamben writes in his critique of Badiou, "No universal man, no Christian can be found in the depths of the Jew or the Greek, neither as a principle, nor as end" (see Agamben 2005, 523). Badiou is explicit in that it is "imperative that universality not present itself under the aspect of particularity," and this is of course linked with the idea of the "truth procedure" as deploying "a purely generic multiplicity" and later as an "address" (see Badiou, 98–106).

52. This was simply and factually the case since across the sprawling European empires, religion was used both as a marker of identity and the basis for the formulation of laws in a wide range of contexts well into the twentieth century.

Works Cited

Agamben, Giorgio. 2005. *The Time That Remains.* Translated by Patricia Dailey. Stanford: Stanford University Press.

——. 2007. *The Kingdom and the Glory.* Translated by Lorenzo Chiesa. Stanford: Stanford University Press.

Anderson-Gold, Sharon. 2001. *Unnecessary Evil: History and Moral Progress in the Philosophy of Immanuel Kant.* Albany: State University of New York Press.

Arendt, Hannah. 1977. "Concept of History." In *Between Past and Future* by Hannah Arendt. New York: Penguin, 1977.

Asad, Talal. 2003. *Formations of the Secular* Stanford: Stanford University Press.

Badiou, Alain. 2003. *St. Paul: The Foundation of Universalism.* Translated by Ray Brassier. Stanford: Stanford University Press.

Blumenberg, Hans. 1983. *The Legitimacy of the Modern World.* Translated by Robert M. Wallace. Cambridge, Mass.: MIT Press.

Curely, Edwin. 2007. "Hobbes and the Cause of Religious Toleration." *Cambridge Companion to Hobbes's Leviathan,* edited by Patricia Springborg, 309–37. Cambridge: Cambridge University Press.

Govind, Rahul. 2011. "Equality, Right, Identity: Rethinking the Contract through Hobbes and Marx." *Telos* 154:75–98.

——. 2015. *The Infinite Double.* Shimla: Indian Institute of Advanced Study.

——. 2021a. "The Deity as Juristic Personality." *National Law School of India Review* 33, no. 2: 150–180.

——. 2021b. "Criminalizing unto Death." *Law, Culture and the Humanities.* October 1.

——. 2023. "From Carl Schmitt to Walter Benjamin: Sovereignty, Mythic-Fate and the Dialectical Leap." In *Assured Self, Restive Self,* edited by Prasanta Chakravarty. New Delhi: Bloomsbury.

Habermas, Jürgen. 1992. *The Structural Transformation of the Public Sphere.* Translated by Thomas Burger. New York: Polity.

——. 2008. *Between Naturalism and Religion.* Translated by Ciaran Cronon. Cambridge: Polity Press.

Hobbes, Thomas. 1994. *Leviathan.* Edited by Edwin Curley. Indianapolis: Hackett.

Hont, Istavan. 1994. "The Permanent Crisis of a Divided Mankind." *Political Studies* 42 (S1): 166–231.

Israel, Jonathan. 2006. *Enlightenment Contested: Philosophy, Modernity, and the Emancipation of Man 1670–1752.* Oxford: Oxford University Press.

Kant, Immanuel. 1983a. "Idea for a Universal History with a Cosmopolitan Intent." In *Perpetual Peace and Other Essays.* Translated by Ted Humphrey. Indianapolis: Hackett.

——. 1983b. "Speculative Beginning of Human History." In *Perpetual Peace and Other Essays.* Translated by Ted Humphrey. Indianapolis: Hackett.

——. 1983c. "Theory and Practice." In *Perpetual Peace and Other Essays.* Translated by Ted Humphrey. Indianapolis: Hackett.

——. 1983d. "To Perpetual Peace: A Philosophical Sketch." In *Perpetual Peace and Other Essays.* Translated by Ted Humphrey. Indianapolis: Hackett.

——. 2001. "Religion within the Boundaries of Mere Reason." *Religion and Rational Theology,* edited by Allen Wood and George Di Giovanni. Cambridge: Cambridge University Press.

Koselleck, Reinhart. 2002. *The Practice of Conceptual History.* Translated by Todd Samuel Presner. Stanford: Stanford University Press.

——. 2004. *Futures Past: On the Semantics of Historical Time.* Translated by Keith Tribe. New York: Columbia University Press.

Lessay, Franck. 2007. "Hobbes' Covenant Theology and its Political Implications." *Cambridge Companion to Hobbes's Leviathan,* edited by Patricia Springborg, 243–71. Cambridge: Cambridge University Press.

Lilla, Mark. 2007. *The Still Born God: Religion, Politics and the Modern West.* New York: Penguin.

Lloyd, Sharon. 2009. *Morality in the Philosophy of Thomas Hobbes.* Cambridge: Cambridge University Press.

Martel, James. 2007. *Subverting the Leviathan.* New York: Columbia University Press.

Martinich, A. P. 1992. *Two Gods of Leviathan.* Cambridge: Cambridge University Press.

Michalson, Gordan. 1990. *Fallen Freedom: Kant on Radical Evil and Moral Regeneration.* Cambridge: Cambridge University Press.

Nelson, Eric. 2011 *The Hebrew Commonwealth: Jewish Sources and the Transformation of European Political Thought.* Cambridge, Mass.: Harvard University Press.

Nirenberg, David. 2013. *Anti-Judaism.* New York: W. W. Norton.

Palmquist, Stephen. 2000. *Kant's Critical Religion.* Vol 2. Aldershot, UK: Ashgate.

Pocock, J. G. A. 1972. "Time History and Eschatology in Thomas Hobbes." In *Politics, Language, Time.* London: Methuen.

Rawls, John. 1997. "The Idea of Public Reason: Postscript." In *Deliberative Democracy: Essays on Politics and Reason,* edited by J. Bohman and W. Rehg, 131–41. Cambridge, Mass.: MIT Press.

Schmitt, Carl. 1985. *Political Theology.* Translated by George Schwab. Cambridge, Mass.: MIT Press.

——. 2007. *The Concept of the Political.* Translated by George Schwab. Chicago: University of Chicago Press.

——. 2008. *Political Theology II.* Translated by Michael Hoelzl and Graham Ward. Cambridge: Polity.

Schwartz, J. 1985. "Hobbes and the Two Kingdoms of God." *Polity* 18, no. 1 (Autumn), 7–24.

Shell, Susan Meld. 2009. *Kant and the Limits of Autonomy.* Cambridge, Mass: Harvard University Press.

Sorel, Tom. 2007. "Hobbes's Moral Philosophy." In *Cambridge Companion to Hobbes's Leviathan,* edited by Patricia Springborg, 128–57. Cambridge: Cambridge University Press.

Stern, Paul. 1986. "The Problem of History and Temporality in Kantian Ethics." *Review of Metaphysics* 39:505–45.

Wood, Allen W. 1999. *Kant's Ethical Thought.* New York: Cambridge University Press.

Zagorin, Perez. 2009. *Hobbes and the Law of Nature.* Princeton: Princeton University Press.

BOOKS RECEIVED

Agamben, Giorgio. *Hölderlin's Madness: Chronicle of a Dwelling Life, 1806–1843.* Translated by Alta L. Price. London: Seagull, 2023.

Ben-shai, Roy. *Critique of Critique.* Stanford: Stanford University Press, 2023.

Blackwell, Maylei. *Scales of Resistance: Indigenous Women's Transborder Activism.* Durham: Duke University Press, 2023.

Blair, Nicholas. *Castro to Christopher: Gay Streets of America 1979-1986.* Brooklyn: powerHouse, 2023.

Boisvert, Raymond D. *Albert Camus and the Philosophy of the Ordinary.* New York: Bloomsbury Academic, 2023.

Bradley, Cisco. *The Williamsburg Avant-Garde: Experimental Music and Sound on the Brooklyn Waterfront.* Durham: Duke University Press, 2023.

Brandl, Mark Staff. *A Philosophy of Visual Metaphor in Contemporary Art.* New York: Bloomsbury Academic, 2023.

Butler, Judith, and Frédéric Worms. *The Livable and the Unlivable.* New York: Fordham University Press, 2023.

Cabrera, Lydia. *El Monte: Notes on the Religions, Magic, Superstitions, and Folklore of the Black and Creole People of Cuba.* Durham: Duke University Press, 2023.

Calirman, Claudia. *Dissident Practices: Brazilian Women Artists, 1960s-2020s.* Durham: Duke University Press, 2023.

Campbell, Timothy, and Grant Farred. *The Comic Self: Toward Dispossession.* Minneapolis: University of Minnesota Press, 2023.

Chalfin, Brenda. *Waste Works: Vital Politics in Urban Ghana.* Durham: Duke University Press, 2023.

Chandler, Nahum Dimitri. *Annotations: On the Early Thought of W.E.B. Du Bois.* Durham: Duke University Press, 2023.

Cotton, Jess. *Critical Lives: John Ashbery.* Chicago: University of Chicago Press, 2023.

Cross, Gary S. *Free Time: The History of an Elusive Ideal.* New York: NYU Press, 2024.

Cohen, Brianne. *Don't Look Away: Art, Nonviolence, and Preventive Publics in Contemporary Europe.* Durham: Duke University Press, 2023.

The Creation of Wittgenstein: Understanding the Roles of Rush Rhees, Elizabeth Anscombe and Georg Henrik von Wright. Edited by Thomas H. Wallgren. New York: Bloomsbury Academic, 2023.

Crip Genealogies. Edited by Mel Y. Chen, Alison Kafer, Eunjung Kim, and Julie Avril Minich. Durham: Duke University Press, 2023.

de Gaynesford, Maximilian. *How to be Radical in Philosophy.* New York: Bloomsbury Academic, 2023.

Eley, Geoff. *History Made Conscious: Politics of Knowledge, Politics of the Past.* New York: Verso, 2023.

Evans, Jennifer V. *The Queer Art of History: Queer Kinship after Fascism.* Durham: Duke University Press, 2023.

Fischer, Michael M. J. *Probing Arts and Emergent Forms of Life.* Durham: Duke University Press, 2023.

Foucault, Michel. *Madness, Language, Literature.* Edited by Henri-Paul Fruchaud, Daniele Lorenzini, and Judith Revel. Translated by Robert Bononno. Chicago: University of Chicago Press, 2023.

Franklin, Cynthia G. *Narrating Humanity: Life Writing and Movement Politics from Palestine to Mauna Kea.* New York: Fordham University Press, 2023.

Fregoso, Rosa-Linda. *The Force of Witness: Contra Feminicide.* Durham: Duke University Press, 2023.

Ghosh, Bishnupriya. *The Virus Touch: Theorizing Epidemic Media.* Durham: Duke University Press, 2023.

Gould, Rebecca. *Erasing Palestine: Free Speech and Palestinian Freedom.* New York: Verso, 2023.

Hammer, Allison K. *Masculinity in Transition.* Minneapolis: University of Minnesota Press, 2023.

Hankins, James. *Political Meritocracy in Renaissance Italy: The Virtuous Republic of Francesco Patrizi of Siena.* Cambridge, Mass.: Harvard University Press, 2023.

Harrison, Olivia C. *Natives against Nativism: Antiracism and Indigenous Critique in Postcolonial France.* Minneapolis: University of Minnesota Press, 2023.

Hawhee, Deborah. *A Sense of Urgency: How the Climate Crisis Is Changing Rhetoric.* Chicago: University of Chicago Press, 2023.

Kaufman-Osborne, Timothy V. *The Autocratic Academy: Reenvisioning Rule within America's Universities.* Durham: Duke University Press, 2023.

Kong, Travis S. K. *Sexuality and the Rise of China.* Durham: Duke University Press, 2023.

Krauss, Chiara Russo. *The Philosophy of Joseph Petzoldt: From Mach's Positivism to Einstein's Relativity.* New York: Bloomsbury Academic, 2023.

Kuhn, Mary. *The Garden Politic: Global Plants and Botanical Nationalism in Nineteenth-Century America.* New York: NYU Press, 2023.

Lawtoo, Nidesh. *Violence and the Oedipal Unconscious: Volume 1, The Catharsis Hypothesis.* East Lansing: Michigan State University Press, 2023.

Lear, Jonathan. *Imagining the End: Mourning and Ethical Life.* Cambridge, Mass.: Harvard University Press, 2022.

Lustig, Kfir Cohen. *Makers of Worlds, Readers of Signs: Israeli and Palestinian Literature of the Global Contemporary.* New York: Verso, 2023.

McAuliffe, Sam. *Improvisation in Music and Philosophical Hermeneutics.* New York: Bloomsbury Academic, 2023.

Mitchell, Lisa. *Hailing the State: Indian Democracy Between Elections.* Durham: Duke University Press, 2023.

Muehlebach, Andrea. *A Vital Frontier: Water Insurgencies in Europe.* Durham: Duke University Press, 2023.

Montemayor, Carlos. *The Prospect of a Humanitarian Artificial Intelligence: Agency and Value Alignment.* New York: Bloomsbury Academic, 2023.

Nash, Mark. *Curating the Moving Image.* Durham: Duke University Press, 2023.

O'Dwyer, Rachel. *Tokens.* New York: Verso, 2023.

Parageau, Sandrine. *The Paradoxes of Ignorance in Early Modern England and France.* Stanford: Stanford University Press, 2023.

Parikka, Jussi. *Operational Images: From the Visual to the Invisual.* Minneapolis: University of Minnesota Press, 2023.

Pfeiffer, Ludwig K. *Sociability and Society: Literature and the Symposium*. Stanford: Stanford University Press, 2023.

Pinkus, Karen. *Subsurface*. Minneapolis: University of Minnesota Press, 2023.

Political Theology Today: 100 Years after Carl Schmitt. Edited by Mitchell Dean, Lotte List, and Stefan Schwarzkopf. Bloomsbury Academic, 2023.

Posthumanism in Practice. Edited by Christine Daigle and Matthew Hayler. Bloomsbury Academic, 2023.

Rarey, Matthew Francis. *Insignificant Things: Amulets and the Art of Survival in the Early Black Atlantic*. Durham: Duke University Press, 2023.

Rodríguez, Juana María. *Puta Life: Seeing Latinas, Working Sex*. Durham: Duke University Press, 2023.

Saxena, Akshya. *Vernacular English: Reading the Anglophone in Postcolonial India*. Princeton: Princeton University Press, 2022.

Settling the Boom: The Sites and Subjects of Bakken Oil. Eds. Mary E. Thomas and Bruce Braun. Minneapolis: University of Minnesota Press, 2022.

Severino, Emanuele. *Law and Chance*. Trans. Damiano Sacco. New York: Bloomsbury Academic, 2023.

Sgarbi, Marco. *The Age of Epistemology: Aristotelian Logic in Early Modern Philosophy 1500-1700*. New York: Bloomsbury Academic, 2023.

Smetona, Matthew J. *Recovering the Later Georg Lukács: A Study on the Unity of His Thought*. Cambridge, Mass.: MIT Press, 2023.

Steinmann, Michael. *Reframing Ethics Through Dialectics: A New Understanding of the oral Good*. New York: Bloomsbury Academic, 2023.

Swarbrick, Steven. *The Environmental Unconscious: Ecological Poetics from Spenser to Milton*. Minneapolis: University of Minnesota Press, 2023.

Sweeney, Megan. *Mendings*. Durham: Duke University Press, 2023.

Taylor, Timothy D. *Working Musicians: Labor and Creativity in Film and Television Production*. Durham: Duke University Press, 2023.

Terada, Rei. *Metaracial: Hegel, Antiblackness, and Political Identity*. Chicago: University of Chicago Press, 2023.

Terranova, Tiziana. *Hypersocial*. Minneapolis: University of Minnesota Press, forthcoming.

Terranova, Tiziana. *After the Internet: Digital Networks between Capital and the Commons*. Cambridge, Mass.: MIT Press, 2022.

Thiong'o, Ngũgĩ wa. *The Language of Languages*. Chicago: University of Chicago Press, 2023.

Tongson, Karen. *Normporn: Queer Viewers and the TV That Soothes Us*. New York: NYU Press, 2023.

Toscano, Alberto. *Late Fascism*. New York: Verso, 2023.

Vernallis, Carol. *The Media Swirl: Politics, Audiovisuality, and Aesthetics*. Durham: Duke University Press, 2023.

Vijay, Ameeth. *Topothesia: Planning, Colonialism, and Places in Excess*. New York: Fordham University Press, 2023.

Žižek Responds! Eds. Dominik Finkelde and Todd McGowan. New York: Bloomsbury Academy, 2023.